AROUND THE WORLD IN
500 FESTIVALS

From Burning Man in the US to Kumbh Mela in Allahabad—The World's Most Spectacular Celebrations

STEVE DAVEY

Skyhorse Publishing

Contents

AROUND THE WORLD IN
500 FESTIVALS

Introduction

I must confess to a touch of personal bias in this book: the Weston-super-Mare carnival – part of England's West Country Carnival circuit, of which the Bridgwater Carnival was and still is the main event – was the first festival I went to. I can still remember as a young child watching open mouthed as each of the massive illuminated floats passed by. I have vivid memories of standing by the side of the road, usually in West Country drizzle, bathed in the waves of noise from the music and the heat from countless light bulbs that provided a brief respite from the winter cold. As a family we would attend every year and be treated to a hot dog. Once the last float had passed, everyone ran for their cars like the start of the Le Mans 24 Hours race in an attempt to avoid the monster traffic jam on the way out of town.

It seemed so extraordinary and so impossibly glamorous that I was totally hooked. It was a festival that gave me my first significant published work in a magazine, too ('Venice Carnival', *Ritz Newspaper,* 1988). When the publisher asked if I knew anyone who could write a story I volunteered in a fit of bravado, which set me falteringly on my path to becoming a writer. Since then I have travelled to as many festivals as possible.

I started going in the 'here-be-dragons' days, when guidebooks barely mentioned festivals, and if they did it was in desultory fashion, more in the spirit of warning people that they might be inconvenienced by the crowds or by the lack of accommodation. Yet like the people of the West Country running for their cars, I went anyway and made the most of the inconvenience and hardships, just so that I could experience the magic. Now, festivals are in vogue, attendances are up and many of the celebrations in this book have their own official Facebook pages.

Since the days of the West Country carnival, I have run with bulls (or more accurately run from bulls) many times, bathed in the Ganges with millions of pilgrims, got drenched at Lao New Year and drunk too much rice wine and fell in a ditch seeing in the Lisu New Year. I have dodged a yak at the Korzok Gustor in Ladakh, and danced with Gypsies at the Pèlerinage des Gitans, along with countless other exploits that often left me somewhat battered and bruised, but in no way chastened by the experience.

Why am I so attracted by festivals? To me they represent the best time to visit a destination. Festivals characterize so many places. Flick through a rack of postcards in almost any city in the world and the majority of images will be of its main festival: in Venice you can't avoid the Carnevale, in Pamplona everything seems to revolve around the Fiesta, and Rio is all about the Carnaval. During festival time people seem more alive, more engaged, often spending much of the year in anticipation of these few days of intense activity. I remember speaking to some young locals at their village fiesta in Spain. They worked in Madrid and said that they

COVER AND PAGE 1
A participant in full body paint at the Mount Hagen Festival in Papua New Guinea, where more than 50 tribes from the Western Highland Province gather for a sing-sing and perform traditional dances and songs.

FRONTISPIECE Horsemanship skills are a highlight at the annual Shoton Festival in Tibet. Originally a religious observance dating back to the 11th century, the Shoton Festival now incorporates a rich tapestry of Tibetan traditional and cultural activities.

OVERLEAF An exuberance of colour and costumes, sound and dance marks the street parades at the Trinidad and Tobago Carnival.

could be away for Christmas or birthdays, but if they didn't go home for the fiesta they were in big trouble with their families. A friend who lived in Pamplona maintains that if someone misses two fiestas in a row they aren't considered a local anymore.

For many of the religious festivals included here, people might plan and save for months, years or even a whole lifetime to attend. Driven by great faith to travel vast distances, enduring privations and often spending large amounts of money, pilgrims appear to team up like ants when viewed from a distance. Yet, up close, a pilgrimage is a collection of unique individuals driven by their own hopes and dreams. Talking to pilgrims and appreciating just how much going to a festival means to them is a humbling experience, even for a hardened old cynic like me.

To create this book we first had to agree on what actually constitutes a festival. By our definition we were only interested in festivals with some cultural significance, with a tradition or history, or that have evolved from historical or cultural events. Commercial events, like the jazz, food or shopping festivals dreamed up by hyperactive PR consultants or brainstormed by tourist boards, were instantly dismissed. We have selected festivals that actually have a true connection with a place and that are unique in some way. A few may have had inauspicious commercial origins, but have since been taken over by the populace and developed an identity of their own.

Wherever possible, we wanted festivals that are held at a particular location, rather than vague national celebrations, so the only mention of Christmas, for example, is at Bethlehem, where it all began. As this is essentially a travel book, we also only wanted to select festivals that are open to anyone, and so have not included events that can only be attended by one particular community, such as the Muslim Hajj.

Of course, I haven't actually been to all the festivals in this book. Going to all the carnivals included here would take over forty years, travelling to one a year. Attending many festivals has given me experience in festival spotting – researching an event and deciding if it's worth going to. Some people will disagree with my selection, be horrified at the omission of their favourite, consider some a little too light-hearted and others too cruel to be included, but I think this list goes a long way towards illustrating the extraordinary diversity in the ways we celebrate our cultural and historical heritages. Certainly, my own personal bucket list of festivals that I am planning to visit has grown significantly. If this book has the same effect on the readers, and encourages them to throw caution to the wind and seek out some of the amazing celebrations I've included, then I will consider it a success.

A NOTE ON DATES
Because many festivals are set by local custom or lunar calendars which do not correspond to the Western solar year, their dates can vary widely. For current dates please check with the local tourist authorities.

Festivals may sometimes not be held for a number of years. This might be the result of wars and international conflicts, legal or civil restrictions or more local issues. Where we expect that this is likely to be a temporary situation, we have still included them in the listing. Please check before making any travel plans.

AFRICA >> EAST AFRICA

> ETHIOPIA

MASKAL
Addis Ababa

Bright yellow Maskal daisies carpet the city squares on Maskal day, when Ethiopian Orthodox Christians traditionally celebrate St Helena's reputed discovery in AD 326 of the True Cross upon which Christ was allegedly crucified. The faithful converge on city squares to light a bonfire commemorating the saint's vision of a trail of smoke that led her to the True Cross. Splendid ceremonial processions of priests and choirboys, ornately dressed in gold-embroidered vestments, circle the pyre before enthusiastic crowds. As the sun sets, torchbearers draw close to light the bonfires, where celebrations continue until dawn.

Where: City squares, especially Maskal Square, Addis Ababa, Ethiopia
When: 27 September (28 September on leap years)

TIMKAT
Gondar

Every January huge and happy crowds of Ethiopian Orthodox Christians gather in Gondar to celebrate the feast of Epiphany by commemorating Christ's baptism in the River Jordan. On the eve of Timkat, which means 'baptism' in Amharic, a replica of the Ark of the Covenant – a casket described in the Book of Exodus – is carefully wrapped in crimson cloth and borne in procession from the royal enclosure to the royal baths. Priests clad in rich vestments lead the procession of pilgrims bearing candles and bamboo crosses. At dawn the water is blessed and sprinkled on the faithful, who are invited to immerse themselves in the pool for a second baptism. Many leap in and splash around joyfully. After a day of singing, dancing and feasting, a lively carnival procession returns the Ark to its sanctuary.

Where: Gondar, Ethiopia
When: 19 January (20 January on leap years)

> KENYA

MAULID
Lamu Island

The tropical island of Lamu comes alive every February with spiritual festivities that draw Muslims from across Kenya to celebrate the birth of the Prophet Mohammed on the 12th day of Rabi-al-Awal (the third month in the Islamic calendar). From sunset until dawn the next day, the faithful pray, sing and chant praises of the Prophet. During the last week of Rabi-al-Awal, the National Museums of Kenya stage fairground-style entertainments and community-building events, from tug-of-war to donkey races. On the final day, men congregate for prayers at the city cemetery, then stroll back along the ancient seafront, reciting religious poems.

Where: Lamu Island, Kenya
When: 12th day of Rabi-al-Awal (3rd month of the Muslim calendar)

> MADAGASCAR

FAMADIHANA
Central Highlands

The Malagasy have their own special way of keeping family ties. Every seven years, the bones of the *razana* (ancestors) are taken from their crypts, cleaned and wrapped in a fresh shroud before appearing as the guests of honour at a party held in their name. The gatherings, which can last several days, are lively affairs with feasting and tomb-side music. Some family members even dance with the shrouded *razana*. The ancient ritual of *famadihana*, or bone-turning, dating back almost 400 years, is believed to bring good fortune to the surviving family members. Today, though, the custom is apparently declining due to the cost of silk shrouds and lavish feasts.

Where: Central Highlands, Madagascar
When: June to September

> MAURITIUS

MAHASHIVRATREE
Gango Talao (Grand Bassain)

A magical night festival glowing with candlelight, the Great Night of the Shiva draws the mainly Hindu population of Mauritius to the Temple of Shiva, overlooking the Ganga Talao. After travelling many miles, more than 400,000 white-clad pilgrims converge on the holy lake, bearing little wooden arches decorated with mirrors, paper and flowers. At the lake, devotees perform *pujas* (acts of worship), such as bathing in the sacred waters and immersing Shiva *lingams* – phallic-like stones, symbolizing divine energy. As night falls, the lake glows with the lights and colours of myriad candles and flowers, set afloat as offerings to Shiva.

Where: Ganga Talao (Grand Bassain), Mauritius
When: February to early March

> SEYCHELLES

CREOLE FESTIVAL
Victoria

If you think that the Seychelles are just about beaches, then this lively celebration of all things creole will change your mind. For generations the Seychelles have welcomed diverse

Ethiopian drummers line up for the religious procession to the royal baths during Timkat, the Ethiopian Orthodox celebration of Epiphany.

cultural influences from around the Indian Ocean, which have produced a unique Seychellois identity, regarded by the islanders themselves as 'creole' or mixed. Reflecting their rich cosmopolitan heritage, the Creole Festival bills itself as the oldest pan-creole event in the world. With dance and music, fashion and food fairs, it certainly offers an exciting medley of Seychellois culture and customs, crafts and cuisine.

Where: Victoria, Seychelles
When: The last week of October
....

> TANZANIA

MWAKA KOGWA
Zanzibar
....

There are many ways to settle scores before the start of the New Year: negotiation, conciliation, forgiveness, even a fist fight. The people of Makunduchi on Zanzibar have been staging a mock fight for more than 1,500 years. The male fighters used to swing clubs for the ceremonial contest, but now hit each other with banana stems in a ritual punch-up that is meant to clear the air before the New Year. While the

battle warms up, the womenfolk stroll around singing songs, some of which poke gentle fun at the fighting men. Once the battlers have worked any rivalries out of their system, the local shaman sets fire to a hut to bring good luck – a cue for the women to prepare a large banquet where guests are welcomed before everyone heads off to dance.

Where: Makunduchi, Zanzibar
When: Four days around the 3rd week of July
....

>> NORTH AFRICA
....

> EGYPT

MOULID OF SAYYID AHMED AL-BEDAWI
Tanta
....

The quiet Muslim city of Tanta fills with pilgrims during Egypt's biggest *moulid* (religious festival), when up to 2 million devotees gather at the city's triple-domed mosque to honour the 13th-century Sufi saint Sayyid Ahmed al-Bedawi. During the eight-day festival, Sufi brotherhoods chant and dance until many slip into a trance, which helps them draw closer to God. At the saint's tomb, children draw near to be blessed, while the sick pray for health, and everywhere food vendors ply the crowds with sugar-coated *hubb el Azziz* nuts (seeds of the Beloved Prophet). On the final Friday, drummers lead pilgrims through the streets in a fervent religious procession.

Where: Tanta, Nile Delta, Egypt
When: Late October
....

SUN FESTIVAL, ABU SIMBEL
Abu Simbel
....

Twice a year, the rays of the rising sun penetrate the entrance of the rock-cut Temple of Abu Simbel, reaching down its 60m hall to light up the statues of the pharaoh Ramses II and the sun gods Amun and Ra. The fourth statue on the left remains in deep shadow, as befits Ptah, god of the underworld.

The dramatic solar effect, first achieved when the temple was built more than 3,000 years ago, was probably designed to coincide with the anniversaries of Ramses's birthday on 21 February, and his ascension on 21 December. Three millennia later, in 1971, the erection of the Aswan High Dam necessitated the relocation of the temple further uphill, where the solar effect now occurs one day later. Outside the temple, the breathtaking light show is celebrated locally with much feasting, dancing and music-making.

Where: Abu Simbel, Egypt
When: 22 February and 22 October
....

> LIBYA

GHADAMES DATE FESTIVAL
Ghadames

After the arduous labour of scaling date palms for the annual harvest, the desert tribes of Arabs and Berbers, including the Tuaregs, celebrate in the old quarter of the stunning oasis town of Ghadames, now a UNESCO World Heritage Site. The bright white limestone city is officially uninhabited, but its relocated residents return every year for the date festival, enjoyed in the ornate splendour of the old quarter among a maze of narrow, shaded streets and squares.
On the final day, the action shifts from the city to the sand dunes for the camel and horse races. After lively displays of daring and skill in and out of the saddle, the desert tribes settle down to a day of peaceful feasting and merrymaking.

Where: The old city of Ghadames, Libya
When: Three days in October

NALUT SPRING FESTIVAL
Nalut, Nafousa Mountain

The desert town of Nalut hosts an annual festival every spring showcasing a Berber culture relatively unaffected by tourism. After a ceremonial flame is lit, regional tribes display traditional customs and skills, from desert horsemanship and camel transport to acrobatic feats. In the old quarter, a local market sells decorative handicrafts as well as culinary delicacies and local produce, such as oil and dates. Bands in local dress play historical Libyan instruments, such as the *zukra* bagpipe and *eddenget* drum, while food vendors keep people fed and watered.

Where: Nalut, Nafousa Mountain, Libya
When: March

> MOROCCO

IMILCHIL WEDDING MOUSSEM
Imilchil

Finding a partner isn't easy for the nomadic Berbers, but the yearly Imilchil Wedding Moussem provides the perfect opportunity to date prospective mates. Up to 30,000 Berbers camp on the outskirts of Imilchil in pitched tents, surrounded by dozens of goats and donkeys. Hopeful brides dress up in their finest outfits and lure potential suitors with their dancing. When a woman views an admirer favourably, she utters the encouraging words, 'You have captured my liver', as the liver, rather than the heart, is considered the seat of true love in Berber culture. Nuptial negotiations then begin in earnest over a cup of mint tea.

Where: Imilchil, Morocco
When: September (variable)

Berber brides-to-be converge on the Imilchil Wedding Moussem in Morocco in search of prospective grooms.

MOUSSEM BEN AÏSSÂ
Meknes

By far the largest and most atmospheric pilgrimage festival in Morocco, the Moussem Ben Aïssâ honours the 15th-century Sufi mystic of the same name, whose devotees are renowned for their evocative music, ritual dances and ecstatic trances. In earlier times, some brothers were known for their death-defying feats, such as eating glass or snakes. These days, though, anyone crunching glass is likely to be a street entertainer. After soaking up the spiritual atmosphere, visitors can enjoy the city's medieval pageantry and *fantasia* cavalry charges as riders gallop towards the crowds, firing into the air before skidding to a halt at the last moment.

Where: Meknes, Morocco
When: The day before the birth of the Prophet 12 Rabi-al-Awal

MOUSSEM OF TANTAN
Tantan

A sort of Saharan Mardi Gras, the Moussem of Tantan is easily the most eagerly awaited gathering of nomadic desert peoples in North Africa. Up to 30 different Arab Bedouin tribes are drawn to the small desert town of Tantan not only to celebrate, but also to preserve Bedouin customs and culture. Lines of camel-wool tents exhibit a surprising array of local metal and leather handicrafts, Saharan culinary arts and even herbal remedies. Outside, dancers swirl and stomp in dazzling dress, while virtuoso riders perform acrobatic feats at full gallop.

Where: Tantan, Morocco
When: May to September (variable)

> TUNISIA

FESTIVAL OF THE OASES
Tozeur

Set among lush palm trees in the old Moorish, sand-coloured city of Tozeur, the Festival of the Oasis attracts Berber and Bedouin tribes from across the Sahara to display their desert traditions. The opening parade is a grand spectacle: resplendent horsemen rein in spirited Arab stallions adorned in dazzling woven saddles; camel-riders, shrouded in tumbling silks, glide past on tall, loping camels; one by one the dance troupes whirl and leap to the rhythm of drum and horn. Over three days of Arabian delights, there's something for everyone, ranging from camel fighting to knife-throwing, from story-telling to snake-charming and dancing. The final camel races across the undulating dunes make for a breathtaking evening.

Where: Tozeur, Tunisia
When: Three days in November or December

FESTIVAL OF THE SAHARA
Douz

Feisty Arab stallions, alluring Bedouin brides and *salughi* hunting dogs – all take a whirl in a compelling show of Saharan cultures and customs. During four days of festivities, thousands of desert nomads witness awe-inspiring camel marathons and equestrian virtuosity. The brilliance of the riders' displays is matched only by the splendour of their robes. The cultural events showcase tribal song and dance and even Bedouin marriages. Poetry, too, plays a role, recounting the history of the Bedouins. A highlight is the poetry contest run by the desert poet Abdellatif Belgacem.

Where: Douz, Tunisia
When: Four days at the end of December

>> SOUTHERN AFRICA

> BOTSWANA

KURU DANCE FESTIVAL
D'Kar, near Ghanzi

Although a fairly modern event, founded in 1997, the Kuru Dance Festival celebrates the very ancient traditions of Botswana's first people – the San, Basarwa or Bushmen. Each year, the festival attracts San from all over the country for a cultural revival of song, dance, music-making and story-telling. During San dances, performers enact specific cultural traditions, such as the *gemsbok* dance of the Gantsi and the *diware* healing ritual of the Hambukushu.

Where: D'Kar near Ghanzi in the Kalahari Desert, Botswana
When: Three days in August

> SOUTH AFRICA

KAAPSE KLOPSE
Cape Town

A flamboyant minstrel carnival, Kaapse Klopse takes off on 1 January every year, when more than 13,000 brightly dressed minstrels jauntily parade through the streets of Cape Town, singing and dancing the New Year in. The custom apparently stems from the time when enslaved Africans celebrated their New Year's Day on 2 January, the 'second new year' (*Tweede Nuwe Jaar*), as they were bound to work on 1 January. Today, the festival kicks off when more than 160 different minstrel clubs (*klopse*) take to the streets. Clad in eye-catching, themed costumes, they prance through the city to the delight of cheering crowds. The festivities, which roll on into January, include street marches and costume competitions.

Where: Cape Town, South Africa
When: New Year's Day

UMKHOSI WOMHLANGA
Nongoma

An ancient Zulu rite of passage steeped in the royal history of the Zulu Kingdom, the Umkhosi Womhlanga reed dance marks a Zulu maiden's passage to womanhood. Up to 10,000 girls gather reeds from the local river and present them to the king in his KwaNyokeni palace as a sign of their loyalty and chastity. It is an honour to take part and, by tradition, only virgins are eligible. If any maiden is less than chaste, her reeds will apparently break, much to her embarrassment. After presenting their gifts, the women put on their finest beadwork to sing and dance before the king, who might choose one of the girls for his wife. Thousands come to watch the stunning display of Zulu culture.

Where: Nongoma, KwaZulu-Natal, South Africa
When: September

A young Kaapse Klopse minstrel sings his heart out in Cape Town.

Love and Marriage

THE RITUALS OF COURTSHIP ARE AS OLD AS TIME. TO HELP YOUNG PEOPLE FIND THEIR PERFECT PARTNERS, AND PRESERVE THE TRADITIONS OF MARRIAGE, COURTSHIP FESTIVALS ARE CELEBRATED IN MANY SOCIETIES AROUND THE WORLD.

ABOVE Young girl carrying a reed to the King's Palace at KwaZulu-Natal during the Zulu Reed Dance Festival.

OPPOSITE Wodaabe men showing off the whiteness of their teeth and eyes at the Cure Salée.

We in the West are spoiled for choice when it comes to ways of finding a partner. The sexes can freely meet, drink and be merry. The Internet means that we are not confined to our local area, and speed dating allows us to break out of our usual circle of friends. In many traditional cultures, though, the options are more limited. Geographical isolation can make finding a partner all but impossible, and cultural restrictions can prevent girls and boys from getting to know each other.

OPPOSITE Berber woman made up to attract a husband at the Imilchil Wedding Festival.

ABOVE Wodaabe men dancing at the Cure Salée.

Many societies rely on courtship rituals. These may just mean formal inquiries, introductions, and unions arranged by families or village leaders, but some cultures have festivals where young people can meet and socialize under controlled circumstances and conduct their courtship without breaking local taboos.

One of the most visually stunning courtship festivals is the Gerewol, held by the traditionally nomadic Wodaabe Fula people of Niger. This is a yearly courtship ritual in which young tribesmen compete for the attentions of single women of marrying age. The most famous Gerewol is the Cure Salée at the town of Ingali, on the southern edge of the Sahara, where the clans gather for the festival, a market and meetings (see p. 31).

The Gerewol includes a beauty pageant in which it is the men who dress up, apply elaborate face make-up, and then dance, sing and pull extreme faces in order to impress the girls with their white eyes and teeth – considered the most beautiful features by the tribe. Once they have attracted a prospective partner there are complex rules about what happens next, including the bartering of a dowry.

The Tuareg, who also attend the Cure Salée, show off their camel riding skills and take part in a mass procession of riders.

In Morocco there is a tradition of wedding festivals among the Berber population. Berber communities who live in remote settlements come together in festivals called

TOP Swazi girls processing to the Umhlanga Reed Dance.

Moussem. These usually commemorate a saint, and involve music, dancing and general revelry. They also allow fathers to show off their daughters. The most famous of these is the Betrothal Festival in the small town of Imilchil in the Atlas Mountains, where Berbers from all over the region congregate in order to meet a partner (see p. 16). Women dress up in traditional finery and the young are free to choose a spouse for themselves. There are no long engagements here: weddings are carried out en masse at the festival, sometimes up to forty at a time.

In southern Africa, in Swaziland, the famous Umhlanga, or Reed Dance Ceremony, is a ritual where young women compete in a pageant to be selected as the next wife of the Swazi king (see p. 28). Thousands of unmarried women travel from their villages to the royal village, where they collect reeds to mend the wall surrounding the queen mother's palace. They then dance for the royal family, and try to attract the king's attention in the hope of becoming one of his many wives. At the last count he had thirteen.

There is also a Zulu Reed Dance Festival that takes place at the palace of the Zulu king at Nongoma in KwaZulu-Natal. Up to 25,000 virgins fetch reeds from the river and dance in front of the king. Again, this is a celebration of chastity and the king will select one of the maidens to be his wife. The common man, unfortunately, doesn't get a look in, so if you are looking for love, this might not be the festival for you (see p. 17).

In Asia, many of the minority hill tribe societies have regular festivals that include courtship elements. New Year celebrations for the Hmong people in Shi'Dong in Southern China all feature games where boys and girls can meet under the supervision of their elders.

The Hmong (erroneously termed Miao by the Chinese) have an entire festival devoted to courtship. At the Sisters' Meal Festival, marriageable women dress in their finery, which includes much silver, collected over the generations (see p. 96). This is supposed to ward off evil spirits, but also traditionally gave women a chance to carry their dowry with them. Some of this jewellery is so heavy that the women can hardly walk. They dance for the menfolk to the strains of the *lusheng*, an ancient form of reed instrument. A man will pass a bowl of rice to a woman who interests him. A return gift with one chopstick means 'let's just be friends', two chopsticks indicates an interest.

In the village of Lisdoonvarna in western Ireland, the annual Matchmaking Festival is billed as the largest singles event in the world. It originates in the tradition of matchmaking, where villages used to have a go-between who would sift through the various romantic options and perform introductions for people living in remote rural communities.

The Lisdoonvarna festival comprises a series of dances, events and then a beauty pageant. In truth, few people nowadays expect a real relationship to grow out of this – most are here for the famous Irish *craic* – but there are still those who make an appointment with the last matchmaker in Ireland, Willie Daly, in the hope of being introduced to the love of their life (see p. 211).

As if confirming that some people think foolhardy and even aggressive behaviour is a way to win over the ladies, there are a couple of festivals where unmarried men fight with each other and even with bulls to secure a wife. At the Usaba Sambah festival in Bali (see p. 148), combatants duel with handfuls of spiky *pandau* leaves to try to draw blood from each other, watched over by the unmarried girls of the village. The Indian Jallikattu tournament, which is part of the Pongal Harvest Festival (see p. 120), sees local men being charged by an enraged bull. The winner of this ritual is the one who

BELOW Fighting to impress the ladies at the Usaba Sambah festival of the Bali Aga people in Indonesia.

BELOW RIGHT The ancient sport of bull-taming called Jallikattu used to be a way to win a bride.

ABOVE Hmong girl weighed down by silver jewellery.

LEFT Hmong in their festival finest at the Sisters' Meal Festival, Shi'Dong.

manages to hold on to the bull for 50 metres. In the past, this meant that he won a bride. Although Jallikattu is now more of a sport than a matchmaking ritual, the prestige still doesn't do the winner any harm in the bridal stakes.

The patron saint of romance is, of course, St Valentine, and the city of Terni in Italy throws the biggest St Valentine's Day festival in the world. There is a feast outside the Basilica where the saint's remains are interred and awards are given to couples who are celebrating gold and silver wedding anniversaries (see p. 208).

OPPOSITE Kalash people dancing, telling sacred stories from their past and performing rituals at the Joshi (spring) festival in Rumbur Valley, Kalasha Desh near Gilgit, Pakistan.

ABOVE Young Kalash girls dancing at the Joshi festival in Bumbaret Valley, Kalasha Desh near Gilgit, Pakistan.

In the remote valleys of northern Pakistan live the Kalash people who are non-Muslim animists. In their culture marriage is frequently by elopement, which often takes place during the colourful Joshi (spring) and the Uchau (autumn) festivals (see p. 144). Festivals happen on different days, attracting people from other valleys. Much mulberry wine is drunk, leading to a raucous atmosphere, with men and women dancing together – a taboo in neighbouring tribal regions of Pakistan. In Kalash society, women enjoy greater equality than their sisters in the surrounding Muslim communities, and if a wife is unhappy with her husband she can divorce him by eloping with another man.

> SWAZILAND

INCWALA
Royal Kraal

One of the last surviving mass ceremonies in Africa, Incwala, or the Festival of the First Fruits, unites the people of Swaziland in an eight-week festival that welcomes the harvest, invokes ancestral blessings and renews the power of the king. While the king retires to meditate in the royal palace, young men trek more than 37km to gather ceremonial branches from the sacred Lusekwane bush, whose telltale leaves apparently wither if touched by impure hands. On the third day, warriors slaughter an ox and dance the *inczuala* near the royal enclosure, encouraging the king to emerge. Eventually he comes out in full regalia, performs a sacred dance and, in a symbolic gesture, tastes the first pumpkin of the harvest. The New Year harvest party can then start in earnest, with joyous feasting, music and dance.

Where: Royal Kraal, Swaziland
When: Late December to January, set by the moon

UMHLANGA REED DANCE
Ludzidzini Royal Village

It's an unforgettable sight to see more than 25,000 brightly dressed Swazi maidens cut reeds twice their height for the prestigious Umhlanga Reed Dance, which occurs at the end of an eight-day festival. On the first day, the girls gather at the queen mother's village, before dispersing to fetch tall reeds as a symbol of tribute labour. On the sixth day, the young women don splendid beadwork dresses and rattling anklets, and parade to the royal court to dance before the king. Many carry bush knives as a symbol of their virginity. On the final day, cows are slaughtered and their meat given to the girls to take home. For many, the ceremony serves to promote respect for the purity of young women.

Where: Ludzidzini Royal Village, Swaziland
When: August to September

> ZAMBIA

KUMBOKA CEREMONY
Limulunga

Loosely translated, *kumboka* means 'getting out of water onto dry land', which is exactly what the Lozi chief does each year at the end of the rainy season, amid the pomp and splendour of a 300-year-old ceremony dating back to the time when the first Lozi migrated to Zambia. Sometime in April or May, the River Zambezi swells and floods the Barotse plains – an unmistakable cue to the chief at Lealui to take to the royal barge and lead his people safely upriver to dry land at Limulunga. Escorted by his entire village in a flotilla of canoes, the barge glides serenely upriver, paddled furiously by boatmen crowned with splendid red turbans. When the flotilla reaches dry land at the end of the day, a huge crowd celebrates with joyful singing and dancing.

Where: Upper Zambezi between Lealui and Limulunga, Zambia
When: From April to May, depending on the rains

LIKUMBI LYA MIZE
Mize

Striking, boldly patterned robes and haunting masks make the Likumbi Lya Mize an event like no other. Every August, the Luvale tribe gather at the palace of the senior chief, or *ndungu*, at Mize to celebrate their heritage at a vibrant cultural fair, with varied displays of local handicrafts and traditional song and dance. A popular highlight that always draws the crowds are the *makishi* masquerades, performed by masked dancers clad in boldly patterned *lakishi* costumes and arresting masks that represent mythical characters and deities. Stemming from boys' initiation rites, the masquerades enact morality stories, imparting practical lessons for life and values to live by. Throughout the event, the festivities spread out on both sides of the River Zambezi, with round-the-clock entertainment and lively market stalls. After much feasting and dancing, the party reaches its climax with a splendid *makishi* procession for the chief.

Where: Mize, Zambia
When: Last week of August

>> WEST AFRICA

> BENIN

GELEDE
South-east Benin and south-west Nigeria

With their shiny, brightly painted wooden masks, the Gelede masqueraders look like supersize dolls coming to life in a magical street drama. Flashing goofy smiles and tear-stained cheeks, they grin, grimace and weep with convincing drama in vivid masquerades dramatizing the legends and history of the Yoruba-Togo of Benin and Nigeria.

Gelede pays tribute to the primordial mother goddess Iyà Nlà and the spiritual role of women in Yoruba-Togo communities. The masquerades enact the legends of the Yoruba-Togo and impart morality messages on more than one level – both for the general public and the initiate. The dramas are often satirical or humorous and evoke cheers from the crowds. Gelede rituals are performed at the end of the harvest, during drought, epidemics and at funerals to stave off the effects of evil witchcraft.

Where: Yoruba areas of south-east Benin and south-west Nigeria
When: The end of the dry season, between March and May

VOODOO FESTIVAL
Ouidah

A high point of the voodoo calendar is the festival at Ouidah, which draws the faithful from as far afield as Nigeria and Togo. At the heart of voodoo, known locally as *vodun* or spirit, is the animistic belief that everything on earth is 'animated' by spirits, whether we can see them or not. A good time to reach them is during voodoo rituals when they are thought to possess masked dancers. Essential to the rituals are fabulously elaborate costumes that help a dancer 'put on the mantle' of a particular spirit. Among the most impressive are the massive, swirling, multi-coloured robes of the Yoruba. Feathered, sequinned and appliquéd into the most extraordinary forms, some even come with matching modern accessories, such as handbags and gloves.

Where: Ouidah, Benin
When: 10 January and the preceding week
....

> CAMEROON

NGONDO
Douala

The coastal Sawa pay an annual tribute to their ancestors on the lush banks of the River Wouri. Martial contests, choral singing, folk dancing and even the election of the next Miss Ngondo showcase the unique coastal culture of the Sawa. The festivities culminate in the Festival of Water, which includes ritual processions to the water's edge and a dramatic dugout race fought between teams of brightly clad rowers. The main action of the ceremony then unfolds as a diver takes a sacred clay pot to the riverbed, where the Sawa ancestors are thought to dwell. After nine minutes, he returns to the surface with a miraculously dry pot, filled with predictions for the year ahead.

Where: Wouri Bay and the banks of the River Wouri, Douala, Cameroon
When: The start of the dry season (November to December)
....

> CAPE VERDE ISLANDS

SÃO VICENTE MARDI GRAS
Mindelo, São Vicente Island

It is a long way from the streets of Rio de Janeiro in Brazil to the islands of Cape Verde, but São Vicente's Mardi Gras has all the verve and atmosphere of Rio's street carnivals. The main event is a flamboyant float parade celebrating the festive season before the privations of Lent. Joyous revellers clad in exuberant costumes sway to the beat of the bossa nova and other vivacious Cape Verde rhythms. In the evening, the festivities rave on with lively dancing, street parties and an electrifying firework display.

Where: Mindelo, São Vicente Island, Cape Verde Islands
When: Two days, generally before Ash Wednesday
....

São Vicente Island throws an exuberant Mardi Gras.

> CÔTE D'IVOIRE

FÊTE DU DIPRI
Gomon

The people of Gomon don't mess around when it comes to chasing evil spirits out of their village. In a purification ritual that has its roots in an ancient mystical cult, families steal naked from their huts at midnight to take part in a communal exorcism rite. When the chief arrives, the villagers dance to the beat of the vibrant drums, and slip into a trance. At first light, celebrants daub themselves with chicken blood and drink hallucinogenic potions. Some cut their stomachs, but their wounds apparently heal quickly. Afterwards, they wash in the local river, smear themselves with white kaolin powder and dress in white, symbolizing purity.

Where: Gomon near Abidjan, Côte D'Ivoire
When: April
....

FÊTES DES MASQUES
Man

For the Dogon, their boldly chiselled masks embody the spirits of the earth and the souls of the dead. Wearing a mask that represents a particular spirit, be it an animal or an ancestor, helps a dancer transform into that spirit. Rich in symbolism, Dogon masks serve varied spiritual purposes. Some are protective, while others help to impart wisdom during morality masquerades. The dances performed by members of the Awa cult serve as funeral rites, or *damas*, with dramatic enactments that symbolically lead the souls of the dead to their final resting place.

Where: Man, Côte D'Ivoire
When: November
....

> GHANA

ABOAKYERE, ANTELOPE HUNTING FESTIVAL
Winneba

If you are a vegetarian, Aboakyere probably isn't for you. It kicks off with a contest between two troops of warriors who compete to capture a live bushbuck. When the dust settles, the winning troop presents its trophy at a colourful royal court. The bushbuck is then slaughtered to mark the start of the festival. Rooted in Simpafo history, Aboakyere commemorates the Simpafo's successful migration from Timbuktu in the ancient empire of Sudan to their current home in Winneba on the central coast of Akanland, Ghana. While giving thanks for their present plenty, they also petition the gods for a bountiful harvest and spiritual guidance.

Where: Winneba, Ghana
When: The 1st Saturday of May

FETU AFAHYE
Cape Coast

In the days of their ancestors, the Oguaa were afflicted by a deadly plague that threatened to wipe out the entire community. They prayed to the gods, who purified the village, which was cleansed of the epidemic. Ever since, the Oguaa have purified their town in a time-honoured ritual that starts with a ban on drumming and fishing while the *omanhene*, or main chief, retires to meditate. A week later he emerges and casts a fishing net into the Fosu lagoon, lifting the ban. After a night of libations and incantations at the lagoon, the people gather in the public square where the *omanhene* sacrifices a bull to seal the purification. The event rounds off with much lively drumming, dancing and musketry fire as the chiefs, clad in fabulous gold and red attire, parade through the streets of Cape Coast.

Where: Cape Coast, Ghana
When: The 1st Saturday in September

HOGBETSOTSO FESTIVAL
Volta Estuary

During the Hogbetsotso (exodus), the Ewe celebrate their ancestors' peaceful escape from an oppressive regime in Notsie, Togo, with a period of ritual peace-making and purification. A spate of energetic cleansing – sweeping and burning the rubbish in every village – starts at the Volta Estuary in Ghana and finishes a few days later with a huge royal durbar at the Mono River in Benin. Royal chiefs, clad in full regalia, are feted by their subjects with singing and dancing, including the local *borborbor*, a lively dance with rapid hand-tapping and elaborate footwork.

Where: Volta, Ghana, culminating at the Mono River, Benin
When: The 1st Saturday in November

> MALI

DEGWAL
Diafarabé

The Degwal, or 'crossing of the cattle', when herdsmen lead their cattle across the river to new pastures, has been celebrated at Diafarabé since the founding of the village in 1818. During the one-day event, local herdsmen compete for the Best Caretaker Prize, awarded for the fattest and healthiest cows. More than a simple contest, though, the Degwal offers nomadic herdsmen the opportunity to reunite with their families and catch up with local news. It is also a prime time for courtship, when unmarried men and women can put on their Sunday best and vet potential mates during the popular *Promenade des Jeunes*.

Where: Diafarabé, Mali
When: A Saturday in November or December, depending on the rains

FESTIVAL AU DESERT
Oursi

An exotic concert among the sand dunes, the Festival au Desert stages both traditional Tuareg and contemporary international music. Although only founded in 2001, it is based on much older Tuareg gatherings, such as Takoubelt in Kidal and Temakannit in Timbuktu, which provided the regional nomads with a location and occasion for socializing and celebrating their culture. Reviving the earlier gatherings, the festival today offers a chance for the Tuareg to congregate, exchange news and resolve clan issues. Alongside the social events, Tuareg families celebrate their culture with song, poetry recitals, dance and camel races.

Where: Oursi, Mali
When: January or February

FÊTES DES MASQUES
Dogon country

Beaded, feathered, tasselled and carved in mesmerizing shapes and patterns, Dogon masks are world-renowned, both for their intricate craftsmanship and their rich symbolism. But though we might well appreciate the aesthetic qualities of each unique creation, Dogon masks are carved for specific ceremonial roles in sacred dance, where they serve varied spiritual purposes, whether to ward off evil, to guide the souls of the dead or to pass on knowledge to the young. The Fêtes des Masque is both a memorial and a celebration – commemorating the spirits of the dead and giving thanks for the harvest. For outsiders, it is a vibrant symbol of Dogon culture. Masked dancers, clad in rich costumes and often on stilts, dramatize the story of the Dogon since the dawn of time.

Where: Villages in Dogon country, Mali
When: Five days in April or May

A Dogon masquerader peforms at the Fêtes des Masques in Mali.

SANKÉ MON
San

In an extraordinary communal fishing rite in the small, dusty town of San, hundreds of townsfolk cast their conical nets into the Sanké Mon pond to celebrate the founding of their town and the start of the rainy season. Locals make their way to the muddy pond by foot, donkey, bicycle and horse-drawn carriage, clasping noisy roosters and stubborn goats that will be sacrificed to the spirits of the pond before the fishing starts.

The fifteen-hour fishing rite is a steamy, joyous scramble to net fish in the shallow waters. The fishing techniques are traditional using small- and large-mesh pocket-shaped nets with which the seasoned fishermen scoop leaping fish out of the churned-up waters of the pond. Immediately after the mass fishing, masked dancers, fabulously adorned in cowrie shell costumes and headdresses, swirl and leap to the sound of drums in the village square – a cue for some spirited dancing and feasting to get underway.

Where: San, Mali
When: Every 2nd Thursday of the 7th lunar month

> NIGER

CURE SALÉE
Ingall

A crucial time for desert people, the Cure Salée (Salt Cure) marks the end of the rainy season, when clans converge on the salt pools near Ingall to refresh their herds before heading south to survive the dry season. Traditionally, the gathering at the salt flats benefitted the desert tribes in other ways, too, by providing medicinal trade and the chance to attract future mates. The Wodaabe, especially, are famous for the Gerewol, a dramatic courtship ritual, when young men show off their charm and stamina by dancing in line for seven days under the burning sun. Male beauty is prized by the Wodaabe, whose women are especially drawn by height, elegant features and white teeth and eyes, which the boys obligingly reveal by grinning and rolling their eyes.

Tuareg women, too, take the opportunity to size up the local talent, while potential mates display their skills as horsemen, musicians and craftsmen.

Where: Ingall, Niger
When: Three days in September

> NIGERIA

ARGUNGU FISHING FESTIVAL
Argungu

At the sound of a gun, up to 35,000 eager fishermen, teamed in pairs, race to the Malan Fada River and plunge into the swirling waters to compete for the biggest fish, which often weigh more than 50kg. During one frenetic hour of frenzied fishing, with nothing but hand nets and flotation gourds, contestants test their skills to the limits. The winning pair earns a million naira prize (c. $800US) and a minibus. The dramatic fishing contest marks the end of a four-day cultural festival, originally conceived in the 1930s as a peace-building ritual between the Argungu and Sokoto peoples.

Where: Malan Fada River, Argungu, Nigeria
When: Mid-February

EYO MASQUERADE FESTIVAL
Lagos

In the hauntingly atmospheric Eyo masquerade, hundreds of white-clad, masked Eyo figures parade round Lagos to commemorate a recently deceased *oba* (king) or other prominent person. The tradition dates back to 1854, when it was first staged as a funeral rite of passage for Oba Akintoye, but the custom is probably older. For the procession, the Eyo are organized into five separate groups, each identifiable by a particular hat. Masked by white *iboju* face cloths, they bear a decorated bamboo staves with which to beat anyone who breaks their taboos, such as smoking, raising an umbrella and, sometimes, even using a camera.

Where: Lagos, Nigeria
When: Variable, decided by the current *oba*

KANO DURBAR
Kano

Kano's royal durbar is the site of a breathtaking cavalry charge every year. At the culmination of the Muslim festivals of Eid-ul-Fitr and Eid-al-Adha, the emir annually hosts a splendid royal durbar. The highlight of the event is a procession of ornately clad cavalry en route to the emir's palace. Quite suddenly, the mounted warriors charge the emir, but stop just in front of him and raise their swords in salutation. The dramatic military ritual dates back to the 19th century, when every town and noble household in the emirate was expected to provide the emir with a mounted guard. Twice a year, regiments were summoned to the emir's durbar where they would be inspected before ceremonially saluting their lord. Today, after the durbar, the festival continues with traditional dancing and drumming.

Where: Kano, Nigeria
When: Eid-ul-Fitr and Eid-al-Adha in the Muslim calendar

Argungu fishermen compete to land the fattest catch during an intense one-hour fishing contest in Nigeria.

OSOGBO FESTIVAL
Osogbo

The Sacred Grove of Osun, ancestral home of the Osogbo, attracts huge crowds to draw water from the River Osun in an ancient fertility rite. The ceremony, unchanged in more than 700 years, forms part of a 12-day cultural celebration of the Osogbo kingdom. It opens with the ceremonial cleansing of the pilgrimage route from the palace to the grove, followed by four days of masquerades and processions honouring the Osogbo gods and ancestors. On the night of the sixth day, a 14th-century 16-point lamp is lit in the palace grounds at 7.00 p.m., burning until 7am the next day in honour of Osanyin, god of healing. On the tenth day, the crowns of all past rulers are blessed in a symbolic reunion of the people with their founders. The grand finale is a spectacular ceremonial parade of the whole community to the Sacred Grove.

Where: Osogbo, Nigeria
When: August

> TOGO

GUIN FESTIVAL
Aneho-Glidji

Unlike the Makunduchi of Tanzania, who start the New Year with a mock brawl (see p. 15), the Guin people mark the turning year with a festival of prophecy. In a ritual that dates back 350 years, Guin priests glean the future by reading the colours of a sacred stone. Red is a sign that the gods are angry, white suggests peace, while blue indicates mixed blessings. On the final two days, a carnival party gets underway, with much dancing, parading and feasting.

Where: Aneho-Glidji, Togo
When: Four days at the beginning of September

A young Muslim warrior, armed with a traditional sabre, waits his turn to pay tribute to the emir at the annual Kano Durbar in Nigeria.

The Power of the Mask

IN LIFE AND IN DEATH, MASKS HAVE FEATURED IN CULTURES ALL OVER
THE WORLD FOR MILLENNIA, USED AS A WAY TO CONCEAL IDENTITY, ADOPT
ANOTHER PERSONA, OR REVEAL A HIDDEN TRUTH. MANY OF THE MOST
THRILLING AND MOVING FESTIVALS INCLUDE THE WEARING OF MASKS.

ABOVE Dogon dancer wearing a traditional wooden mask, Mali.

OPPOSITE Masked *cham* dancer at the Phayang Tsedup, Ladakh, India.

Masks were used in the ancient Greek cult of Dionysus and in the Saturnalia festivals of ancient Rome – the word 'persona' is derived from the Latin for mask. Adopting a different persona allowed people to break social mores without fear of being identified: a major motive for the wearing of masks during festivals throughout history.

Arguably, the continent with the greatest tradition of masks is Africa, more specifically West Africa. Predominantly used for rituals and ceremonies, the skills of mask-making are often closely guarded secrets, reserved only for an elite group of craftsmen. Masks are powerful, empowering the wearers to portray spirits or animals, sometimes adopting their character in a trance as if possessed by the mask.

The Dogon people who live in Côte D'Ivoire and Mali are famous for their mask-making, holding important Fêtes des Masques, which are rich in symbolism (see pp. 29 and 30). Carved in wood, masks are created specifically for each festival and used only once before being retired. They represent natural spirits and dead ancestors and are used to act out morality themes running through the history of the Dogon people.

Masks are often used for social control and cohesion, as they are an effective way of conveying messages to the masses. In this way the mask-makers can often control the population, which is why the secrets of their craft are so restricted. Similarly masks that embody the spirits of the dead, such as those used in the Ouidah Voodoo Festival in Benin (see p. 29), allow people to interpret and even control the wishes of powerful ancestors. Many of the most spectacular masks at the Ouidah festival originate from the Yoruba people who are found in south-west Nigeria and south-east Benin. The Yoruba tradition of mask-making (along with that of the Fon people) is celebrated in the Gelede Festival (see p. 28). Gelede is a fertility cult dedicated to Mother Earth, and masked

OPPOSITE Masked Dogon dancers on stilts, Mali.

RIGHT Gelede dancers with brightly coloured masks acting out the legends of their people, Benin.

ABOVE Masked *cham* dancers at the Thak Tok Tse Chu festival, Ladakh, India.

ABOVE RIGHT Masked dancers in the courtyard of the Korzok Gustor, Ladakh, India.

characters are used to mime morality tales for the villagers. These stories induce great hilarity, but the entertainment carries strong underlying messages. Often the meanings of individual masks and masked dances are heavily codified and difficult for the uninitiated to interpret. This is deliberate, as the masks each represent precise characters, and their symbolism is a guarded secret for initiates of the Gelede religion only.

In Zambia, masked *makishi* dancers appear at the Likumbi Lya Mize festival to act out morality lessons for boys during their initiation into adulthood. They use different masks to enact particular stories, life lessons and values for the young men to live by as they grow up (see p. 28).

Masks are also used to scare and intimidate. With their unmoving expressions masks can remove all traces of humanity, enabling the wearer to adopt a different and often malevolent persona and frighten others into a particular behaviour. A perfect example is the Eyo Masquerade in Lagos. Cloaked and masked with white face cloths, the Eyo parade around the city bearing bamboo staves with which they beat people for breaking various taboos (see p. 32).

Masks play a significant role in Tibetan Buddhism, the major religion of Tibet, Bhutan and the Indian region of Ladakh. Here Buddhist monks make masks from painted wood and plaster to represent various deities, demons and historical characters such as kings and *lamas* (monastic teachers of Buddhist *dharma*). The monks wear the masks to perform *cham* dances, in which they act out historical, religious and moral themes to watching pilgrims. The rhythmic dance moves are often accompanied by horns and repetitive drum beats. The masks are colourful and grotesque, and many old ones are displayed at monasteries throughout the year.

The most famous of the dances take place at the Paro Tse Chu in Bhutan (see p. 120), and the Hemis festival in Ladakh (see p. 122), but most monasteries in these regions will have at least one festival a year featuring *cham* dances. At the Korzok Gustor Festival on the shores of the remote high-altitude Lake Tsomoriri (see p. 124) the dances last over two days. In the courtyard of the ancient and rickety Korzok Gompa, masked monks dance around with slow and repetitive movements. In the galleried shadows of the courtyard hundreds of Chang-pa nomads sit watching, seemingly transfixed. The faces of many of the older pilgrims are scored with the lines of old age. They seem familiar with the dances, and eagerly anticipate the livelier moments, such as the Black Hat Dance, when monks enact the killing of an apostate king by a monk in the middle ages.

Many Catholic carnivals feature masked characters. Sometimes, such as in the Carnaval de Barranquilla in Colombia (see p. 98), they are educational and convey moral messages; at other times they are mischievous and even fearsome characters who dominate the carnival celebrations, their masks allowing them to misbehave with impunity.

BELOW Masked dancers at the Korzok Gustor, Ladakh, India.

Belgium has a long history of mischievous carnival characters. At the Carnaval de Binche up to a thousand masked characters called *Gilles* run riot during processions,

ABOVE LEFT *Gille* mask at the Binche Carnival, Belgium.

ABOVE RIGHT *Blanc Moussi* mask at the Stavelot Carnival, Belgium.

hurling out 'lucky' oranges (see pp. 188–9). The *Gilles* in their wax masks are unique to the town, derived from characters created by a local writer. Similarly unique, the *Blanc Moussis* of the Stavelot Carnival dress in white shrouds and hide behind masks as they roam through the town grunting and hitting people with inflated pigs' bladders (see p. 198). But not all of the masked carnival groups seek to cause such chaos. In contrast, the *cliquen* (groups) of the Basel Carnival wear masks as a kind of uniform, and process in the carnival parades playing piccolos and drums and carrying large lanterns made of wood and canvas (see p. 234).

The Catholic Church in South America is not averse to using masked characters to encourage the faithful to follow its doctrines. The Fiesta de la Tirana in Chile (see p. 90), La Diablada at Puno in Peru (see p. 92) and Los Diablos Danzantes at Yare in Venezuela (see p. 93) all feature variations of the Dance of the Devils, in which dancers wear fearsome, evil masks. The dances are strictly formalized and, after running riot through the town, the devils often undergo some degree of repentance, signifying the triumph of good over evil. The characters of the devils are often influenced by indigenous pre-Christian religions, and similar characters appear throughout the Andean region.

ABOVE Los Diablos
Danzantes, Yare,
Venezuela.

BELOW *Kurent* mask of the
Kurentovanje festival,
Slovenia.

Devilish characters also feature in carnivals in Eastern Europe. Folkloric characters dressed in hairy sheepskin costumes and adorned with horned or grotesque masks are a feature of Catholic carnivals in Croatia, Hungary and Slovenia. The *Zvončari* of the Rijeka Carnival (see p. 174), the *Busós* of the Busójárás Festival in Mohács in Hungary (see p. 175) and the *Kurents* of Kurentovanje (see p. 177) appear to mix characters symbolizing evil with regional folk characters that are said to have originated during the invasion of the region by the Ottoman Turks.

Sometimes masks are less about adopting another character and more about concealing your own, often for somewhat nefarious reasons. For Roman Catholics, the run-up to the period of abstinence of Lent sees people allowed a certain amount of bingeing. While this would normally mean gorging on

ABOVE *Touloulous* at the Mardi Gras in French Guiana.

OPPOSITE Masks at the Carnevale di Venezia.

foods that you will subsequently give up, in some carnivals it has escalated to full-on licentiousness. People normally expected to act with decorum suddenly indulge their baser natures. In some cases this has included priests and nuns, who would use a mask to conceal their identities so that they could party with impunity.

This freedom of action lies behind the adoption of masks that we see in the Carnevale di Venezia and the carnivals it has influenced in other Italian cities, such as Putignano and Viareggio (see pp. 204–5) Carnival in Venice dates back to the thirteenth century, when the wearing of masks allowed the notable citizens to cavort with anonymity, breaking any vows and social conventions. Over the years five basic mask styles have evolved, some out of historical functions, like the *Medico della Peste* (the Plague Doctor), a long-beaked mask created by a doctor treating plague victims to help him avoid infection, and the full-face *Bauta*, which was designed to facilitate anonymous civic decision-making.

At certain points in history, the wearing of masks was considered to be so subversive that it was banned. At the Mardi Gras carnivals in in French Guiana, women dress as characters called *touloulous* (see p. 91). Completely disguised with masks, gowns and even gloves, they traditionally enjoy the opportunity to flirt and even fornicate without being recognized – proof that the custom of using the mask for sexual anonymity is alive and well.

Junkanoo troupes clad in wildly imaginative themed costumes go 'rushing' through the crowds on Boxing Day and New Year's Day.

THE AMERICAS >> CARIBBEAN

> BAHAMAS

JUNKANOO
Nassau

A striking street parade, or 'rush-out', with roots in the slave plantations, Junkanoo is traditionally celebrated in towns across the Bahamas every Boxing Day and New Year's Day. The festival probably originated in the 16th and 17th centuries when plantation slaves celebrated their allotted two days' annual leave with a party that reminded them of their African roots. The celebration grew into a festival with African masks, bright costumes, drums and brass horns. Junkanoo has since developed into a full-blown carnival procession with elaborate costumes, themed music and competition prizes, but still reflects its African roots in the prevailing bold colours and pulsating rhythms of goatskin drums, shrill whistles, horns and cowbells.

Where: Nassau, Bahamas
When: 26 December and 1 January; Junkanoo summer in June and July

> BARBADOS

CROP OVER
Bridgetown

Crop Over sprang out of the sugar plantations of the 17th century when, after the crop had been reaped, the exhausted slaves chilled out with a party. As the sugar industry declined in the 1940s, so did Crop Over, but it was revived in 1974 as a cultural festival, which has grown in popularity ever since. Today, a variety of parades culminate in the *Grand Kadooment*, a carnival procession with lively costumes and floats that pulse through the streets to the strains of calypso music and the rhythms of steel pan bands. A particular attraction is Bridgetown Market, a three-day fair displaying Bajan handicrafts and culinary delicacies.

Where: Bridgetown, Barbados
When: From May to the 1st Monday in August

> BONAIRE

RINCÓN DAY
Rincón

Rincón Day is the ideal time to savour the unique culture of Bonaire, with its subtle mix of Dutch, Spanish and African traditions. The warm terracotta hues of the historical village of Rincón provide a welcoming setting for the festivities, which coincides with the current monarch of the Netherlands' birthday celebrations. The whole island is invited to a welcoming street party, with lively floats and gyrating dancers in vivid national dress. Festivities run from mid-morning until midnight, allowing revellers time to enjoy the local music and dance, sample the local cuisine and handicrafts, and immerse themselves in all things Bonaire.

Where: Rincón, Bonaire (formerly Netherlands Antilles)
When: 30 April

> CAYMAN ISLANDS

PIRATES WEEK
Grand Cayman

Pirates Week is a perfect example of a festival originally conceived to boost tourism but now a major cultural event in its own right. At its heart is the mass parade of pirate floats, differently themed each year to stimulate competition. The day is filled with street dances, games, local cuisine, parades and sports events, while the night brings its own delights with fireworks and dancing under the stars. During the 11-day event, each of the Cayman Islands hosts a Heritage Day, showcasing aspects of its own unique culture.

Where: Grand Cayman, Cayman Islands
When: Eleven days in November

> CUBA

HAVANA CARNIVAL
Havana

Every summer, Cubans take to the streets for an explosive show of colour and sound during one of the country's oldest festivals. With roots in the Cuban sugar plantations, the carnival evolved from the street celebrations held by African slaves on religious holidays. Each neighbourhood in the city forms its own *comparsa* (ensemble). Preparations start months ahead, with floats to build, costumes to produce and dances to practise. The outcome is a Caribbean extravaganza. A special Cuban feature are the seaside concerts on the Malecón waterfront, where people can enjoy Cuban delicacies against the backdrop of a Caribbean sunset.

Where: Havana, Cuba
When: July to August

PROCESSION DE SAN LÁZARO
El Rincón

As patron saint of the poor and sick, San Lázaro attracts thousands to his shrine. Pilgrims crawl on bloodied knees, walk barefoot for miles or drag themselves along on their stomachs – for the faithful, the greater the suffering, the greater the reward. Some seek material help, others hope to banish evil spirits and illness, or come to give thanks. Along the route, the faithful shower the emaciated saint with flowers, candles and coins. Although the pilgrimage was once banned by the Communist authorities, up to 50,000 people now complete the journey each year.

Where: Santuario de San Lázaro, El Rincón, Cuba
When: 17 December

> DOMINICAN REPUBLIC

FIESTA DE MERENGUE
Santo Domingo

More than anything else, the Fiesta de Merengue is a celebration of dance, especially the Merengue – the Dominican Republic's national dance. Although the fiesta was instigated only recently in 1967, it was immediately taken to the hearts of the people, who dance all over the city, in the streets, in the squares, in the bars and along the Malecón seafront. The festivities open with a colourful parade of dignitaries, dancers and bands before the concerts start in earnest. Related cultural events unfold along the boulevards, with handicraft exhibitions, market fairs and impromptu parties. People can enjoy the spectacle from a distance, or let the rhythm take over and join in.

Where: Santo Domingo, Dominican Republic
When: From the last week of July to the 1st week of August

Flamboyant troupes brighten the streets during the Havana Carnival.

> HAITI

FÊTE GEDE
Port au Prince

The *loa* spirits of Haitian *vodou* (voodoo), known locally as *gede*, run wild during Fête Gede (Festival of Spirits) on I and 2 November, when the faithful flock to the National Cemetery of Port au Prince to honour Baron Samedi, father of the *gede*. Devotees bring candles, flowers, food and chilli-laced rum. It might be the rum or it might be the chilli peppers, but things soon hot up. Revellers become possessed and dance salaciously. Some even rub laced rum over their naked bodies while in a trance, and glance around with a lecherous glint in their eyes.

Where: National Cemetery, Port au Prince, Haiti
When: 1–2 November

SAUT D'EAU VOODOO FESTIVAL
Saut d'Eau, Ville Bonheur

The sacred waters of the Saut d'Eau fall have attracted Haitian pilgrims every summer since 1847, when an apparition of the Virgin Mary appeared on a nearby palm tree. The faithful bathe in the river to wash away their sins, drive off evil and restore their health. Many leave their clothes in the water or toss them in the air, shedding their 'old skins'. As Christian and pagan creeds are often interwined in Haiti, many of the pilgrims hold mixed beliefs, part Catholic, part voodoo. They honour not only the Virgin but also the *loa* water spirits of voodoo, and some devotees become possessed. In a unique blend of Christianity and animism, the bathing takes place amid drumming, dancing and the scent of herbs mixed to please the *loa*.

Where: Saut d'Eau, Ville Bonheur, Haiti
When: 14–16 July

> JAMAICA

ACCOMPONG MAROON FESTIVAL
St Elizabeth

At the turn of each year, thousands of Maroons flock to the historical village of Accompong to celebrate their heritage and freedom. The Maroons were runaway slaves who settled in Jamaica's hilly interior in the 17th century and later fought the ruling British for their freedom. The festival also commemorates the birthday of the Maroon hero, Captain Cudjoe, who negotiated a peace treaty in 1739. The sound of a conch shell signals the start of the festival at the Peace Cave. The action then shifts to a sacred feast of succulent pork, followed by chanting and dancing long into the night.

Where: Accompong, St Elizabeth, Jamaica
When: 6 January

> PUERTO RICO

ACABE DE CAFÉ
Maricao

If you are a coffee junkie, then the Acabe de Café is definitely for you. A celebration of the coffee harvest in Puerto Rico, the three-day festival draws coffee-loving Puerto Ricans every February. Although not formally founded until 1978, the festival stems from old rural traditions of harvest thanksgiving. Today, the event has widened to include a cultural and historical dimension with an arts programme of live folk music and local handicrafts, along with exhibitions of coffee tools and utensils and all manner of coffee-flavoured foods and drinks.

Where: Maricao, Puerto Rico
When: Three days (Friday to Sunday) in February

> SINT MAARTEN

SINT MAARTEN CARNIVAL
Philipsburg

Carnival comes to the small territory of Sint Maarten for a fortnight just before the rainy season. After the startlingly early dawn parade of *J'ouvert* (daybreak) at 4am one day at the end of April, the festivities begin in earnest, with a round of feasting, singing and dancing to the sound of steel bands and horns, while street booths ply the crowds with island delicacies. The main event – the Grand Carnival Parade of floats filled with revellers in fancy dress – is carefully timed to coincide with the Dutch monarch's birthday celebrations. The festival culminates in the traditional burning of the carnival king, marking the close of festivities for another year.

Where: Philipsburg, Sint Maarten
When: Two weeks from mid-April

> TRINIDAD

TRINIDAD CARNIVAL
Port au Spain

Carnival came to Trinidad in the 1770s with the French planters and their slaves. Banned from their masters' lavish costumed balls and masquerades, the slaves developed their own vibrant version of carnival called *Canboulay,* short for the French *cannes brulées* (burnt cane), after the burning sugar cane that they carried in procession amid spirited chanting and drumming.

With the abolition of slavery in 1863, freed slaves could now participate in carnival, which they transformed with their own evolving *Canboulay,* mythologies and customs – from stick-fighting to tamboo bamboo bands, from African drums and cowbells to steel pans, from calypso to soca music.

Today, cultural contests on Sunday, Monday and Tuesday play a central role in the carnival, with intense competition to be named Calypso Monarch or Band of the Year. Modern revellers sport flamboyant feathered and sequinned fashions and enjoy exuberant partying. Street floats and parades resounding with soca music swing through the city long into the night.

Where: Port au Spain, Trinidad
When: Monday and Tuesday before Ash Wednesday

A sunny reveller, clad in dazzling fancy dress, exudes the bubbly spirit of Sint Maarten's extravagant springtime carnival.

Girls in striking folk dress strut down the streets on stilts during the Trinidad Carnival in the Republic of Trinidad and Tobago.

Carnival!

FOR MOST PEOPLE THE WORD CARNIVAL CONJURES UP THE UNABASHED
SEXUALITY OF RIO. PNEUMATIC WOMEN, BARELY DRESSED AND SPORTING
SPECTACULAR FEATHERED HEADDRESSES, GYRATE AND PUMP TO THE
SOUND OF STEEL DRUMS IN THE ELABORATE PROCESSION OF FLOATS IN THE
SAMBADROME. HOWEVER, THE TRUE ROOTS OF CARNIVAL
GO FAR BACK INTO HISTORY.

ABOVE Dancer at the Trinidad and Tobago Carnival.

OPPOSITE Enormous themed float at the Carnevale di Viareggio, Italy.

The traditions adopted by the people of Rio originated in the Caribbean islands of Trinidad and Tobago (see p. 46). They were brought to the islands by French plantation owners who settled with their slaves at the end of the eighteenth century. The French organized masquerade balls (*mas*) in the tradition of the European carnival. The slaves weren't allowed to join in the party and so organized their own celebration called *Canboulay*, after the French phrase *cannes brulées* meaning burnt cane, which parodied the slave owners' celebration. The use of steel pan drums evolved from a prohibition on stick-fighting, which the slaves circumvented by using sticks to hit pots and pans, in the process using remembered themes and rituals from Africa. Gradually *canboulay* evolved into the familiar Caribbean version of carnival.

As well as Rio, a number of celebrations around the world, particularly the Notting Hill Carnival in London (see p. 239), copy the style, dance and music of the Caribbean carnival. However, these festivals, often held in the summer months, seem to have shed their religious roots and become purely secular occasions. A true carnival, on the other hand, has a very specific religious significance and can only happen at a certain time of year. Carnival is based on the licence granted by the Church in the period leading up to the fasting and self-denial of Lent, during which the faithful avoid certain rich foods and luxuries, notably meat. The forty-day period of Lent represents the time Jesus was tempted in the wilderness, culminating in the Passion of Good Friday and the Easter Sunday Resurrection. In the Western Church, Easter Sunday is the first Sunday after the March (spring) equinox, and so the dates for both Easter and carnival can vary by as much as a month.

OPPOSITE Costumed performer at the Sambadrome, Rio Carnival, Rio de Janeiro, Brazil.

BELOW Sambadrome, Rio Carnival, Rio de Janeiro, Brazil.

TOP *Mamutzones* mask of Il Carnevale di Samugheo, Sardinia, Italy.

ABOVE Horned *Zvončari* character at the Rijeka Carnival, Croatia.

Although Lent and Easter are observed by all Christian denominations, Carnival celebrations are predominantly Roman Catholic. Carnival is thought to have originated in Italy and spread across Europe and then the rest of the world with Catholicism, but in order to win over local populations, the Church incorporated elements of existing pre-Christian folklore and rituals. In the Carnevale di Samugheo, for example, a goat character called S'Urtzu is dragged around town and then killed (see p. 204), and the Croatian Rijeka Carnival and Hungarian Busójárás Festival have similar masked folkloric characters called *Zvončari* and *Busójárás*, which are part of a pagan tradition. This willingness to adapt to local customs has meant that carnival has evolved into an eclectic and varied series of celebrations. Of the 500 festivals chosen here, forty are carnivals, and each has developed its own unique observances and flavour.

The official start of the carnival season varies by culture and country. In Germany it can be as early as 11 November, the number eleven being associated with foolishness. This is the official start of the Cologne Carnival (see p. 201), when a council is formed to plan the events. Some carnivals last for a few weeks, but most hold their most significant events in the week leading up to Ash Wednesday, the official start of Lent.

The days leading up to Lent all have their own names depending on local traditions. The day before Ash Wednesday is know as Mardi Gras, Shrove Tuesday or Fat Tuesday, as this is often the last day to eat rich food before the start of fasting. In German carnivals, this is known as *Fasnacht* – the night before the start of the fast. Monday is called Fat Monday, Shrove Monday or occasionally Crazy Monday. In the Eastern Christian and Greek traditions this day is often known as Clean Monday.

There are a number of theories about the derivation of the word carnival. Some say that it derives from the Latin words for meat and goodbye – *carne* and *vale*. Another interpretation is that the word derived from the phrase *carne levare*, which means 'to put away meat'. Yet another links carnival to its pre-Christian origins. In the same way that Christianity aimed to appeal to converted populations by the adoption of many of the pagan Yule traditions into the Christian festival of Christmas, many believe that carnival incorporated pre-Christian winter solstice rituals that were celebrated in ancient Greek and ancient Roman society and claim it comes from the Latin *carrus navalis* (wagon of ships), referring either to the ancient Babylonian Ship of Fools or the Ship of Isis, which was a part of the ancient Roman festival of Navigium Isidis.

In Babylon, the Ship of Fools was a decorated ship on wheels that was pulled to the temple of the god Marduk. Adapted from the religion of the Ancient Egyptians by the Romans, the Ship of Isis was a chariot decorated to look like a ship. These are the forerunners of the extravagant floats that we enjoy today. Impressive parades of floats can be seen at the Carnevale di Viareggio (see p. 205), where they can be 20 metres

BELOW Masked character of Mrs Fritschi, Lucerne Carnival, Switzerland.

ABOVE Parade of the Maastricht Carnival, Netherlands.

long and weigh 40 tonnes, and the Chienbäse in Switzerland (see p. 234), where twenty wagons topped with great bonfires are pulled through the town. Carnival celebrations often incorporate elements of the Greek cult of Dionysus, which also featured a boat as a part of the celebration of the transition of winter to spring, and the Roman Saturnalia festival, which revered Saturn, the Roman god of peace and plenty.

Another feature of the Saturnalia was the temporary overturning of the natural order. Masters served their slaves, men dressed as women and the lower classes got to rule over the elite. At Saturnalia a character was elected to run the festival, creating his own bizarre rules. This is believed to be the forerunner of Prince Carnival, a character like the Prince of Fools of the Maastricht Carnival in the Netherlands (see p. 209) that features in many European carnivals. This elected regent is often symbollically dispatched at the end of the festival; such a fate befalls Joselito Carnaval at the Carnaval de Barranquilla in Colombia (see p. 91), whose ceremonial burial marks the close of festivities.

Many carnivals have adopted the overturning of the natural order as a theme. In the Montevideo Carnival (see p. 93) white people disguise themselves as black and vice versa, and in the history of the Carnevale di Venezia (see pp. 204–5) the ruling elite cavorted with ordinary citizens, and priests and nuns took part in the general licentiousness. It was this suspension of the natural order that prompted the rise of the carnival mask, in part to help people to adopt another persona, but mainly to conceal their activities from their peers.

Although only supposed to involve an element of feasting on the foods that people would subsequently be giving up for Lent, many carnivals feature conduct that would never be sanctioned by the Church. In the past carnivals like Venice were hotbeds of secret sexual liaisons. At the Mardi Gras in French Guiana and the Apokreas (the Greek Orthodox Carnival) at Patras women still don masks so that they can be sexually provocative at carnival balls without being recognized (see pp. 91 and 203).

Some carnivals go out of their way to be offensive. At the Aalst Carnival in Belgium floats and parades are designed to offend, and men dress up in drag as strange characters called *Voil Jeanetten* (Dirty Jennies), who run around town pushing prams (see p. 188). At Tirnavos in Greece, ironically on Clean Monday, people carry, wave and even sit on giant phalluses, to much drunken hilarity (see p. 204).

Memorable characters appear in a number of different carnivals. The Maastricht Carnival features an old woman called the *Mooswief*, and the Lucerne Carnival is based on the imaginary Fritschi family (see pp. 209 and 235). Some feature groups of strange figures who run riot during carnival time, causing chaos and mocking the populace, often behind the anonymity of masks. At the Stavelot Carnival in Belgium, figures called the *Blanc Moussis* go crazy, hitting locals with inflated pigs' bladders, and at the Viano de Bolo in Spain *peliqueiros* run through the streets getting up to mischief (see pp. 198 and 225).

Sometimes carnivals involve activities that can only be described as bizarre. Rather than just eating food before Lent, some revellers like to throw it, such as in the flour fights of Apokreas at Galaxidi and the meringue fights of the carnival at Vilanova i la Geltrú in Spain and (see pp. 203 and 220). The Carnaval de Panamá features water fights (see p. 57), whereas the Apokreas in Messini culminates in ritual mock hangings, commemorating an old woman who was executed by Ottoman invaders (see p. 203).

RIGHT Flour fight during Apokreas in Galaxidi, Greece.

>> CENTRAL AMERICA

> BELIZE

NATIONAL DAY
Belize City

Belize's National Day doesn't just celebratethe country, but also commemorates the naval Battle of St George's Caye, fought between English and Spanish fleets in 1798, when a vastly outnumbered force of British soldiers, locals and slaves defeated the Spanish without any losses. Ever since, the victory has been celebrated with varied religious services, parades and carnivals before and after National Day on 10 September. Highlights include the Queen of the Bay Pageant and Citizens' Parade on National Day. Around the main action, a day-long fair is held in Central Park, while live bands play local music along the beach.

Where: Belize City, Belize
When: 10 September

> EL SALVADOR

BOLAS DE FUEGO
Njapa

If you chanced upon the Bolas de Fuego (Balls of Fire) unexpectedly, you'd be forgiven for thinking that you had strayed into a gang fight. Two teams of agile youths, their faces smeared in war paint, fling and dodge flaming balls of fire. Some say that it all started in 1658, when the local volcano, El Playon, spewed out blazing balls of fire. Others say that the custom commemorates the defeat of the Devil by the village's patron saint, fire-breathing San Jerónimo. However it started, the firefight continues today in earnest. Preparations begin a month ahead, when rags are rolled into balls, tied with wire and soaked in kerosene. On 31 August, the balls are lit and hurled, often hitting their target at point-blank. The only reason that the revellers do not immolate each other is that they soak themselves in water beforehand.

Where: Njapa, El Salvador
When: 31 August

> GUATEMALA

ALL SAINTS' DAY KITE FESTIVAL
Santiago Sacatepéquez

Spiralling up through the clouds, rainbow-coloured kites drift silently over the horizon on All Saints' Day in the historical town of Santiago Sacatepéquez. Down below, people mill around the crowded cemetery with eyes fixed on the rising kites, which are thought to carry messages from the living to the souls of the dead. Crafted from nothing but tissue

Multi-coloured kites take to the skies on Guatemala's All Saints' Day.

paper, cloth and bamboo, the remarkable airborne creations display ornate patterns conveying religious, folkloric and, increasingly, political messages. The high autumn winds can carry the kites far, but often rip through their fragile paper. Even if they survive their flight, the kites will be burnt at the end of the day, symbolically laying the spirits to rest.

Where: Santiago Sacatepéquez, Guatemala
When: 1 November

FIESTA DE SANTO TOMAS
Chichicastenango

In a breathtaking twist on pole-dancing, a pair of Guatemalan daredevils climb a 30m pole and leap off – precariously attached to the pole by nothing more than a rope around their ankles. As the *voladores* (flyers) plummet headfirst, the rope attached to their ankle unwinds from around the pole, spinning them safely to the ground. After these nail-biting antics, a party atmosphere spreads through the city with parades of revellers clad in Mayan masks and costumes. Fusing both native and Spanish Catholic traditions, the fiesta welcomes the Mayan winter messenger Olentzero while also honouring Santo Tomas on the last day of festivities.

Where: Chichicastenango, Guatemala
When: The week leading up to 21 December

QUEMA DEL DIABLO
Guatemala City

The devil might well lie in the details, but in Guatemala he also lurks in the dirt according to the locals who believe that evil lingers in dusty corners and under beds. To turf him out before Christmas, they roll up their sleeves on 7 December for a thorough 'winter clean'. Every cranny is swept and scrubbed. All old, worn and unwanted things are piled high on the street. A paper devil is often tossed on top before the rubbish is torched. The sky turns grey with smoke and the air thickens with soot, much to the chagrin of the environmentalists, but the Guatelmalans sing and dance in celebration.

Where: Guatemala City, Guatemala
When: 7 December

> NICARAGUA

EL GÜEGÜENSE
Diriamba

A compelling, satirical comedy, *El Güegüense* was created in the 16th century as a protest against Spanish colonial rule. Combining both Spanish and Amerindian dramatic traditions, the plot involves a series of encounters between the colonial authorities and native rebels, led by the wily old hero El Güegüense, who cleverly outwits his masters. The play is performed by locals clad in elaborate costumes and expressive, brightly painted wooden masks. As the festival coincides with the feast of San Sebastián, patron saint of Diriamba, performances of El Güegüense are interspersed along the processional route of the saint through the streets.

Where: Diriamba, Nicaragua
When: 17–27 January

The ancient Mayan ritual of *Palo Volador* (pole-flying) is a cultural and thrilling highlight of the Fiesta de Santo Tomas in Guatemala.

> PANAMA

BLACK CHRIST FESTIVAL
Portobelo

No one knows exactly how or why the life-sized statue of *El Nazareno* (the Black Christ) arrived in the small coastal town of Portobelo, but few pilgrims doubt the seemingly miraculous events that have since occurred. Soon after its mysterious appearance during the 17th century, the plague devastating Panama subsided. Ever since, pilgrims have flocked to worship *El Nazareno*, an ebony-coloured wooden effigy clad in the blood-red robes of the Via Dolorosa (Christ's route from Jerusalem to Calvary). The celebratory pilgrimage today attracts more than 60,000 devotees, many of whom walk the 85km route from Panama City – though the truly devout crawl the last kilometre on their hands and knees.

Where: Portobelo, Panama
When: 21 October

EL CARNAVAL DE PANAMÁ
Panama City

The Panama City Carnival is a wet and wild affair, notorious for its playful *mojaderas* (showers). The water fun starts early on Saturday morning when everyone is doused, whether by fire hose, water-bombs or simple buckets. Equally famous for its concerts, El Carnaval de Panamá showcases every type of Panamanian music, from salsa to reggae and tipico. Other highlights include the lavish floats and costumed parades, especially of Panamanian beauties in *pollera* dress. The glitzy festivities spill out into the squares, avenues and discos, until Tuesday's climax with the Grand Parade.

Where: Panama City, Panama
When: For four days before Ash Wednesday

FIESTA DE SANTA LIBRADA
Las Tablas

As the patron saint of poor married women, Santa Librada is particularly popular in the rural town of Las Tablas. Pilgrims adorn the saint's statue in shiny paste jewellery. Each piece symbolizes particular wishes, requested or granted. On Friday, the richly decorated effigy is borne through the town and honoured at mass. The festivities then take to the streets with folk music and dancing. A celebration of folk culture predominates with a parade of women in national *pollera* dress. Lively competitions for the best folk hats and skirts highlight the exotic regional costumes of Panama.

Where: Las Tablas, Panama
When: Thursday to Sunday in late July

>> NORTH AMERICA

> CANADA

CALGARY STAMPEDE
Calgary

Ambitiously billed as the 'Greatest Outdoor Show on Earth', the Calgary Stampede does in fact offer ten action-packed days of rodeos, parades and fairs celebrating the Wild West. At the heart of the show, the rodeo dangles rich prizes of up to $100,000 for varied contests, from bareback riding to steer wrestling. Outside the ring, spectacles abound, with chuckwagon racing a popular attraction. Meanwhile, the less equestrian can sit back and watch stage shows, concerts and farming exhibitions, and there is a Native American village to explore. First held in 1912, the event was created by cowboy entertainer Guy Weadick, who wanted to preserve the old traditions of America's frontier history. The only puzzle is why it is staged in Canada.

Where: Calgary, Canada
When: Ten days in July

CARNAVAL DE QUEBEC
Quebec

Carnival is usually associated with sultry hot days and revealing costumes. In Quebec the season, if not the mood, is quite a bit cooler. The carnival mascot, Bonhomme Carnaval, a cheerful, red-capped snowman, leads the snowy activities. Uniquely, icy attractions include the snow sculptures lining Carnival Street and Bonhomme's sparkling ice palace. Among the key events are two stunning night parades, complete with lavish floats and marching troupes. Varied festive activities fill the carnival fortnight with concerts, masquerade balls, funfairs and events celebrating local traditions, such as canoe and dog-sled races.

Where: Quebec, Canada
When: Two weeks leading up to Lent

CURVE LAKE POWWOW
Curve Lake Indian Reserve, Ontario

At the Curve Lake Powwow, First Nations gather for an annual reunion, to catch up with old friends, make some new ones, honour their ancestors and preserve their tribal heritage. The gathering opens with the Grand Entry, led by tribal chiefs, honoured guests, veterans bearing tribal staves, and dancers in full regalia. Two days of tribal song and dance rituals dramatize the mythic and historical stories that express the spiritual and social values of the individual tribes.

Where: Curve Lake Indian Reserve, Ontario, Canada
When: Two days in September

The Curve Lake Powwow is the annual gathering of many First Nation tribes who come together to celebrate their heritage in song and dance.

> MEXICO

CINCO DE MAYO
Puebla

Celebrated mainly in the state of Puebla, Cinco de Mayo (5 May) commemorates the unlikely victory of an outnumbered Mexican army over French forces at the Battle of Puebla in 1862. The triumph is replayed today with a parade of soliders in period costume. A variety of colourful floats also display cultural themes, such as *talavera* ceramics, reflecting Puebla's fame as the City of Tiles, while women parade in tasseled hats and ruffled skirts. For Mexican-Americans living in the USA, Cinco de Mayo has evolved into a celebration of Mexican heritage and culture. Street parades, *mariachi* music and picnicking take place on both sides of the Mexican border.

Where: Puebla, Mexico
When: 5 May

DIA DE LOS MUERTOS
Oaxaca

The Day of the Dead is celebrated all over Mexico, but nowhere is it more atmospheric than in Oaxaca, where native animistic and Spanish Catholic beliefs mingle in a uniquely Mexican commemoration of the souls of the dead. Quite simply, the city becomes obsessed with death and life after death. Shops sell coloured sugar skulls and all sorts of *calaveras* (skeletons) made of wax, wood and candy. Families spend the night at the cemetery and often leave offerings of food and trinkets at the graveside to nourish and welcome the souls of their loved ones. Children are especially honoured on 1 November (Catholic All Saints' Day), while adults are remembered on the following day (Catholic All Souls' Day). Despite the solemn theme, the mood is celebratory, with singing and dancing, as many native Mexicans believe that the souls of the dead return every year to visit their loved ones.

Where: Oaxaca, Mexico
When: 31 October to 2 November
....

FERIA NACIONAL DE SAN MARCOS
Aguascalientes

Mexico enjoys more than one national fair, but the one at Aguascalientes is much the largest and oldest, dating back to 1828. Initially a celebration of the wine harvest in November, it has now moved to 25 April, the feast day of San Marco, and has evolved into a general agricultural fair, showcasing local livestock and produce. Particularly popular events include bullfights, cockfights and a *charreada*, or Mexican rodeo. A large fairground caters for the whole family with rides, fair games and market stalls, while art-lovers can gravitate to the cultural fair with its recitals and plays, alongside exhibits of local arts and crafts.

Where: Aguascalientes, Mexico
When: Three weeks around 25 April
....

FESTIVAL OF THE ASSUMPTION OF THE VIRGIN
Huamantla

The people of Huamantla honour the Virgin in their own special way by laying a marvellous 7km floral carpet for her procession on Assumption Day. Running parallel to the spiritual ceremonies are the more worldly festivities of a Mexican fiesta – from cockfights to fairground rides, from donkey races to rodeos. After working up an appetite, revellers can sample local Tlaxcalan fare at the food market. On the last day, 20 bulls are let loose for La Huamantlada, the Mexican version of Spain's Running of the Bulls, in which the city's bravest race before the bulls.

Where: Huamantla, Mexico
When: 15–20 August
....

GUELAGUETZA
Oaxaca

The Zapotec civilization once dominated the Oaxaca Valley, from 7 BC until the arrival of the Spanish in 1521. For the ancient Zapotecs, reciprocal offerings, or *guelaguetza*, were a regular part of social and religious life. The Guelaguetza festival, held each summer, originally petitioned the gods, especially the corn deity Centeotl, for abundant rain and a bountiful harvest. The festival today combines a folk celebration of Zapotec culture with a Spanish Catholic overlay honouring the feast of the Virgin of Mount Carmel on 16 July. The festivities open with traditional dancing, with both men and women clad in striking costume such as the imposing demilune plumes sported by the men in the *danza de la pluma*. Other highlights include parades of bands, feasts of local cuisine and pre-Columbian crafts.

Where: Oaxaca and surrounding towns, Mexico
When: The last two Mondays in July
....

NOCHE DE BRUJAS
Catemaco

Rooted in a rich *mestizo* (mixed) heritage, the subtropical city of Catemaco has a long history of magic, combining native Indian, medieval Spanish and African practices. The city's magical tradition was unexpectedly modernized in 1970 when a local *brujo* (shaman) set up a witchcraft convention that soon attracted New Agers from all over Mexico. The idea took off, drawing shamans, witches and healers to perform a mass cleansing ceremony, which has since evolved into a major tourist attraction staged on the Cerro Mono Blanco Hill. Despite its commercial aspects, the ritual still represents a unique Mexican counter-culture.

Where: Catemaco, Mexico
When: The 1st Thursday and Friday in March
....

NOCHE DE RABANOS
Oaxaca

Although it gives every appearance of a tourist event created by the local agricultural board, the Noche de Rabanos (Night of the Radishes) has been staged in Oaxaca's main plaza during the Christmas Vigil market since 1897. Venerating the humble radish, which was brought to Mexico by the Spanish in the 16th century, the event showcases radishes that have been sculpted by craftsmen. Many represent seasonal themes, such as the Nativity, but some portray national celebrities. To be large enough for sculpting – up to 50cm long – the radishes are harvested late. Although the event lasts only a few hours, it is a unique ode to a humble vegetable, attracting thousands of visitors every year.

Where: Oaxaca, Mexico
When: 23 December
....

Days for
the Dead

MANY PEOPLE AROUND THE WORLD VENERATE THEIR ANCESTORS, CREATING

SPECIAL SHRINES IN THEIR HOMES FOR THE SPIRITS OF THE DEPARTED,

CONSULTING THEM, AND EVEN GIVING THEM GIFTS. LITTLE WONDER, THEN,

THAT SOME CULTURES TAKE IT A STEP FURTHER AND CREATE FESTIVALS

ENTIRELY DEVOTED TO THE DEAD.

ABOVE Malagasy celebrants jubilantly carry the bones of their ancestors, which they
have wrapped in fresh shrouds, at Famadihana, a funerary tradition that
takes place every seven years to honour the dead.

OPPOSITE A massive kite is held steady before being released to join the
hundreds of other beautifully crafted kites that will hover over the cemeteries
of Santiago in Guatemala on All Saints' Day.

In the northern hemisphere, many festivals of the dead take place in the autumn, when the light of summer gives way to the darkness of winter. With most originating in the days before electricity, it is natural that people's thoughts turn to the spirits of the dead as the nights start drawing in.

Cultures that believe that the spirits of the dead can still have an effect on the temporal realm have a vested interest in keeping those spirits happy, to ensure that their actions are at least benign, and at best positive. Some will do this by giving the spirits gifts, others by celebrating with a party. In Madagascar, the tradition of Famadihana, or bone-turning, involves disinterring the bones of ancestors every seven years, throwing them a monster party and then wrapping them in a new shroud and burying them again. It is a joyful occasion, and the living dance with the freshly wrapped bones of their ancestors in a ritual that is supposed to bring good fortune to surviving family members (see p. 14).

Many faiths revere the memory of dead saints, but the Catholic Church takes this a step further with a vast pantheon of saints whose countless relics can be found in churches all over the world. It is said that some saints have so many body parts credited to them that they must have had completely different physiques from the rest of us mere mortals. In the past, as many as seven churches claimed to house the head of St John the Baptist.

It is no great surprise, then, that many Christian churches have special feast days for all their saints (All Saints' Day on 1 November), and the souls of the dead (All Souls' Day on 2 November). Cultures that blend elements of the Catholic religion with their existing pagan traditions of revering the dead often choose these feast days on which to hold their own festivals.

OPPOSITE A night-time scene, aglow with burning candles, at a cemetery in Mexico where families spend the evening chatting and picnicking at the graves of their loved ones on the Day of the Dead.

RIGHT A Famadihana attracts not only family and friends, but also the whole village. This event, at which ancestors are honoured, is an opportunity for a great celebration, and no one wants to miss out on the party.

ABOVE On sale during the festival of Dia de los Muertos in Ecuador are *guaguas de pan*, pastries made from sweetened bread dough in the shape of babies.

ABOVE RIGHT Children in Mexico join in the Day of the Dead festivities by participating in costume competitions for the best and scariest outfit.

OPPOSITE A threatening devil figure dances his way through the crowds to celebrate the Day of the Dead in Mexico.

At the All Saints' Day Kite Festival at Santiago in Guatemala (see p. 56), people construct large colourful kites, up to 10 metres in diameter. These generally have a religious or folkloric theme. The kites are flown in the cemetery to keep the spirits of the dead happy before being burnt as offerings. Ecuador holds its Dia de los Muertos (Day of the Dead) on All Souls' Day (see p. 91). In a custom that originated in pre-Christian Andean culture, people visit their relatives' graves, picnic and party and leave small gifts, flowers and trinkets for them. In Oaxaca state, Mexico's version of the same event is a full-on celebration of death (see p. 58). People buy papier-mâché skulls and skeletons as well as all sorts of death-related paraphernalia and confectionary. As in Ecuador, people visit cemeteries, eat food, sing songs and leave treasured possessions as gifts. They visit the graves of children on All Saints' Day, and adults on All Souls' Day.

At the Fête Gede (see p. 45), adherents of the Haitian voodoo religion also go to the cemetery at Port au Prince to make offerings, but these are to Baron Samedi, the king of the *gede* (Loa spirits), who are believed to go on the rampage during the festival. The *gede* are somewhat frisky, and as well as leaving offerings of food and chilli rum, some of the devotees appear possessed by them, dancing lasciviously and rubbing their naked bodies with the rum.

Some cultures believe that the spirits of the dead can have valuable messages to give to the living, and have created elaborate rituals to consult them. At the Guin Festival in Togo (see p. 32), voodoo priests read a sacred stone to ascertain what the year holds

for the people. The stone's colour bears the gods' messages. The Ngondo festival in Cameroon (see p. 29) sees a man dive with a clay pot to the bottom of a river where the ancestors are believed to live. He stays down for as long as possible – sometimes as long as nine minutes – before surfacing, after which the pot is divined for messages from beyond the watery grave.

Many cultures believe that the nature of the send-off will affect the deceased's passing into the afterlife. The Toraja people of the Indonesian island of Sulawesi will store the body for months until they have saved enough for a lavish funeral. During this time the 'deceased' are referred to as sick and not dead. On the day of the funeral, many guests are invited, animals are sacrificed and a large and cheerful funeral party is thrown before the body is interred in a cave, or hung from a cliff face (see p. 148).

Sometimes people think that the spirits of the dead will harm them, and so try to drive them away. During the Fête du Dipri in Côte D'Ivoire (see p. 29) people carry out strange and bloody exorcism rites. Women and children run naked from their huts, entering trances and dancing, drinking potions, cutting themselves and smearing themselves in kaolin.

Although Halloween is now seen as a festival for children to dress up in scary costumes and go trick-or-treating, its roots are a mix of paganism and early Christian festivals of the dead. The name is a contraction of All Hallows' Evening, which is the day before All Saints' (Hallows) Day. The pagan influences on Halloween are said to originate from the Celtic festival of Samhain, which marks the end of the harvest season

BELOW A lavish and intricately painted 'temple' houses the coffin which will be processed by family members of the deceased to its final resting place.

when the door to the 'other world' is opened for the souls of the dead to enter. They are welcomed with gifts of food. The tradition of dressing up is believed to come from the early Christian belief that All Hallows' Evening was the last chance for the spirits of the dead to visit vengeance on the living, so people disguised themselves from vengeful spirits.

The Festival of Near Death at Las Nieves (see p. 221) in Galicia, Spain, is not a festival for the departed; it's a celebration for the nearly departed. Anyone from the town who has had a near-death experience in the previous year, whether through illness or accident, is loaded into an open coffin by their family and paraded around the town. If you don't have any family to hand, you are expected to carry your own coffin. The festival is held on the feast day of St Marta de Ribarteme, the patron saint of resurrection, and the coffins are carried around the local cemetery before everyone returns to town for a celebratory party. A statue of the saint is carried around while the locals chant 'Virgin Santa Marta, star of the north, we bring you those who saw death'.

Undoubtedly, the oddest festival for the dead is the Frozen Dead Guy Days of Nederland in Colorado (see p. 70). A macabre series of death-related events is held to remember the bizarre story of Bredo Morstøl, a Norwegian grandfather whose frozen body was found in a shed in Nederland. Coffin races, Dead Guy lookalike competitions and a deathly slow parade are amongst the morbid events held on this very special day for the dead.

BELOW A ghoulish character in snowy Nederland, Colorado, remembers one Norwegian grandfather at the Frozen Dead Guy Days festival parade.

SPRING AND AUTUMN EQUINOX
Chichén Itzá

The snake-trick never fails to draw the crowds to the Mayan city of Chichén Itzá at the time of the equinox. Huge crowds marvel as an ancient Mayan spectacle unfolds on the steps of the Temple of Kulkulkan, the snake-god. At around 4.00 p.m., the sun casts a ripple of light that looks like a giant snake slithering down the steps of the pyramid, where it links up with the stone head of a plumed snake. The effect lasts for just a couple of days but is most dramatic on the actual day of the equinox. To capture the sun's light so effectively, the 30m step pyramid was orientated with extreme precision by the Mayan astronomers and architects. The arresting light show has become something of a New Age happening, which is likely to grow in popularity over the next several decades as the alignment will only last until 2048.

Where: Temple of Kulkulkan, Chichén Itzá, Mexico
When: Spring and autumn equinoxes

VANILLA FESTIVAL
Papantla

Vanilla and pole-dancing don't usually go hand in hand, but both take centre-stage at Papantla's Vanilla Festival. The mountain town of Papantla lies at the heart of Mexico's vanilla-growing region, where the vanilla orchid *Vanilla planifolia* has been harvested for centuries for its sweet-smelling pods, the source of one of the world's best-loved flavours. The festival celebrates the local produce with a tempting panoply of beverages and treats, including the local *xanath* liquour and ice cream, as well as more unusual vanilla-based products, such as scent and handicrafts woven from vanilla pods. Perhaps the biggest crowd-pleasers, though, are the local folk dances, especially the *danza de los voladores*, an ancient Nahuatl and Totonac ritual, in which *voladores* (flyers) leap off a 30m pole and spiral down, attached by a long rope wound around the pole (see p. 257). According to myth, the daring ritual promotes fertility and honours the sun. As with other native Amerindian ceremonies, the Vanilla Festival is now linked to a Catholic feast, in this case Corpus Christi (Body of Christ), an occasion for all the children to be blessed.

Where: Papantla, Mexico
When: Feast of Corpus Christi (Usually June)

> USA

ALBUQUERQUE BALLOON FIESTA
Albuquerque

For nine carefree days in October, the sky over Albuquerque fills with multi-coloured hot-air balloons drifting silently across the desert landscape. Billing itself as the largest hot-air balloon event in the world, the festival hosts up to 800,000 visitors, 750 balloons and at least as many pilots every year. Some of the most spectacular sights occur at night when inflated balloons tethered to the ground glow like gas lamps, creating a sea of bobbing lights. For the people left on the ground, varied diversions include a balloon chainsaw-carving contest and fireworks displays. If the wind is too strong, though, no balloons will be launched.

Where: Albuquerque, USA
When: Nine days in October

ALOHA FESTIVALS
Hawaii

Exotic *lei* garlands of orchids, carnations and tuberoses fill the streets, festoon the floats and adorn everyone in sight during the fragrant Aloha Festivals. Created in 1946 as a cultural celebration of Hawaii's unique island traditions, events are staged across the achipelago's six main islands: Kauai, Maui, Oahu, Lanai, Molokai and Big Island. The festivities open with the investiture of the festival *ali'i* (royals), accompanied by the tooting of conch shells and traditional Hawaiian *hula* dancing. Highlights include floral parades, marching bands and processions of *pa'u* riders, each in the distinctive colours of their island. Along the route, market stalls offer Hawaiian handicrafts and tasty local fare. Run by hundreds of dedicated volunteers, the festivals attract enthusiastic visitors each year.

Where: Events all over Hawaii, USA
When: September

Participants at the investiture of the Festival *ali'l* (royals) at one of the Aloha festivals that takes place on the six main islands of Hawaii.

ANNUAL MOONING OF AMTRAK
Laguna Niguel

Way back in 1979 at the Mugs Away Saloon by the railway tracks in Laguna Niguel, Orange County, California, a local by the name of K.T. Smith wagered a drink for the next person who would moon (bare his backside to) the next railway train to pass by. It cost him a few drinks but started a tradition. From small beginnings, large crowds now turn up to moon passing trains during the summer mooning season. A number of trains roll by, so you will have plenty of time to join in – and down a few drinks in between. As mooning has sometimes got out of hand, the local police now attend to prevent excessive nudity and lewd behaviour.

Where: Laguna Niguel, USA
When: A Saturday in mid-July
....

ATLANTIC ANTIC
New York City

Once a year, about a mile of Atlantic Avenue in Brooklyn (from Hicks Street to Fourth Avenue) is transformed into a vast street festival. There is a lively street fair and almost all the entertainment you could wish for, including concerts by live bands. The Atlantic Antic is a great family event with an entire street block devoted to the kids, who will be torn between pony rides, face-painting, storytelling and other tempting activities. A popular attraction for the whole family is the vast and varied food market with myriad mouth-watering delicacies from around the world, reflecting the cosmopolitan mix of people who make New York their home.

Where: Brooklyn, New York City, USA
When: End of September or beginning of October
....

BRIDGE DAY
Fayetteville

You don't have to be mad to take part on Bridge Day, but it helps to have a good head for heights. For more than 20 years, adrenaline junkies have flocked to the New River Gorge Bridge in West Virginia to find fresh and enthralling ways of flinging themselves off. At 267m, the bridge was the highest in the world when opened in 1977. In its honour, Bridge Day was inaugurated three years later. On the big day, the road is closed to traffic and entirely given over to around 400 bravehearts. Among them, BASE jumpers sky-dive with fast-opening parachutes, while rapellers bound tirelessly up and down on 215m ropes. Bungee jumping from the bridge is, however, now forbidden.

Where: Fayetteville, USA
When: The 3rd Saturday of October
....

BURNING MAN
Black Rock City, Black Rock Desert

Burning Man is the ultimate New Age festival, attracting tens of thousands of people to the Black Rock Desert for a week of happenings, self-expression and partying. People dress up – or rather dress down – in highly personal gear. Many wear little or nothing at all. Overnight, the party-goers erect a temporary, self-sufficient desert town – Black Rock City – complete with solar-powered lighting. Everyone is then free to create artworks, moving sculptures or mutant vehicles or cycle around the desert meeting and greeting fellow travellers. On the last evening, the giant wooden effigy of a man, symbolizing summer, is ceremonially burned and Black Rock City is dismantled until next year.

Where: Black Rock Desert, Nevada, USA
When: The last Monday in August to the first Monday in September
....

CALLE OCHO FESTIVAL
Miami

Once a year, Calle Ocho (Southwest 8th Street) turns into Little Havana and throws the largest Latino street party in America, attracting more than a million people. The main event is the final Block Party, when up to 24 blocks of Southwest 8th Street host dancing, feasting and just about every style of Latin music, played on up to 30 stages. In 1988 the festival was the scene of the world's longest *conga* dance line of almost 120,000 people. In the lead-up week to the Block Party visitors can enjoy the hottest jazz at the Carnival on the Mile, along with the intensely competitive Domino Tournament, reflecting the game's popularity in Cuba and Little Havana.

Where: Miami, USA
When: One month in February to March
....

FANTASY FEST
Key West

The eclectic community of Key West in the Florida Keys throws an annual street party every October to celebrate the counter-culture that has made the island its home. Originally set up by two civic-minded businessmen to boost trade, it has grown into a genuine community celebration. Events range from charity balls to drag queen contests. Mainstream USA this is not: the highlight of the ten-day event is the parade of the newly elected conch king and queen, who lead a line of comical floats, reflecting the Fantasy Fest's refusal to take itself too seriously. Like New Orlean's Mardi Gras (see p. 72), it draws out-of-towners with its light touch, attracting more than 100,000 visitors in recent years.

Where: Key West, USA
When: The last week of October
....

FROZEN DEAD GUY DAYS
Nederland

Coffin races? Dead Guy parades? Without doubt, Frozen Dead Guy Days caters for a niche market. It all started in 1989 when the Norwegian Trygve Bauge shipped his late Grandpa to the USA, where he was cryogenically frozen at the Trans Time facility. When Trygve was deported for overstaying his visa in 1993, he shipped Grandpa off to his mother's house in Nederland, Colorado, where the body was stored in her Tuff shed, much to the chagrin of the local council, who evicted her. Fearing that her father might thaw after her eviction, she spilled the beans to the local press. When the story broke, townspeople with a wry sense of humour dreamt up Frozen Dead Guy Days. The most jaw-dropping events include a slow-motion Dead Guy parade, a Dead Guy lookalike contest and a tour of the Tuff shed.

Where: Nederland, USA
When: The 1st full weekend in March, from Friday to Sunday

GREEN RIVER RENDEZVOUS
Pinedale

The Green River Rendezvous dates back to the 1830s, when the local mountain men, trappers and Native American Indians who lived in the wilds of Wyoming would meet once a year in a valley below the Green River to trade skins and pelts for guns and tools. In celebration of the skills and culture of the mountain men, the Green River Rendezvous relives their heyday during the 19th century. For one wild weekend, the rural town of Pinedale steps back in time, with costumed pageants and Native American encampments that replay the daily dramas of the trappers, travellers and Indians who have now slipped into mythology.

Where: Pinedale, USA
When: The 2nd full weekend in July

GROUNDHOG DAY
Punxsutawney

In early Europe, farmers watched keenly for signs of spring at the end of a cold winter. The second day of February was a turning point when badgers emerging from their burrows might herald spring, if they hung around, or another bout of winter if they were scared by their shadows into scurrying back inside. The legend travelled with German settlers to Pennsylvania, where the New World's groundhog took over the badger's role. Today, the folklore has become part of popular culture, especially since the blockbuster film *Groundhog Day* (1993). The Punxsutawney Groundhog Club, formed in the 1880s, divines the weather with the help of Punxsutawney Phil, a tame groundhog.

Where: Punxsutawney, USA
When: 2 February

HALLOWEEN
Salem

Despite its scary undertones, Halloween is popular all over the United States. From coast to coast, kids dress up and knock on doors to trick-or-treat. One of the most atmospheric places to celebrate Halloween is Salem in Massachusetts. Famed for its witch trials of the 1690s, the city has embraced Halloween like no other. Festive events last all month, with tour parties and Halloween balls.

Where: Salem, USA
When: 31 October

IDITAROD TRAIL SLED DOG RACE
Anchorage

A gruelling race by dogsled across more than 1,770km of windswept ice and tundra in Alaska, the Iditarod is one of the toughest trials on earth. Teams of up to 16 dogs face extreme blizzards, whiteout, sub-zero temperatures and gale-force winds. Although the Iditarod started out in 1973 as an event to test the best dogsled teams, it evolved into today's hotly contested feat of endurance, which lasts up to 17 days and runs from Anchorage to Nome on the Bering Sea. The ceremonial start, when the ribbons are cut and the dogs take off, is the most exciting moment. An honorary musher leads the way before teams head off every two minutes. After a spirited run through cheering crowds in downtown Anchorage, the race proper is restarted the next day at Willow Lake and continues all the way to the sea.

Where: Anchorage to Nome, Alaska, USA
When: Starts on the 1st Saturday in March

JUKE JOINT FESTIVAL
Clarksdale

Describing itself as 'half blues festival, half small-town fair and all about the Delta', the Clarksdale Juke Joint Festival is a celebration of the blues – past, present and future. More than 100 acts perform over the weekend, mostly playing Mississippi or Southern blues. By day, open-air concerts resound from a dozen small stages. At night the action moves indoors to the city's surviving juke joints and blues clubs at more than 20 venues. Film shows, pig-racing and fairground amusements round off the weekend.

Where: Clarksdale, USA
When: Long weekend in April

JUMPING FROG JUBILEE
Angels Camp

The prolific American novelist Mark Twain first made his name with his short story, *The Celebrated Jumping Frog of*

Calaveras County (1865), based on a tale he had heard at the Angels Hotel in the Californian Gold Rush town of Angels Camp. Since then, jumping frogs have been the celebrities at Angels Camp, which now hosts an annual Jumping Frog Jubilee at the county fair each May. More than 4,000 fans watch hundreds of California bullfrogs compete for the longest leap. After an initial round of heats, the top 50 frogs take their places in the Grand Final on Sunday, known locally as International Frog Jump Day. Around the jumping, other events celebrate America's master storyteller with readings from his fiction, a Mark Twain lookalike contest, and costume competitions based on popular characters from his novels.

Where: Angels Camp, USA
When: Four days in May (Thursday to Sunday)
....

JUNETEENTH
Galveston
....

On 18 June 1865, 2,000 Federal troops marched into Galveston to enforce the abolition of slavery on the Confederate State of Texas. On the following day, Union General Gordon Granger read out the Emancipation Proclamation of 1863, marking the official ending of slavery in the United States. Freed slaves rejoiced in the streets with jubilant celebrations that spread through the country. The festive tradition survives today on Juneteenth (merging June and 19), also known as Freedom Day or Emancipation Day. During a fairly open-ended festival,

running from 9 June to 19 June, events range from historical tours to costumed re-enactments and stirring speeches. But it is also a time for thanksgiving and fun, with park picnics, street parades, joyous family gatherings and singalongs of traditional tunes. You can even catch rodeos, street fairs and cookouts with assorted African-American foods.

Where: Galveston, USA
When: 9–19 June
....

MIGHTY MUD MANIA
Scottsdale
....

The Mighty Mud Mania is a perfect example of an event that was originally created for quite specific commercial reasons but then transformed into a community festival. It started off as a promotional stunt for local Arizona company Johnson's Wax in 1976, when 300 locals wearing pristine white T-shirts were smeared in mud, then washed in Johnson's Wax 'Shout' Spray. The citizens took to the mud and turned the event into a festival, which now runs as the climax to Scottsdale's summer events. Mud-filled obstacle races soon have contestants swinging over mud pits, rolling around in mud baths and building mud castles. Grown-ups are free to get stuck in too. There's a rival mud festival, four years younger than the Scottsdale event, in Kingman, Arizona.

Where: Scottsdale, USA
When: Saturday in June
....

A competitor and his team of dogs set off on the punishing race across Alaska.

NALUKATAQ
Barrow

After a fruitful whaling season the Inuit Inupiat peoples of Alaska have a unique way of celebrating and giving thanks; they toss each other high into the air with a blanket made from the skins of bearded seals. The blanket toss is only a part of the festival, which serves to maintain the strong bonds within the community, as the successful whaling boat captains distribute frozen whale meat and blubber to their neighbours. The Nalukataq is considered so important that different villages stagger their celebrations so those from other communities can attend. The largest celebrations though are held in the settlement of Barrow, which also features feasting, traditional dances to an accompaniment of drums and singing. Some dances are for everyone to join in, othertimes they are displays to keep local traditions alive.

Where: Barrow, Alaska, USA
When: Usually the third week of June

NEW ORLEANS MARDI GRAS
New Orleans

Gold, green and purple – the festive colours of Mardi Gras – set the streets aglow in New Orleans every spring. With its glitzy pageants and irrepressible revelry, the Big Easy's Mardi Gras is a benchmark across the world. In French, the term *Mardi Gras* means Fat Tuesday, the last chance before Lent to consume rich food and drink. The lead-up to the big day involves a fortnight of masked balls and extravagant parades, the best occurring in the last week. The streets fill with a sea of masked revellers, swirling around the *krewe* floats and marching bands. Among the most arresting are the Mardi Gras Indians in their towering feather headdresses – essentially Africans, but dressed as Native Americans to honour the Indians who helped African slaves before their emancipation in 1863 (see p. 79).

Where: New Orleans, USA
When: Two weeks leading to Ash Wednesday

PASADENA DOO DAH PARADE
Pasadena

A spoof parade dreamed up in a California bar in 1978 as a counter-culture alternative to the traditional formality of the Pasadena Rose Parade, the Pasadena Doo Dah Parade now attracts thousands to its irreverent spectacle. It has also spawned copycat events in Columbus, Ohio, and Capital City, New Jersey. The event features groups that dress up as wild, ironic, absurd or farcical characters, including the Lawn Mower Drill Team, the Bastard Sons of Lee Marvin and the Men of Leisure Synchronized Nap Team. The parade's signature band, Snotty Scotty and the Hankies, entertains the crowds with unpredictable music and lyrics, such as the evocative *It's a 'Hi, Buddy' World*.

The irrepressible atmosphere spills over into impromptu parties where you can carry on the fun.

Where: Pasadena, USA
When: Variable – Autumn or Winter; or nearest Saturday to May Day

PRIDE FESTIVAL, NEW YORK
New York City

Both festive and serious, the New York Pride Festival celebrates lesbian, gay, bisexual and transgender (LGBT) culture. Many Gay Pride marches occur around the world but the New York event remains one of the largest. Like other gay pride festivals, it is staged during June to commemorate the police raid on the Stonewall Inn, New York, in 1969, which provoked a revolt against police treatment of gay people. During a month of varied Gay Pride festivities, some events express a carnival spirit, with farcical elements, such as drag queens, while other activities might be more activist in tone – marching for equal gay rights or throwing charity balls for AIDS. At the end of it all, a lively and irrepressibly proud parade strides through the streets of New York.

Where: New York City, USA
When: Various events in June

Gay Pride paraders march to their own drumbeat in New York City.

RED EARTH
Oklahoma City

Shawnee and Tisimshian, Hopi and Cherokee – more than 100 Native American tribes from across the continent gravitate to the Red Earth arts gathering each year, where up to 1,200 artists display their diverse and dynamic heritage. Although only founded in 1986, the festival has already grown into the foremost native cultural gathering in the USA. Red Earth opens with a Grand Parade on Friday morning, when tribal representatives clad in full regalia parade through Oklahoma City. Over the next three days, exhibitions showcase contemporary and traditional painting, sculpture, beadwork and ceramics, while ritual dance competitions display the originality and creativity of tribes across America.

Where: Oklahoma City, USA
When: Three days in early June

REDNECK GAMES
East Dublin

When Atlanta was awarded the Summer Olympic Games in 1996, there were many jokes about rednecks running the games. The proud citizens of East Dublin in Georgia decided to do just that, and the Redneck Games were born – a spoof Olympics to send up the media image of rednecks as reactionary low-brows. Since then, the Redneck Games have grown in fame and popularity. Events include the Hubcap Hurl, (a skit on discus throwing), Bobbin' for Pig's Feet and Redneck Horseshoe, where lavatory seats, rather than horseshoes, are thrown. You can enjoy the Mud Pit Belly Flop and the distinctive sound of the Armpit Serenade, alongside redneck bands, beer and food. Best of all, it's all in the name of charity... *Yee haw!*

Where: East Dublin, USA. (The Redneck Games have been skipped for a couple of years, but a similar event is held in Hebron, Maine)
When: A Saturday at the end of May or the beginning of June

ROADKILL COOK-OFF
Marlington

If you've ever craved porcupine stew, deer sausage or teriyake marinated bear, the Roadkill Cook-off offers the best menu in town. This offbeat recipe contest began in 1991 when organizers of the Pocahontas County Autumn Harvest in Marlington, West Virginia, thought it might draw the punters in for the main event. It very quickly became the main event, attracting up to 10,000 visitors annually to submit and sample the tastiest roadkill dish around. The rules remain simple. The main ingredients must be authentic roadkill – animals hit by a speeding car, such as squirrels, snakes or deer – but judges will deduct points for any gravel left on the dish.

Where: Marlington, USA
When: The last Saturday of September

ROSWELL UFO FESTIVAL
Roswell

Conspiracy theorists and UFO buffs gather at the city of Roswell in New Mexico for the annual UFO Festival to debate the unresolved mystery of the 1947 incident when Roswell Army Air Field reported the crash of a flying saucer 48km away, but later revised their statement, claiming instead that the object had been a weather balloon. The incident provoked a controversy and a cult that continues to inspire popular culture. An alien theme runs through the whole festival, with extra-terrestrial parades and costume contests for people and their pets. Sci-fi experts can debate the evidence of life beyond Earth but, with cute green aliens welcoming the punters in, the Roswell UFO Festival is probably more tongue-in-cheek than the conspiracy theorists would have us believe.

Where: Roswell, USA
When: The weekend nearest 4 July

SWEETWATER RATTLESNAKE ROUNDUP
Sweetwater

Hunting down and rounding up rattlesnakes was a traditional survival skill in the rural Midwest, but roundups today are more often carried out for money and entertainment. Snake-handlers are paid a bounty for captured snakes, which are milked for their venom and placed in a pit at the local fair before the fascinated gaze of more than 30,000 spectators. Eventually, the snakes will be killed for their flesh and skin. Related entertainments at this Texas festival include tips on snake-handling and a feast of rattlesnake delicacies.

Where: Nolan County Coliseum, Sweetwater, USA
When: The 2nd weekend in March, from Thursday to Sunday

WORLD COW CHIP CHAMPIONSHIP
Beaver

Civic pride is a strange thing. In 1970 the old frontier town of Beaver, Oklahoma, decided to put itself on the map and wondered if throwing dried cowpats might be the way to do it. The game took off and a rival competition developed five years later at Sauk City, Wisconsin. The rules of the game are fairly simple. All 'chips' must be locally produced and at least 15cm in diameter. Contestants choose two chips and try to chuck them further than anyone else. The record to date for the furthest throw is an amazing 56m. The contest culminates in a week of communal activities in honour of the early pioneers who settled in Beaver in the late 19th century, when dried cow dung served as vital fuel.

Where: Beaver, USA
When: April

A Slice of Americana

AMERICAN FESTIVALS NEVER FAIL TO SURPRISE WITH THEIR UNPREDICTABLE MIX OF WIT AND WACKINESS, GRAVITAS AND FRIVOLITY, OLD AND NEW WORLD CULTURES AND CREEDS. THE BREADTH OF THE LAND IS MATCHED ONLY BY THE DIVERSITY OF ITS PEOPLE AND THEIR EQUALLY VARIED FESTIVALS, RUNNING ALL THE WAY FROM CHEROKEE DANCES AND LATINO STREET PARTIES TO SPOOF OLYMPICS AND CARNIVALS *À LA FRANÇAISE*, SPICED WITH THE HOTTEST RHYTHMS OUTSIDE AFRICA. EVERYTHING IS POSSIBLE IN THE LAND OF THE FREE.

ABOVE A wildly glam horn player leads the spoof Pasadena Doo Dah Parade, dreamt up as a playful alternative to the stifling formality of America's more conventional festivals.

OPPOSITE The Big Easy's Mardi Gras Indians reflect America's rich cosmopolitan heritage, combining African, Native American and French traditions. Clad in fabulous, often handmade costumes, New Orleans' Black Indians honour the Native Americans who helped runaway slaves 200 years ago.

The popular vision of America as a cross-cultural melting pot comes dramatically to life in vibrant festivals across the fifty states of the Union. At the top of the continent, near the North Pole, the gruelling Iditarod recalls the dogsled treks of the native Inuit and early European settlers as they forged a route across the Alaskan wilderness. In the deep South, in steamy New Orleans, a louche and glitzy Mardi Gras combines Old World French, African and Amerindian traditions with the vivacious currents of a modern American city to produce a dynamic fusion of cross-cultural jazz, dance and masquerade that can only be experienced in America. Between the two extremes, a wealth of festivities celebrates American irony, enterprise, courage and imagination.

ABOVE Huskies strain at the leash to compete in the Iditarod Trail Sled Dog Race, a strenuous trek across the Alaskan wilderness from Anchorage to Nome on the Bering Sea. The 1,770km trail partially retraces the dogsled mail route blazed by gold-diggers in the 1900s.

'*American* irony?' you might wonder, raising a quizzical eyebrow. The British, who pride themselves on their ironic wit, are often fond of lamenting their American cousins' apparent lack of it, but no one who has ever witnessed the Pasadena Doo Dah Parade in California or the Redneck Games in Georgia could possibly doubt its existence. The US variety, though, is not a pale reflection of the drier-than-dry British brand, but decidedly more vibrant and offbeat, with lashings of unashamed irreverence and a liberal helping of slapstick. Take the Redneck Games. When Atlanta was chosen to stage the 1984 Summer Olympic Games, there were snide mutterings about a bunch of 'rednecks' – poor White southern farmers – running the Olympics. The Statist carpings soon galvanized the southern town of East Dublin in Georgia to stage their own Redneck Games – a playfully ironic send-up of the contests that rednecks might be expected to

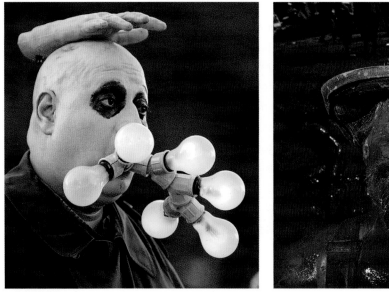

ABOVE A playful Doo Dah reveller, made-up as manic Uncle Fester, sets bulbs alight with his natural magnetism. One of the mad and macabre Addams Family characters, Fester and his clan satirize the all-American family – an ideal butt for the ironic wit of Doo Dah Paraders.

ABOVE RIGHT None the worse for his mud dip, the Redneck Games' torch-bearer L-Bow emerges from his dive in the Mud Pit Belly Flop contest.

enjoy. During one madcap day of redneck frolics, car hubs, rather than discuses, are spun haphazardly, parodying the athletic grace of Olympic discus throwers, while lavatory seats, rather than horseshoes, are tossed in the Redneck Horseshoe, and anyone might discover a hidden talent for armpit serenading (see p. 73). In a similar but rather more satirical vein, the Roswell UFO Festival, which celebrates the unresolved 'sighting' of a UFO at Roswell Army Air Field in 1947, manages to combine credulity with tongue-in-cheek humour, appealing in one stroke to both conspiracy geeks and alien fashion fans (see p. 73).

The historical Roswell 'sighting' last century is close enough for many people to remember. But the histories of more distant events need to be carefully pieced together and preserved, such as the labyrinthian route by which the legend of a weather-divining badger in Celtic Europe reached the shores of the New World and turned into the modern media event that is Groundhog Day (see p. 70).

History, though, is a relative thing and especially so in America. Certainly, compared to the Old Worlds of Africa, Asia and Europe, dating back several millennia, the USA might well seem quite a 'new' country, since the first permanent European settlers did not arrive until the seventeenth century. Long before they turned up, though, the original Native American tribes had been roaming the length and breadth of the North American continent for at least 10,000 years – possibly longer if they came across the Bering land bridge from Asia, as some experts believe. On the great plains and mountains, in the rainforests and deserts, they developed rich, distinctive cultures enshrined today in a wealth of heritage festivals, such as Red Earth in Oklahoma, where more than 1,200 Native American Indian artists from both ends of the States gather for a dynamic display of their living arts (see p. 73).

The arrival of European settlers more than four centuries ago heralded an eventful stretch of history, marked by major milestones, such as the taming of the Wild West, the American Civil War (1861–5), the emancipation of slaves (1863), the push for human rights and the rise of commercial enterprise – all now celebrated in a variety of festivals across the States. America's epic frontier story, for instance, is preserved with verve – and hundreds of hooves – in the aptly named Calgary Stampede, which showcases the now mythic life of the American cowboy and the ol' Wild West. On a quieter note, the Green River Rendezvous recaptures a less familiar aspect of America's frontier past, when the grizzled men of the mountains emerged from their solitary retreats to barter and carouse in the Green River Valley running through the wilds of Wyoming (see p. 70). Although today's rendezvous is probably much more sedate than the original drunken revelry, it helps preserve a unique slice of American history.

As the European settlers pushed out across the continent, a multitude of towns sprang up in their wake, and with them came civic pride. For modern Americans, pride in their city is still a big thing and many dream of putting their town on the world map. In an enthusiastic bid to outstrip the competition, city councils and enterprising townsfolk have brainstormed long and hard to come up with some remarkably imaginative, even outlandish, ideas for world-class events that could thrust their town into the limelight. The World Cow Chip Championship, for instance, dreamt up by the proud citizens of Beaver, Oklahoma, certainly put their city on the map, albeit for the rare honour of hosting a cowpat tossing contest (see p. 73).

OPPOSITE TOP At the Calgary Stampede a female rider demonstrates her horsemanship skills in the arena.

OPPOSITE BOTTOM Flamboyant party-goers join the fanciful masquerades at Key West's irrepressible Fantasy Fest, which draws more than 100,000 revellers to its counter-culture celebrations.

ABOVE The old German custom of observing the movement of hibernating animals for signs of winter's end has been enthusiastically embraced in Punxsutawney, Philadelphia. Here the weather-divining groundhog is held high for public admiration.

In the Home of the Brave almost anything is possible. The indomitable frontier spirit that drove early settlers to push out the boundaries re-emerges today in extreme sports, such as the Iditarod, a punishing 1,770km dogsled race across the perilous snowfields of Alaska (see pp. 70). Demanding similar courage, Bridge Day is a breezier event – though hardly a breeze – at the top of the 267km-high New River Gorge Bridge in Virginia, where the dauntless try out alternative ways of flinging themselves into the gorge (see p. 69).

On a more universal note, the same resolute spirit is reinforced on Freedom Day, otherwise known as Juneteenth, when Americans across the continent celebrate the hard-won battle against slavery, and salute the abolitionist heroes of the past (see pp. 70).

In a country renowned for its spirit of enterprise, it is hardly surprising that some American festivals should have started out as trade boosts, such as the counter-culture Fantasy Fest in Key West, Florida, or as corporate party ideas, such as the uplifting Albuquerque Balloon Fiesta in New Mexico (see p. 68). What is more intriguing is how some purely commercial sales stunts were taken up by the townsfolk and turned into full-blown communal celebrations. Mighty Mud Mania in Scottsdale, Arizona, for instance, arose out of a cleaning manufacturer's promotional event to dislodge mud from white shirts. Although the Arizonian mud probably proved too tough to shift, the stunt was a hit with the townsfolk, who have since taken mud frolics to new levels of delight (see p. 71).

ABOVE Black Rock Desert revellers discover new ways of exploring love and art through a love-themed artwork at the alternative New Age Burning Man festival in Black Rock City, Nevada.

LEFT Brightly coloured hot-air balloons are tethered, waiting for optimum weather conditions for their ascent at the Albuquerque Balloon Fiesta in New Mexico.

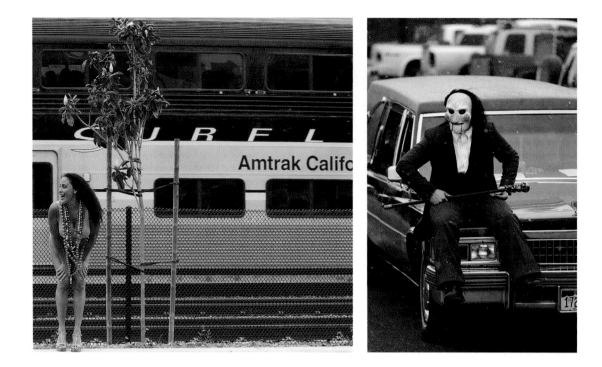

ABOVE Obliging mooners brighten up the mundane commute for passengers on trains lucky enough to pass by the Mugs Away Saloon in Laguna Niguel, California.

ABOVE RIGHT It's not everyday that you spot a ghoul perched on the hood of a hearse, but in springtime Nederland, Colorado, it's not such an uncommon sight during Frozen Dead Guy Days.

OPPOSITE AND INSET Scenes of another world at the Burning Man festival in Black Rock Desert. A week-long voyage of discovery offers 'burners' the chance to experiment with self-expression, self-sufficiency and new ways of 'gifting'.

The playful undercurrents that run close to the surface of many American festivals sometimes burst through in exuberantly wacky events. Burning Man, a week of New Age happenings and curious creations in the Black Rock Desert, Nevada, is every *dharma* bum's delight. Put on your glad rags – or take them off for the desert heat – and hit the road less travelled for an entirely new type of meaningful experience (see p. 69).

Roadkill Cook-off and Frozen Dead Guy Days, though, pander to a decidedly more acquired taste. But, if you've ever hankered after marinated snake or deer sausage, head for the Virginian Roadkill Cook-off contest, which offers a cultivated menu of choice game, with a difference – it must have been hit by passing traffic. Even more exclusive is the taste for coffin races and blue ice-cream laced with sour gummy worms – just a couple of the macabre treats in store on Frozen Dead Guy Days in Colorado. 'What, dead *and* frozen?' you might wonder (see p. 70).

Rather more prankish, the Annual Mooning of Amtrak sounds like the type of 'bright idea' that anyone might have at the end of a long stag or bar night, only to discard in the cold light of the morning after. It started in a railway saloon, where a merry Californian wagered a drink for the next person who dared to bare his backside to a passing train. The brainwave took off and is now a popular summer spectacle drawing thousands every year to shed their inhibitions, along with their pants, in a moment of playful abandon. Passing trains even slow down to allow passengers a 'decent' view – only in America (see p. 69).

>> SOUTH AMERICA

> ARGENTINA

LA FIESTA DE LA TRADICION
San Antonio de Areco

The mythic appeal of the Spaghetti Western *gaúcho* (cowboy) draws Latino cowboys and their spirited horses from all over Argentina to savour the genuine article at La Fiesta de la Tradicion. The main events take place at the weekend in the Parque Criollo where *gaúchos* gather around a bonfire and listen to folk songs over a beefy dish of freshly grilled *asado*. Sunday kicks off with an impressive parade of mounted cowboys in traditional dress. A highlight of the day is the *jineteada gaúcho* rodeo. Young horses are tied to a post, blindfolded and tormented to a frenzy, at which point a brave cowboy mounts. When the horse is released, the rider hangs on for dear life as he is bucked around the arena – usually for no more than 15 seconds – before falling off.

Where: San Antonio de Areco, Argentina
When: Ten days, early November

MANCA FIESTA
La Quiaca

Popularly known as the Pot Party, after the fine clay pots on sale, the Manca Fiesta dates to pre-Columbian times, when locals from the neighbouring highland villages gathered to barter for essential goods for the winter. Living at an altitude of 3,400m, the villagers have clung to many of their traditions, including weaving llama wool, making clay cooking pots and raising *burros* (donkeys). Today, the fiesta stages a large market fair offering local handicrafts, such as llama ponchos and clay pots, alongside tasty fare, folk music and dance.

Where: La Quiaca, Argentina
When: The 3rd Saturday to the end of October

TANGO FESTIVAL
Buenos Aires

Think of Buenos Aires and you will probably think of the tango. The city is virtually synonymous with this most passionate of dances. During the Tango Festival, Buenos Aires goes even more tango crazy, with shows, classes and mass *milongas*, or dances – in fact, the festival opens with a massive open-air *milonga* of more than 10,000 dancers tangoing through the cobbled streets. The festival climaxes with the *Mundial de Tango* (Tango World Championship), a contest between the finest dancers in the world – and a fantastic opportunity to see the tango as it should be seen.

Where: Buenos Aires, Argentina
When: Last half of August

VENDIMIA FESTIVAL
Mendoza

Vendimia, which roughly translates as grape harvest, celebrates Mendoza's successful wine industry during the first weekend of March. Although the festival began in 1936, *vendimia* festivities date back to the 17th century. On Friday, the first day of the festival, Mendoza's 18 regions are represented by 18 queens, who process through the streets aboard extravagant, vine-themed floats. The queens, in regional dress, toss harvest gifts into the crowds, who cheerfully compete for ripe grapes and gourds. Another parade of royal floats sets off on Saturday morning, escorted by mounted *gaúchos*, decorated veterans and dancers from all over Argentina. On the final day, the Acto Central folk music show unfolds in the Frank Romero Day Greek theatre and the winning queen is announced.

Where: Mendoza, Argentina
When: First week of March

> BOLIVIA

FIESTA DE LA VIRGEN DE LA CANDELARIA
Copacabana

Bolivia's patron saint, the Virgen de la Candelaria, is so widely revered for her miracles that her feast day attracts pilgrims from Peru and all over Bolivia – even new vehicles arrive to be blessed with beer. Held in the scenic town of Copacabana on the shores of Lake Titicaca, the pageant is a colourful mix of pagan and Christian customs. While the Virgin is worshipped in her basilica, folk parades snake through the rural streets, with local Aymara dancing. Finally, bulls are led to a stone corral where anyone brave or drunk enough leaps into the arena, often jumping out just as fast.

Where: Copacabana, Bolivia
When: 2 to 5 February

FIESTA DE SAN MIGUEL
Uncia

However you want to disguise it, the Fiesta de San Miguel involves a good punch-up. The mythic fight between good and evil is played out in the ritualistic *El Tinku* (encounter), where performers swing their arms wildly, inevitably hitting each other. It starts off calmly enough but, as more beer is consumed, serious punches are thrown. Tinku dances play a part in the wider celebration of the town's Catholic patron saint, San Miguel, who according to folklore, defended Uncia by breathing fire at the devil. In his honour, lavish processions of up to 36 native dance groups sweep through the streets to the sound of drums and pipes.

Where: Uncia, Bolivia
When: 29 September (Sometimes nearest weekend)

Splendid Toba warriors, dressed as fiery devils, perform the dynamic *diablada* (dance of the devils) at the Oruro Carnival in Bolivia.

ORURO CARNIVAL
Oruro

Swirling ponchos, jingling *cascabeles* and horned *diablos* – all take a whirl in Bolivia's most spectacular pageant at which more than 28,000 folk dancers and 10,000 musicians showcase Andean heritage. Originally a prehistoric Ito celebration of the earth mother Pachamama, the carnival was transformed under Spanish rule into a Catholic ritual on Candlemas but retained its native undercurrents. The highlight is a 20-hour procession along the 4km pilgrimage route to the shrine of the Virgin of Socavón, who appeared in Oruro's silver mines in 1789. Ending on a triumphant note, masqueraders enact the 16th-century Spanish Conquest and the Archangel Michael's victory over the Devil.

Where: Oruro, Bolivia
When: Friday before to Monday after Ash Wednesday

PHUJLLAY, TARABUCO
Tarabuco

With a name meaning 'play', the Phujllay is bound to be fun. The playful theme alludes to the movement of blossom in the wind at harvest time, which hints at the festival's original role as a Yampara harvest celebration. After the Spanish Conquest in the early 16th century, the Phujllay evolved as part Catholic carnival and part memorial. During the festival, a wooden fortress is erected and showered with offerings of fruit, bread and baked sweets for the Andean earth mother Pachamama. Dancers, wearing Conquistador helmets and spurs, circle around the tower. A feature of the event are the local, brightly coloured, hand-woven ponchos, shawls and skirts that take months to produce.

Where: Tarabuco, Bolivia
When: The 3rd Sunday in March

TINKU
Macha

Some parties end up in a fight, but at Tinku that is the whole point. An ancient Andean tradition of the Quecha and Aymara, *El Tinku* is a mock battle, symbolizing triumph over a foe, rival or some other threatening force. The festivities kick off amicably enough as men and women from different communities start dancing. The women then form circles and chant, while the men gather within the circle, crouch and throw out ritualized, rhythmic punches. Predictably, the fight often gets out of control and turns into a genuine brawl, where people are hurt and even killed. Police sometimes have to break up the fights with tear gas. Any bloodshed, though, is regarded as an offering to Pachamama, goddess of plenty and fertility.

Where: Various locations in the Potosi region, especially Macha, Bolivia
When: The 1st fortnight in May

> BRAZIL

BOI BUMBÁ
Parintins

Boi bumbá, which roughly translates as 'beat-the-bull', gives an Amazonian twist to the heart-warming Brazilian folktale of the death and resurrection of a village *boi* (ox). At Parintins, the tale is told in multi-media, with giant puppet shows, musical plays, masked dances and lively street parties. The outcome is a magical show for the entire community. The main action takes place at the open-air Bumbódromo stadium, where two teams act out the story over three consecutive nights, generating six varied performances. Based on their outfits and performance, the teams are judged by their *galeras* (fans). After the winner is announced, the event culminates with a parade at the Bumbódromo and a round of parties in the streets and bars of the festival town.

Where: Parintins, Brazil
When: The last weekend in June

BUMBÁ MEU BOI
São Luis

Originating in the days of slavery, Bumbá Meu Boi commemorates the story of a slave who killed an ox that was later resurrected. The folktale is a popular one, enacted in many parts of northern Brazil. In São Luis, the festival also loosely celebrates St John the Baptist, although local folklore predominates, with street troupes in costumes representing characters from Brazil's frontier history. Festivities take place throughout the island city with jaunty street parades marching to the rhythms of Amazonian and Afro-Brazilian music.

Where: São Luis, Brazil
When: 13–30 June

CÍRIO DE NAZARÉ
Belém

Reputed to be the world's largest Catholic procession, the Círio de Nazaré attracts up to 2 million pilgrims annually. After a solemn mass, the procession starts at dawn led by a floral cart bearing a small wooden statue of the Virgin of Nazareth. Devotees trail after the Virgin along the 3.6km route from Belém Cathedral to the Nazaré Basilica, where the 300-year-old statue will be displayed for a fortnight. Many devotees compete to help the teams of barefoot *promesseiros* tow the cart and, in the equatorial heat and emotional excitement, hundreds faint. After the procession, a large fair offers local produce with singing and dancing.

Where: Belém, Brazil
When: The 2nd Sunday in October

FESTA DE IEMANJÁ
Rio Vermelho

A magical sea ceremony, the Fiesta de Iemanjá draws crowds of white-robed *candomblé* devotees to the beaches of Rio Vermelho every February. With roots in African mythology, which came to Brazil with slavery in the 16th century, the tradition revolves around Yemoja, mother goddess of the Yoruba people of West Africa. Over the years, native and Spanish elements fused, transforming the deity into the mermaid-like Iemanjá, also known as Lemanjá. The custom of making offerings started in 1923 after a poor fishing harvest prompted fishermen to offer the goddess gifts in the hope of better catches. Today, homage starts at dawn as villagers place their offerings in baskets that are ferried out to sea by a flotilla of up to 300 fishing boats.

Where: Rio Vermelho, Salvador, Brazil
When: 2 February

LAVAGEM DO BONFIM
Salvador

In 1773 some Brazilian slaves were instructed to wash the Bonfim Church in Salvador, in preparation for the feast of Christ. Many of the slaves were *candomblé* – an animistic Afro-Brazilian cult – but came to identify with Christianity. Merging their creator god Oxalá with Christ, they cheerfully continued washing the church of their own accord, much to the chagrin of the Catholic Archbishop of Salvador. Hoping to quash their mixed devotions, he banned the slaves from washing the interior, but allowed them to clean the steps and forecourt. To this day, the church remains stubbornly closed while white-clad *candomblé* wash the steps and courtyard to the sound of joyous African singing and drumming.

Where: Salvador, Brazil
When: Thursday before the 2nd Sunday after Epiphany in January

Sweet-smelling gifts of flowers and scent are ferried out to sea for Iemanjá, goddess of the sea, at Rio Vermelho in Salvador, Brazil.

NEW YEAR CELEBRATION
Copacabana, Rio de Janeiro

On New Year's Eve in Brazil, more than 2 million *Cariocas* dressed in white gather on the beach at Copacabana to make offerings to Lemanjá, goddess of the sea. Some send their gifts in little model boats, while others set white flowers and candles afloat on the waves. On the stroke of midnight, thousands of flowers are tossed into the sea beneath a shower of fireworks. The veneration of the West African deity Lemanjá, or Iemanjá, came to Brazil with African slaves during the 16th century. Over the years, her worship evolved as part of the Afro-Brazilian religion Umbanda, which is related to *candomblé*, but developed its own spiritist dimension in the last century.

Where: Copacabana, Rio de Janeiro, Brazil
When: 31 December

RECIFE AND OLINDA CARNIVALS
Recife and Olinda

Overlooking the ocean on the east coast, the two adjacent cities of Recife and Olinda hold two of the best carnivals in Brazil, but the really good news is that you can enjoy both, as they are only a 20-minute cab ride apart. Evolving side by side, the two cities share a carnival style, with pulsating rhythms and exotic costumes, greatly inspired by the cultures of the African and Indian tribes enslaved under Portuguese rule. Popular at the Olinda event are the giant papier-mâché puppets towering stiffly above the crowds. Everywhere, revellers fill up the streets, cheering the puppets on and swaying to the rhythms of drums and horns. In Recife, the highlight is the Parade of the Rooster of the Early Hour on Saturday morning. Thousands of visitors join the 4km procession, moving to the strains of the local *frevo*, with its distinctive blend of Amerindian and African *maracatu* rhythms.

Where: Recife and Olinda, Brazil
When: Friday to Shrove Tuesday

RIO CARNIVAL
Rio de Janeiro

With up to 2 million people and more than 330 musical *bandas* on the streets every day, the Rio Carnival is one of the largest in the world. Carnival came to Brazil with the Portuguese and their lavish masked balls in the 16th century, but would soon take on a distinctly Brazilian quality inspired by African and Amerindian music and dance, such as the *samba*. Today, the main ticketed parades occur in the Sambadrome while glitzy balls are held in the Copacabana Palace. Outside, more impromptu recitals and parties spread along the sandy beaches long into the starlit night.

Where: Rio de Janeiro, Brazil
When: Four days to Shrove Tuesday

Leaping to the feverish rhythm of *frevo*, a carnival celebrant at the festival in Olinda, Brazil, passes the small traditional parasol back and forth beneath his legs.

SALVADOR CARNIVAL, BAHIA
Salvador da Bahia

More intimate and open-ended than the world-class Rio Carnival, Salvador da Bahia's version pulses through the sultry streets of the city gathering crowds into its vibrant vortex of merry-making. The parades are led by tram-like, 60m-long trucks, known as *trios eléctricos* and organized by *blocos* (carnival troupes). Oufitted with high-wattage sound systems linked to a band atop the truck, the musical trains throb with deafening sound. Down below, a long rope held by guards cordons off a safe arena around the truck, which you can enter by buying a *bloco*'s *abada* T-shirt. The biggest *blocos*, such as the Camaleão, might attract up to 4,000 people dancing, singing and partying. Outside the rope, crowds can grow quite rowdy. For tourists who prefer an altogether more elevated view, *camarote* balcony grandstands line the streets in the Campo Grande neighbourhood. The riotous fun climaxes on Ash Wednesday with a lively parade led by the celebrated Brazilian musician Carlinhos Brown.

Where: Salvador da Bahia, Brazil
When: The week before Ash Wednesday

> CHILE

FIESTA DE LA TIRANA
La Tirana

Every summer, the sleepy village of La Tirana awakes to the sound of pounding feet as more than 200 dance troupes go through their paces to the delight of up to 250,000 pilgrims. In a fusion of native pagan and Spanish Catholic cultures and rituals, the fiesta combines traditional folk dance with the cult of the Virgen del Carmen (Our Lady of Mount Carmel). A highlight of the event is the *diablada* (dance of the devils), a ritual for exorcizing demons. Sporting fearsome horned masks and striking devil suits, the prancing *diablos* whirl to the rhythm of drums and pipes, while the troupe leader sets the beat with whistle toots. At church, the faithful worship, while outside, a fair displays local crafts and cuisine.

Where: La Tirana, Chile
When: 12–17 June; 16th is the main day

> COLOMBIA

CARNAVAL DE BLANCOS Y NEGROS
San Juan de Pasto

The playful chaos of this piebald festival dates back to a slave revolt in 1607, when rebels demanded a day off and were granted the fifth of January. To join in the fun, the slave owners painted their faces black. The slaves responded in kind the next day by whitening their faces with powder.

The custom has been cheerfully carried on ever since, with everyone in the city covering everyone else with chalk, grease, flour or talc. The entire carnival lasts from 28 December to 6 January, but the last two days are the most eventful, when revellers runs wild, blackening and whitening each other on subsequent days. Don't think that you can avoid joining in – everyone gets covered in something white or black, whether they like it or not.

Where: San Juan de Pasto, Colombia
When: 28 December to 6 January

CARNAVAL DEL DIABLO
Riosucio

A true product of its time, the Carnaval del Diablo arose in 1847 after two warring towns, one native Indian and one of mixed black and white ancestry, were persuaded under threat of eternal damnation to pool their resources and merge into one new town – Riosucio. In memory of their hard-won amnesty, the Carnaval del Diablo overturns reality every two years for six wild days under the reign of the Devil, who is ceremonially burnt at the end. Before then, the merrymaking spreads through the streets, with lively parades of *comparsas* (troupes), many masquerading as handsome devils. At the heart of the carnival, huge, fearsome and fiery, the Devil looms over the festivities, there to remind everyone to keep the peace or be damned.

Where: Riosucio, Colombia
When: 4–9 January, only in odd years

Revellers can expect to be smeared, dusted or painted in something black or white during the lively Carnaval de Blancos y Negros.

CARNAVAL DE BARRANQUILLA
Barranquilla

Set in the sun-splashed streets of a bustling port city, the Carnaval de Barranquilla offers a heady mix of African, Spanish and Latin American spectacles and sounds, from *cumbia* and *porro* to *fandango* and *merecumbés*. Colombia's prime folklore celebration, it opens with the folkloric *Batalla de las Flores* (Battle of the Flowers), a six-hour parade of flower floats led by the carnival queen and a retinue of folk characters, from dancers to fire-breathers. On Sunday, the Grand Parade of masqueraders meanders through the packed streets. Perhaps the most haunting – the towering *gigantonas* and hooded, long-nosed *marimondas* – act out traditional stories. Spectators can also enjoy a variety of folk dances, among them the spirited Spanish *paloteo*, African *congo* and Amerindian *mico y micas*. Monday and Tuesday resonate with the sound of massed bands until the symbolic burial of Joselito Carnaval, who is mourned by everyone.

Where: Barranquilla, Colombia
When: Saturday to Shrove Tuesday

> ECUADOR

ALL SOULS' DAY
Ecuador

Roads are blocked off on All Souls' Day in Ecuador as solemn processions wend their way to the cemeteries to honour their loved ones. Celebrated countrywide, but especially in the provinces, the Catholic tradition dictates that it is a time to pray for the souls of the departed. In more rural villages, cemeteries fill up with mourners who spend the whole day at the graveside, weeding and cleaning the tombs, then picnicking and leaving food offerings for the deceased. The rural graveside customs probably stem from the traditions of the early Andeans, who believed that the spirits of the dead live close by in a parallel world. Since the spread of Christianity, mixed customs have evolved, with some Amerindian families attending Catholic mass and some Catholic priests blessing the offerings of food.

Where: All over Ecuador
When: 2 November

CARNAVAL AT CUENCA
Cuenca

If you're travelling through Cuenca during carnival week, watch out for water-bombs. Ecuador celebrates the festive week before Lent with a unique tradition of water fights, otherwise known as 'playing carnival'. In Cuenca, the water games are particularly wild, with *diablillos* (little devils) hurling not just water but also flour and eggs. A favourite carnival pastime among children is to aim water pistols at anything that moves, but especially at *gringos* (white people).

The custom dates back to the days before the Spanish invasion in the early 16th century, when some natives, such as the Huarangas, threw flour, flowers and perfumed water at each other to celebrate the second moon of the year. With the spread of Catholicism, the pagan water rite was absorbed into the pre-Lenten carnival tradition.

Where: Cuenca and all over Ecuador
When: Week leading up to Ash Wednesday

> FRENCH GUIANA

MARDI GRAS
Cayenne

As you might expect from the city that gave us Cayenne pepper, its Mardi Gras is rather a spicy affair – and not just the food, but also the dance and masquerades. Soot-blackened *nèg'marrons* play runaway slaves, while white-clad *jé farin* dust children with baker's flour, and vampirish *sousouri* paint the town red. On Saturday, the hot 'dancings' are electrified by the appearance of *touloulous* – glamorous masked women, shrouded in glitzy silks and satins – who swing and flirt anonymously with whomever they choose. The *touloulous*, named after the colourful crabs that hide in the sand, lead the action until daybreak. After the night-time twirls, revellers can recharge their batteries with traditional *blaff*, a broth of fish and shrimp spiced *à la créole*. On Sunday afternoons, the costumed parades set off again, led by flamboyant floats and ringing brass bands.

Where: Cayenne, French Guiana
When: The week after Epiphany to Ash Wednesday

> GUYANA

MASHRAMANI (MASH)
MacKenzie

The catchy Amerindian word *mashramani*, meaning 'celebration of a job well done', perfectly conjures up the spirit of this festival and what it celebrates – nothing less than the birth of the Republic of Guyana in 1970. One of the most spectacular events in Guyana, Mashramani, or Mash for short, offers a breathtaking show of float parades, calypso competitions and dizzying street dancing, against a backdrop of the wall-to-wall sounds of steel drums and calypso bands. Highlights include the spirited masquerade bands that leap and somersault in an impressive display of acrobatic dance routines, reflecting Guyana's African heritage. In true carnival spirit, a king and queen are crowned every year, which might seem ironic for a festival celebrating the birth of a republic, but no one takes carnival royals too seriously.

Where: MacKenzie, Guyana
When: 23 February

> PERU

FIESTA DE LA CANDELARIA
Puno

Honouring Puno's patron saint, the Virgin of the Candles, the Fiesta de la Candelaria is a dynamic fusion of creeds and cultures, blending the Catholic cult of the Virgin with the Andean worship of the earth mother Pachamama. Although a religious festival on the surface, it is at heart a cultural celebration of the dance, music and dress of the Quechua, Aymara and Altiplano peoples. More than 200 native dances are performed involving 40,000 dancers and 5,000 musicians, not to mention the many thousands of dressmakers, embroiderers, mask-makers, jewellers and cobblers. The festival goes out in style on 9 February with a lavish Grand Parade that takes hours to pass through the city.

Where: Puno, Peru
When: The 1st fortnight of February

INTI RAYMI
Sacsayhuamán, Cusco

In an epic display of Inca culture, Inti Raymi re-enacts the ancient Festival of the Sun when the Incas honoured their sun god Inti, the source of all life. Since 1944, the original ceremony has been imaginatively reconstructed at the ancient ruins of Sacsayhuamán near Cusco, based on the chronicles of El Inca Garcilaso de la Vega (1539–1616) and enacted by native performers to the sound of the local *sampoña* (panpipes), *quena* (flutes) and *bomba* (drums). The central nine-hour ceremony occurs on 24 June, although several days of processions and street parties precede the main event. Authentic versions of Inti Raymi are still celebrated among the Quechua people today, with traditional music and costume, such as the dramatic *aya huma* mask.

Where: Cusco, Peru
When: 24 June

LA DIABLADA
Puno

The Devil prowls around Lake Titicaca under the guise of *la diablada*, a dramatic masked dance performed by *diablos* wearing devil suits and intimidating horned masks. With roots in both Spanish and Andean cultures, *la diablada* combines the traditions of Christian morality plays with pagan dance ceremonies, such as the *llama llama*, which honoured the gods of the lakes, rivers, caves and mines. The origins of the dance, whether Bolivian or Chilean, are keenly debated. Whatever the verdict, *la diablada* offers a unique blend of Christian and native Amerindian rituals.

Where: Puno, Peru
When: The week before 5 November

Against a backdrop of Inca ruins, local actors dramatize the ancient Inca Inti Raymi (Festival of the Sun) at Cusco, Peru.

LORD OF MIRACLES
Lima

The most revered icon of the city of Lima has enjoyed a charmed life, having survived a great earthquake in the 18th century and all attempts to destroy it. Known as the Lord of Miracles, it depicts the Crucifixion of a dark-skinned Christ, apparently a copy of a mural painted by an Angolan slave in the 17th century. Every October, in a ritual more than 200 years old, the Lord of Miracles is paraded through the streets in a 2t silver litter borne by the Brotherhood of Incencers. Thousands of pilgrims, many barefoot and clad in penitential purple, trail behind, singing and praying all the way.

Where: Lima, Peru
When: 18–28 October

VIRGEN DEL CARMEN
Paucartambo

The quiet mountain village of Paucartambo fills with the sounds of fiesta on the feast of the Virgen del Carmen (Our Lady of Mount Carmel), a spirited local festival renowned for its folk dances and exotic masks. As with many Christian cults in the Andes, it expresses a creative synthesis of Christian and pagan traditions. The Virgin Mary is part mother of God and part Pachamama, Andean earth mother. After mass, she is borne through the milling crowds, closely guarded by masked *cojuntos* (troupes). Different *cojuntos* enact folktales celebrating Andean heroes and fabulous creatures, such as the bear-like *Ukukus*. Cavorting around, the demonic *Saqra* try and disrupt the proceedings, but the Virgin banishes them from the town. The triumphant procession climaxes in a joyful explosion of fireworks and dancing through the night.

Where: Paucartambo. Peru
When: Three or four days around 16 July

> SURINAME

OWRU YARI
Paramaribo

The old year is seen out with a bang in the capital of Suriname, where the Chinese tradition of firecrackers livens up the occasion, leaving the streets carpeted in red fireworks paper and the air thick with the scent of gunpowder. The aim is to scare off the old spirits, ready for a fresh start in the New Year. The party continues into the night, getting more raucous as midnight approaches, culminating in a furious salvo as the clocks strike the magic hour.

Where: Paramaribo, Suriname
When: 31 December

> URUGUAY

FIESTA DE LA PATRIA GAÚCHA
Tacuarembó

The picturesque Lake of the Sandpipers is the idyllic setting for a cultural celebration of the *gaúcho* (cowboy) tradition. Although founded in 1985, the fiesta showcases a 200-year-old history. After the carnival royals are elected, lively processions take off on spirited horses. Much of the action unfolds in a rodeo stadium where gifted *gaúchos* display their virtuoso skills of the *rodeo*. Related leather crafts and grilled cuisine can be sampled while enjoying vivid displays of native dance and dress.

Where: Tacuarembó, Uruguay
When: The 1st week of March

MONTEVIDEO CARNIVAL
Montevideo

The roots of the Montevideo Carnival lie in the cruel days of slavery, when African slaves sought consolation and found inspiration in their native song, dance and music, which they were able to revive on rare holidays. The upbeat festival reflects many features inspired by African culture, not least the drum-based *candombe* rhythm. Another vestige of slavery is the practice of *lubolos* (painting white people black), which is not meant as an insult but as an effort to take part and break down barriers. A highlight is the *Desfile de las Llamadas* (Parade of the Calls), a lavish parade with elaborate floats, exotic costumes and resonant *candombe*. The tradition harks back to the days when slaves called to each other across the crowds with their *tambores* (drums).

Where: Montevideo, Uruguay
When: Monday and Tuesday before Ash Wednesday

> VENEZUELA

FIESTA DE SAN JUAN BAUTISTA
Barlovento

The sound of the Fiesta de San Juan Bautista is the sound of the tall *culo e' puya* drums beating out the rhythms of the African soul. As with many festivals in the Americas, the vibrant mix of Spanish, Amerindian and African traditions stems from the days when slaves kept their culture alive with music and dance. After a night resounding with music, a statue of St John the Baptist is borne through the streets to the rhythmic beat of the drums and the strains of improvised songs expressing the joys and sorrows of life. Many wear white, representing the *Santarismo* faith, an animistic religion with roots in the Yoruba culture of West Africa. The night of the saint is regarded as particularly magical, a propitious time to look into the future and cast a few good luck spells.

Where: Barlovento, Venezuela
When: 24 June

DIABLOS DANZANTES DEL YARE
St Francisco de Yare

The timeless struggle between good and evil is a recurring theme in Latin American festivals. On Corpus Christi in Yare, red-clad demons leap and whirl through the town. Despite their grotesque masks, they are adorned with crosses and rosaries, intended to protect the dancers from the evil they embody. In front of the church, the demons thrash around in a symbolic contest between good and evil. It's a close-run thing but at the eleventh hour, the *diablos* kneel in penitence, before dancing off to the rhythm of the *bamba*.

Where: St Francisco de Yare, Venezuala
When: Corpus Christi, May/June

>> ASIA

> CHINA

BAI TORCH FESTIVAL
Zhangjiajie

The flaming centrepiece of the Bai Torch Festival is a giant torch, which blazes in the village square to honour the god of fire and scare off evil. Although the festival is celebrated throughout south-west China, the Bai stage a particularly elaborate spectacle. On the eve of the festival, the 20m torch is fashioned from pine and bamboo and strung with auspicious banners, lanterns and fireworks.

The next morning, the Bai don traditional costume and proceed in a torchlit procession to honour their ancestors at the communal tombs. As night falls, young men set the torch alight to the sound of drum rolls, firecrackers and cheers. People circle the torch three times for luck and compete to catch the auspicious burning bamboo. Across the village, houses light up with torches, while in the darkness amber torchlight flickers through the fields as people scare away pests. The ceremony culminates with traditional torch-playing as young men and women joyfully greet each other with torches that blaze when sprinkled with inflammable powder. The flare is thought to banish evil and bestow good luck.

Where: Bai communities, Zhangjiajie, China
When: The 24th 25th day of the 6th lunar month

CHEUNG CHAU BUN FESTIVAL
Hong Kong

A million miles from the soaring skyscrapers of the financial district, a quaint bun festival takes place every year – usually in early May – on the outlying island of Cheung Chau. The buns in question are attached to 20m-high bamboo poles in front of Pak Tai Temple, which young men race up to snatch as many of the buns as they can. Until recently it was a free-for-all but now the competition is regulated for safety reasons – and the buns are made of plastic. Legend has it that the festival originated in the 18th century, when islanders prayed for deliverance from pirates. Nowadays it extends over a week, during which islanders stop eating meat and throw themselves into parades and ceremonial dances – then gather for the bun-snatching spectacle.

Where: Hong Kong, China
When: Early May

CHINESE NEW YEAR
Hong Kong

No one celebrates New Year quite like the Chinese. In cities all over China, and in Chinatowns all over the world, they throw unforgettable parties on the first day of the first lunar month, between late January and late February. But the biggest and best occurs in Hong Kong, where the main event is a huge night parade of floodlit floats around the Tsim Sha Tsui area of Kowloon. On the stroke of midnight, thousands descend on the Sik Sik Yuen Wong Tai Sin Temple, where Buddhism, Taoism and Confucianism are all practised, to make offerings and wishes for the future.

Then focus turns to the celebrated Hong Kong skyline and harbour, which are lit up in a firework display of dazzling pyrotechnics.

Where: Hong Kong, China
When: The 1st day of the 1st lunar month

CORBAN FESTIVAL
Xinjiang Uygur Autonomous Region

In the days leading up to the festival, dozens of Chinese sheep, cattle and goats can be seen being herded into pens and loaded into vans, and crowded into bazaars across north-west China, in preparation for the Muslim feast of Corban, which means 'sacrifice'. The ceremonial slaughter of livestock enacts the legend of the pious Muslim Ibrahim who had been commanded by Allah to sacrifice his son but was spared at the last moment by the appearance of an angel bearing a sacrificial goat. Ever since, Muslims have shown their obedience to Allah during Corban by ritually sacrificing goats and other livestock. Before the feast, the faithful gather in mosques for prayer and later celebrate with dancing and singing, while the young let off steam by racing horses – and chasing after goats.

Where: Xinjiang Uygur Autonomous Region, China
When: From the 10th to 13th day of 12th Muslim month of Dhu al-Hijjah

DUANWU JIE
Hunan Province

Horned, crested, fanged and scaled – there's no mistaking a dragon boat. A resplendent flotilla skims along the Mi Lo and Yangtze Rivers every year during Hunan's spirited Dragon Boat Festival. It all started in 278 BC when the Chu poet Qu Yuan drowned himself in protest at the invasion of his beloved country by the hated Qin state. As he was popular among the locals, many fishing boats sped after him, while well-wishers on the bank beat drums to scare off evil spirits, and tossed *zonghi* rice parcels into the river to enlist the aid of the dragon god of the ocean. Ever since, the Chinese have remembered Qu Yuan (see p. 96). In Hunan, they celebrate the poet in their own special way by racing dragon boats while beating drums furiously to ward off evil spirits, and feasting on *zonghi* washed down with sweet rice wine. The evening finishes off with dancing and another round of rice wine beneath a shower of sparkling fireworks.

Where: Mi Lo and Yangtze Rivers, Hunan Province, China
When: The 5th day of the 5th lunar month

An ice extravaganza where more than 20,000 cubic metres of snow and ice are used by the world's best ice sculpture artists to make 1,500 amazing sculptures.

HARBIN INTERNATIONAL ICE AND SNOW FESTIVAL
Harbin

Certainly there is no better place than Harbin for the making of ice sculptures – the raw material lies around in abundance during the winter, when the city's sparkling Ice and Snow Festival is held. Harbin's celebration of all things frozen is surprisingly modern; it started in 1963, was suspended during the Cultural Revolution (1966-76) and resumed in 1985. But its origins go back to the Qing Dynasty (1644–1912), when local fishermen fashioned ice lanterns by hollowing out a bucket-shaped block of ice and placing a candle inside. Nowadays, for a month starting in early January, experts craft elaborate and increasingly large sculptures that are displayed throughout the city but principally on two exhibition sites where they are imaginatively illuminated at night.

Where: Harbin, China
When: One month from 5 January

PO SHUI JIE
Jinghong

A lively and rather wet New Year festival, much in the spirit of Thailand's soggy Songkran Festival, Po Shui Jie is celebrated with happy abandon by the Dai people of north-west China. Clad in traditional dress, old and young carry water buckets and urns to the local Buddhist temple. After ritually bathing the Buddha figures, everyone joyfully douses everyone else, symbolically washing away the old year and splashing on the blessings of the coming year. Predictably, water fights can turn from respectful sprinklings into full-blown drenchings, but the greater the deluge, the greater the rewards.

Where: Jinghong, China
When: Mid-April

QIANG NEW YEAR FESTIVAL
Qiang

Since the Wenchuan earthquake in 2008, when many Qiang stone villages were destroyed, the Qiang New Year celebration has been listed by UNESCO as an Intangible Cultural Heritage in Need of Urgent Safeguarding. As the Qiang have not developed writing, their 1,000-year-old culture has been kept alive by word of mouth and ancient ritual, of which the New Year is a prime example. It is a time not only for thanksgiving – for the harvest and the bounty of nature – but also for preserving Qiang heritage through *salang* dances and chanted epics. The elders and *shibi* (priests) lead the festivities with the sacrifice of a goat to the gods of the earth, after which everyone gathers around for a day of communal feasting, chanting and merrymaking.

Where: Qiang, China
When: The 1st day of the 10th lunar month

GRAND SUMMONS, LABRANG MONASTERY
Xiahe

Labrang Monastery, built in the early 18th century, is a holy site for Tibetans, who make up a sizeable part of the population of Gansu in north-west China. A centre of both worship and learning, the monastery boasts thousands of figures of the Buddha, from large to thimble-sized, and every year hosts a series of seven 'summons ceremonies' that draw monks and pilgrims from the surrounding grassland areas. The biggest, known as the Grand Summons, which takes place from January to February, stages a succession of events including the Freeing of Captive Animals Festival, the Sun-Bathing Buddha Festival and a masked *cham* dance. During this period the monks gather six times a day in the Grand Sutra Hall to recite Buddhist scriptures.

Where: Labrang Monastery, Xiahe, China
When: From the 3rd to 17th day of the 1st lunar month

GRAND SUMMONS, TAR MONASTERY
Qinghai Province

The mountain monastery of Tar is a mecca for Buddhist *lamas*, who obey the quarterly summons to gather for a concentrated period of spirituality during eight chant-filled days of prayer, meditation and philosophical debate. Pilgrims and tourists also come to marvel at the monastery's treasures, such as its elegant religious murals and unique relief embroidery. Particularly spellbinding are the *vijra* masquerades designed to protect *dhama* (virtue). Tar is also renowned for its winter butter sculptures, a tradition learnt from the Tibetans but taken to dizzying new levels by the Tar monks (see pp. 00). Other highlights include the parade of a golden buddha and the ceremonial unfurling of the monastery's silk *thanka*, a symbolic image used in meditation.

Where: Tar Monastery, Qinghai Province, China
When: From the 14th to 15th day of the 1st and 4th lunar months; the 7th to 8th day of the 6th lunar month; and the 22nd to 23rd day of the 9th lunar month

SISTERS' MEAL FESTIVAL
Shi'Dong

If you live high in the mountains, it isn't always easy to find a mate, which is why the Sisters' Meal Festival is a magnet for many young villagers of the ethnic Hmong scattered among the highlands of South-east Asia and southern China, where they're known as Miao. Families come by boat, van and on foot for the most popular party of the year. Many carry heavy baggage containing the girls' spectacularly ornate silver jewellery, including towering phoenix coronets, high silver chokers, tasselled breastplates and aprons of silver plaques. Bedecked in their glittering heirlooms, the girls are literally draped in silver from head to foot. The party warms up along the river, where the young women swirl in a measured dance to the mellow sound of the bamboo *lusheng*, beaten by a pair of obliging grandmothers. Handsome youths in royal blue tunics and red caps stand around gazing admiringly at the girls, until moved to hand out a rice parcel or two. If the parcel is returned with two chopsticks, they're in luck. While the younger generation get acquainted, the elders make the most of the day-long markets, chinwags with old friends and noisy cockfights.

Where: Shi'Dong, Guizhou, China
When: The 15th and 16th day of the 3rd lunar month

TUEN NG FESTIVAL
Hong Kong

Otherwise known as the Dragon Boat Festival, this quintessentially Chinese waterborne celebration commemorates the poet Qu Yuan, who drowned himself more than 2,000 years ago in protest at corrupt rulers. Dragon boats – large war canoes with a dragon's head on the bow and a dragon's tail trailing from the stern – are hugely eye-catching vessels. In the 1980s Hong Kong fishermen organized an international race and, since then, interest in dragon-boat racing has taken off across Asia. But nowhere is it more widely attended than in Hong Kong, which has over 30,000 regular participants and hosts various events throughout the year. The most spectacular, and traditional, is the Tuen Ng Festival in June, when the racing is accompanied by the making and eating of rice dumplings.

Where: Hong Kong (and all over China, see p. 94)
When: Double 5th (5th day of the 5th month of the Chinese calendar)

YI TORCH FESTIVAL
Sichuan

The Yi have a unique way of despatching their demons. When last troubled by a devil, their ancestors chased him off with fire by binding torches to the horns of their goats

and driving the obliging creatures into the demon's lair. Since then, the Yi have celebrated their victory over evil by lighting torches for a night of merrymaking.

In recent years the tradition has widened to include daytime events as well, such as concerts of instrumental music and varied sporting contents – from archery to bullfighting and wrestling. To round off the festivities, crowds gather round bonfires and dance the hours away beneath a glittering shower of fireworks.

Where: Sichuan, China
When: The 24th to 26th day of the 6th lunar month

ZIGONG LANTERN SHOW
Zigong

All over China, the town of Zigong is synonymous with lanterns. The people here have been creating traditional Chinese lanterns and putting on elaborate lantern displays since the Tang Dynasty (618–907). Held as a part of Sichuan's Spring Festival, the month-long Zigong Lantern Show features thousands of exquisitely fashioned Chinese lamps, both traditional and contemporary in style. Most are crafted from thin bamboo strips covered with painted silk or coloured paper. Although each lantern is a delight in its own right, some of the most spectacular displays involve clusters of lanterns artfully bundled together in the shape of dragons, dinosaurs or temples. Today many lanterns are illuminated by electricity rather than by candlelight, which can cause blackouts during peak lantern time. The dazzling light show provides the ideal backdrop for trade fairs and conferences.

Where: Zigong, China
When: Around the Spring Festival, from early February to March

> JAPAN

ASAKUSA SANJA MATSURI
Asakusa, Tokyo

'Take up thy shrine and walk' sums up this exuberant festival, which takes place over the third weekend of May in the Tokyo neighbourhood of Asakusa. Thousands of devotees shoulder *mikoshi* (portable shrines) and parade through the streets adjoining the Asakusa Shrine, watched by more than a million people. There is a religious basis to the event – celebrants honour the spirits of the three men who founded the Senso-Ji Temple in the 7th century – but the festival has a reputation for being wild and sometimes drunken and takes place against an unrelenting background noise of drumming. The most feverish moments are when the shrines are jolted, the action is believed to intensify the power of the deities carried within the shrines.

Where: Asakusa, Tokyo, Japan
When: The 3rd full weekend in May (Friday to Sunday)

CHICHIBU YOMATSURI
Chichibu City

This one's a real winter warmer, based around the city's Shinto shrine. Huge floats – weighing up to 20t – are on display at the 2,000-year-old Chichibu Shrine before being pulled through the streets up to the plaza in front of the city hall. Decorated with lanterns, tapestries and gilded wood, some floats are big enough to stage *kabuki* theatre. The climax, during which participants are guaranteed to work up a sweat, is when the floats are hauled up a steep slope to the plaza on the final evening. The reward is a spectacular firework display lighting up the winter sky.

Where: Chichibu City, Japan
When: 2 and 3 December

DAIROKUTEN-NO-HADAKA MATSURI
Yotsukaido

Mud-slinging takes on new meaning at this so-called 'naked' festival, which is part of the Shinto religion. These muddy events occur all over Japan but one of the biggest and best takes place in Yotsukaido, south-east of Tokyo, in late February. There is method in the apparent madness. Youths wearing only *fundoshi* – loincloths – run from the Musubi-jinja Shrine to the nearby lake, where they cover themselves and each other in mud before returning to the shrine to give thanks for the rains and pray for a good harvest. Water and earth are symbols of plenty for without them the rice would not grow. And so for one day in the year mud, glorious mud gets the recognition it deserves.

Where: Musubi-jinja Shrine, Yotsukaido, Japan
When: The 3rd weekend of February

DORONKO MATSURI
Nagahama, Kochi City

If you're passing through Nagahama in April, it would be wise to beware cheerful women bearing mud. The Doronko Matsuri is nicknamed the Hen-pecked Mud Festival with good reason. The women, armed with dollops of the sticky brown stuff, chase after their menfolk to smear their faces in mud. If they manage to hit their mark, the muddied man will enjoy good health throughout the coming year. It all starts quite soberly with a rice-sowing ritual, during which women in farming dress solemnly plant rice in a paddy field. Things soon liven up, though, as laughing women rush up to intended recipients to perform a little 'muddying', for which favour the grimy guys duly express their gratitude. The 400-year-old custom, centred around the Wakamiya Hachimangu Shrine, quite possibly stems from ancient fertility rites or from a thanksgiving ritual after the eradication of an epidemic.

Where: Nagahama, Kochi City, Japan
When: April. Similar Festival in Shirokawa, Ehime in July

Giant lantern-lit floats set the city aglow during Chichibu's Night Festival.

GION MATSURI
Kyoto

In Kyoto, the beautiful former imperial capital, July is given over to one of the most famous festivals in Japan, named after the Gion district in which it takes place. The highlight is a spectacular procession of 32 elaborately decorated floats, some 25m high. The festival is said to date from the 9th century, when it was inaugurated to appease the gods after an outbreak of disease. Borne along in the triumphal procession is a local boy who has been chosen as a 'divine messenger' and is forbidden to set his feet on the ground for four days, until he has been paraded through the city.

Where: Kyoto, Japan
When: Throughout July. Parades on 17 and 24 July

HADAKA MATSURI
Saidaiji-naka

It sounds like a Shinto variant of the English Eton Wall Game. A priest throws two holy sticks from a window above a crowd of 9,000 loincloth-wearing men who fight each other for possession of the sticks. The wonderfully absurd and dramatic spectacle unfolds in the Saidaiji-naka district of Okayama on the third Saturday of February. The sticks are just 20cm long and 4cm in diameter, so getting and hanging on to one is a bit like finding a needle in the proverbial haystack, but the lucky man who manages to do so, and then succeeds in placing it upright in a box of rice, is said to be blessed with a year of happiness.

Where: Saidaiji-naka, Japan
When: The 3rd Saturday of February

HAKATA GION YAMAKASA
Hakata, Fukuoka

Brawn, stamina, speed and grace in equal measure are demanded on 15 July when runners bear decorative floats through the city of Fukuoka during a 750-year-old ceremony. Brawn and stamina are needed to bear the weight of 1t floats along a 5km circuit. Speed is vital if your team is to win the race. Grace is the final challenge, perhaps the hardest, as the runners, clad only in loincloths and short *happi* shirts, strain and grimace to bear their load, let alone look good. The richly decorated floats are displayed at street corners from 1 July, but the main race takes place on 15 July, when up to a million spectators turn up to cheer on the sporting runners.

Where: Hakata, Fukuoka, Japan
When: 10–15 July

HOUNEN MATSURI
Komaki

In Europe we content ourselves with springtime maypoles, but in the small town of Komaki they celebrate fertility and the promise of a rich harvest by parading a giant wooden phallus through the streets – all 2.5m of it. As if that were not enough, revellers tuck into free *saké* and ostentatiously lick phallic-shaped lollypops as the *membrum virile* makes its way to one of two Shinto shrines in Komaki, depending on whether it is an odd or even year.

Where: Komaki, Japan
When: 15 March

KANAMARA MATSURI
Kawasaki

A strange one, this – in the industrial city of Kawasaki, they celebrate the Festival of the Steel Phallus in which said object is paraded through the streets amid predictably ribald and drunken revelry. In recent years the event has been somewhat taken over by the city's transvestite community and by incredulous foreign tourists, but its origins are ancient and complex. Prostitutes once venerated the male member at a local shrine, and prayed there for protection against sexually transmitted diseases.

Where: Kawasaki, Japan
When: First Sunday in April

KANTO MATSURI
Akita City

Hundreds of skilled performers give a new meaning to pole dancing every summer in the northern city of Akita during a Shinto offering for a good harvest. A *kanto* is a bamboo pole, which can be as long as 12m and as heavy as 50kg. Suspended at the top of the pole, up to 46 paper lanterns, symbolizing bags of rice, sway precariously. The trick is to hoist the pole aloft and keep it upright for as long as possible, whether grasped single-handedly or balanced on the forehead, shoulder or hip. It all takes place to a furious accompaniment of drums, flutes and chanting spectators.

Where: Akita City, Japan
When: 3–6 August

A sea of pink blossom above and a sea of admirers below. Picnicking beneath the *sakura* (cherry blossom) is a centuries-old custom that is avidly followed today, and the ceremonial viewing of cherry blossoms is one of the most important dates on the Japanese calendar.

KONAKI SUMO
Tokyo

The Japanese proverb, *Naku ko wa sodatsu* ('Crying babies grow fast'), helps explain this rather bizarre 400-year-old tradition, in which student sumo wrestlers, each grasping a squirming baby, face each other, and wait to see which child will howl first. If being held by a sumo wrestler isn't enough to start any baby wailing, a Shinto priest is on hand to scare the little ones with loud shouts and waving arms. If it's a draw, the baby who cries loudest is deemed the winner and will enjoy good health. After all the *konaki* (crying), prayers are said for the babies. The event is held in temples all over Japan but is particularly popular at the Sensoji Temple in Tokyo, which attracts almost 100 babies every April.

Where: Sensoji Temple, Tokyo, Japan
When: April

NACHI-NO-HI MATSURI
Kumano Mountains, Nachisan

Fire, water and the number 12 are the principal elements of this beautiful and mysterious ritual that takes place at the sacred Nachi-no-Otaki Falls. On 14 July, 12 portable shrines – 6m tall and fashioned to represent the waterfall – are carried on the shoulders of devotees to the Kumano Nachi-taisha Shrine where they encounter men carrying 12 50kg pine torches representing both the 12 gods said to dwell in the Kumano Mountains, and the 12 months of the year. A ritual dance ensues in which the floats are almost, but not quite, set alight in a symbolic purification. Shrines and torches are then taken to the awesomely high, 133m waterfall for the climax of the ceremony, when the water spirit is invoked to bestow his blessings.

Where: Kumano Mountains, Nachisan, Japan
When: 14 July

OKOSHI DAIKO
Hida-Furukawa

Once night falls, a giant drum – the *Okoshi Daiko* – positioned on top of a wooden tower is carried through the streets of Hida-Furukwa by hundreds of men wearing only loincloths. Sitting astride either end of the drum are two men who strike it in turn. Following the *Okoshi Daiko* are 12 teams from different neighbourhoods, each carrying a smaller drum, a *Tsuke Daiko*, attached to a pole. As the streets become congested, and the crowds more rowdy, the 12 teams jostle and shove each other as they attempt to achieve prime 'pole position' – as close as possible to the *Okoshi Daiko*. If you're in the crowd, stand well back as spectators have been known to get dragged into the argy-bargy.

Where: Hida-Furukawa, Japan
When: 19 and 20 April

OMIZUTORI
Nara

In a country of ancient religious festivals, this is one of the oldest, dating back to the 8th century. Omizutori, which means 'drawing sacred water', refers to a specific event in a series of rituals that take place over two weeks in March in the town of Nara. Each evening priests carry giant torches up to the balcony of Nigatsudo Hall in Todai-ji Temple and shower embers down on to the crowds below – ironically, in order to bestow upon them a safe and happy future. Finally, they descend from the balcony to draw water from a well at the base of the temple that is said to be dry at every other time of year and to have restorative powers.

Where: Todai-ji Temple, Nara, Japan
When: The 1st fortnight in March; water drawn on 13th

ONBASHIRA MATSURI
Nagano

This festival doesn't happen very often – once every six years, in the Chinese years of the Monkey and Tiger – but when it does, the participants celebrate for two months. *Onbashira* translates as 'honoured pillars' and involves the ceremonial felling and planting of four huge tree trunks in a symbolic renewal of the four temples that make up the Shinto shrine of Suwa Taisha in Nagano. The trees, measuring up to 17m long, are ceremonially felled in the mountains and dragged down towards the shrine with ropes. As the huge logs skitter over rough terrain, adventurous young men demonstrate their bravery and devotion by riding them down the mountainside. At the shrine, the logs are hoisted vertically, with many of the riders still clinging on and singing as they rise.

Where: Lake Suwa, Nagano, Japan
When: Every 6 years, in the years of the Monkey and Tiger

SAKURA MATSURI
Tokyo

Nothing touches the Japanese more than the annual flowering of the cherry blossom, symbolizing the arrival of spring. All over the country people flock to gardens and parks at the optimum time (the end of March to mid-April) for impromptu parties and celebrations. In some places the gatherings have grown to the point where they have become festivals in their own right. Nowhere is this truer than in Ueno Park in Tokyo, where the pink blossoms of 600 Yoshino cherry trees are lit up at night by more than 1,000 lanterns, to the delight of many thousands of residents, out-of-towners and tourists who flock there to soak up a quintessentially Japanese spectacle.

Where: Tokyo, Japan
When: The end of March to mid-April, depending on the blossom

SHUNKI REITAISAI AND TOSHO-GU
Nikko City

The warriors – or at least men dressed in resplendent samurai costumes and burnished body armour – strut their stuff twice a year at the Spring and Autumn Parades of a Thousand Samurai Warriors (mid-May and mid-October) of this pretty mountain town, which is a registered UNESCO World Heritage Site. The samurai procession, also including Shinto priests, is a re-creation of the funeral cortège of the first Shogun of Tokugawa, who died in 1616. After the main event, there is plenty more samurai action, with mounted archers firing at targets at full gallop, while traditional floats, music and dance add to the festive atmosphere.

Where: Nikko Toshogu Shrine, Nikko City, Japan
When: Spring (17–18 May) and autumn (16–17 October)

TAKAYAMA MATSURI
Takayama

Twice a year, in spring and autumn, the historic city of Takayama takes to the streets for its seasonal *matsuri* (festival). By far the most popular, the spring festivities, welcoming in the new season, are based around the Hie Shrine in the southern half of the old town, while the autumn events are concentrated on the Hachiman Shrine to the north. In both cases, tall and colourful floats – said to be some of the most beautiful and imaginative in the whole of Japan – are prepared and paraded through the streets to the sound of drumming and the enthusiastic applause of the many visitors that the festivals attract.

Where: Takayama, Japan
When: Spring (14–15 April) and autumn (9–10 October)

TENJIN MATSURI
Osaka City

Courtly Japan comes back to life in the country's most spectacular historic pageant. For two days in late July, Osaka commemorates Tenman Tenjin, the patron god of learning and art, in a series of sumptuous events that include traditional theatre, *kagura* music and *bunraku* puppetry. The highlight is the procession of 3,000 people, dressed in the style of the medieval imperial court, who take to more than 100 boats and sail along the river past brightly lit pavilions. As dusk falls, the boats light up with fires to illuminate the course of the river. After a traditional firework display, there is a charming local touch – a demonstration of rhythmic handclapping that is unique to Osaka. The custom recalls the culture of the Edo period of Tokyo (*c*.1603–1868), brought vividly to life in the woodblock prints of *ukiyo-e* (pictures of the Floating World).

Where: Tenman Shrine, Osaka City, Japan
When: 24 and 25 July

TOKA EBISU
Osaka City

Dedicated to good fortune in business, the Toka Ebisu is celebrated throughout Japan, but nowhere more vigorously than in the Kansai region that includes Kyoto and the noted commercial centre of Osaka City. In the latter city, between 9 and 11 January, upwards of a million people flock to the Imamiya Ebisu Shrine to pray to Ebisu, patron deity of business, for success in commercial enterprise. The landmark Ebisu Bridge over the Dotonbori River was originally built for worshippers visiting the shrine. Markets sell good-luck charms in the form of oval coins, sea bream and rice bales, all propitious for enterprise.Alongside the spiritual and trade activities, there is a parade of geishas and *fuku-musumes*, which translates as 'good-luck girls'. Of the 3,000 girls who apply each year to take part – only 40 are chosen for their personality and intelligence.

Where: Imamiya Ebisu Shrine, Osaka City, Japan
When: 9–11 January

YAMAYAKI
Nara City

What better way to see in the New Year than set fire to an old volcano? In late January Buddhist monks light a torch at the Kasuga Taisha Shrine and process to the foot of Mount Wakakusayama, where they set the slopes alight. As the flames race up the side of the mountain, a firework display adds to the pyrotechnics. Some say this act of ritualized arson has its origin in an 18th-century land dispute; others reckon that it was simply the best way to shoo away wild boar and kill off insects. Whichever, it makes for an unforgettable spectacle.

Where: Mount Wakakusayama, Nara City, Japan
When: The 4th Saturday of January

YUKI MATSURI
Odori Park, Susukino, Sapporo

The city that hosted the Winter Olympics in 1972 had been putting on an impressive snow show well before then. From small beginnings in 1950, the annual Yuki Matsuri (Snow Festival), held over a week in February, has grown into a global event attended by more than 2 million people. They come to marvel at the hundreds of intricate statues and tableaux made of ice and snow and displayed at various venues across the city. There's also a competitive element these days as teams from around the world enter a snow sculpture contest – strictly in a spirit of international fraternity, of course.

Where: Odori Park, Susukino, Sapporo, Japan
When: One week in February

> MONGOLIA

NADAAM
Ulan Bator

....

When the Mongol armies swept across Eurasia during the middle ages, they were renowned for their bravura riding and archery, which can be glimpsed today during Mongolia's popular sporting contest. With roots in the nation's martial heritage, Nadaam features archery, wrestling and riding, with up to 1,000 mounted riders. In their heyday, Mongol archers let loose a barrage of arrows at full gallop. Today the targets are static, but the archers still display uncanny accuracy in hitting hundreds of them. The wrestling match imposes no time limits – the winner is the one left standing.

Where: Ulan Bator, Mongolia
When: 11–13 July
....

> SOUTH KOREA

BORYEONG MUD FESTIVAL
Daecheon Beach, Boryeong City

....

The perfect excuse to get very muddy with a bunch of strangers, most in beach attire, the Boryeong Mud Festival is everyone's idea of fun. Although originally conceived as a marketing gimmick for Boryeong Mud Cosmetics, it quickly grew into an international event that now attracts more than 2 million summer visitors. Muddy delights include mudslides, mud wallows and even a mud prison.

Where: Daecheon Beach, Boryeong City, South Korea
When: Two weeks usually including the 1st and 2nd weekends in July
....

GANGNEUNG DANOJE FESTIVAL
Gangneung

....

South Korea's oldest folk festival, rooted in ancient shamanic rites, Gangneung Danoje originally petitioned the sky god for a fruitful harvest, plentiful fishing and a peaceful, healthy community. Some local festivities continue today with the Yeongsin Parade and lively masked dances, such as the Gwanno Gamyeongeuk, alongide international cultural events, such as China's Sichuan Opera. More sportive activities include *sireum* wrestling and tug of war.

Where: Gangneung, South Korea
When: Two weeks including the 1st and 2nd weekends in July
....

LOTUS LANTERN FESTIVAL
Seoul

....

A delight for the eye and soul, the Lotus Lantern Festival is steeped in Buddhist symbolism. At its simplest, lighting a lantern brings light to the dark corners of life. Celebrating the Buddha's birthday, the festival opens with a parade of more than 100,000 people, many in splendid *hanbok* dress, each bearing a lantern glowing with rainbow-coloured light. Anyone can join in and make their own lanterns with the help of street stalls. Lanterns come in all shapes, not just lotuses, but also dragons, tigers and even elephants. Starting at Dongdaemun Gate, the radiant parade snakes through the streets of Insadong before finishing at Jogye-sa Temple. En route, temple dishes sustain the pilgrims, while visitors can take brass rubbings and enjoy a post-parade party.

Where: Seoul, South Korea
When: Birthday of Lord Buddha in lunar calendar (usually May)
....

Wrestling is one of the 'Three Manly Skills' promoted by Genghis Khan to keep his army fit. The art is still popularly practised and wrestling competitions are a highlight of Nadaam in Mongolia's Ulan Bator.

There's nothing quite like a beach mudbath to raise a smile in Boryeong City, South Korea.

Madness
and *Matsuri*

MOST PEOPLE THINK OF JAPAN AS A MODERN, COOL, TECHNOLOGICALLY SOPHISTICATED COUNTRY WHERE THE PEOPLE ARE FORMAL, RESERVED AND POLITE. WHILE THIS IS UNDOUBTEDLY PART OF THE TRUTH, IT TAKES NO ACCOUNT OF JAPAN'S *MATSURI*, OR FESTIVALS. UNINHIBITED, BOISTEROUS, RAUCOUS AND SOMETIMES EVEN VIOLENT – WELCOME TO THE MADNESS OF *MATSURI*!

ABOVE Impeccably turned out with her whitened face and extravagantly styled hair, this geisha offers one of the iconic images of Japan.

OPPOSITE A posse of titans is needed to manoeuvre and process these massive floats through the city of Fukuoka at the Hakata Gion Yamakasa.

OPPOSITE A celebrant wears the traditional *fundoshi* (loincloth) and *happi* (straight-sleeved coat) at the Hakata Gion Yamakasa.

In many festivals around the world, the normal rules of behaviour are suspended for a few glorious hours or days. Japan is no exception, with its extraordinary tradition of *hadaka matsuri*, or naked festivals. These events are held in many places all over the country. The participants – always male – are not completely naked, but wear *fundoshi* (loincloths). As well as the element of nudity, some sort of fighting or violent competition often features. It is almost as though people seek release from their day-to-day lives by, however briefly, doing something completely alien to them.

The *hadaka matsuri* are not recent inventions, set up just for fun. Many date back hundreds of years and are rooted in the Shinto religion, an ancient form of nature worship. (Shinto is associated with life-affirming celebrations. It is said that in Japan

ABOVE With the promise of a year of happiness, men wrestle for the two holy sticks thrown into the crowd by a Shinto priest at the Hadaka Matsuri at Saidaiji-naka.

you are born a Shintoist and die a Buddhist.) The Hakata Gion Yamakasa (see p. 98) at Hakata near Fukuoka is over 750 years old. As well as loincloths the celebrants wear short traditional coats called *happi*. They carry a number of one-ton floats in a race around the town. Bizarrely, this is not just a race – people are also judged on their style and elegance – something that is rather difficult to carry off in a loincloth.

The Okoshi Daiko at Hida-Furukawa is another naked festival that involves a dozen teams of men chasing a drum tower through the streets (see p. 99). They fight and jostle each other to get closest to the drum right through the night. Contrary to the usual rules of politeness and decorum in Japan, the competitors sometimes even brawl with bystanders in the heat of battle.

TOP An immensely popular event, the Festival of the Steel Phallus is held each year at the Kanayama shrine in Kawasaki paying homage to the penis as a symbol of virility and fertility.

OPPOSITE TOP The firework display at Chichibu Yomatsuri is spectacular, lasting over two hours.

OPPOSITE BOTTOM Towering floats festooned with lanterns add to the magic of this December festival of the Chichibu Shrine.

The most famous of all of the naked festivals – and one that involves a colossal battle between participants – is the Hadaka Matsuri at Saidaiji-naka (see p. 97). This is essentially a fight between up to 9,000 individuals who try to grab lucky wooden charms that are thrown into the mêlée by Shinto priests. This tradition dates back over five hundred years when paper scrolls called *go-o* used to be thrown, but these were easily torn in the ensuing chaos.

Some of the fighting that takes place at naked festivals involves nothing more harmful than a good dollop of mud. The Dairokuten-no-Hadaka Matsuri at Yotsukaido sees the loincloth-wearing masses run from the Musubi-jinja Shrine to a nearby lake, where they liberally smear each other in mud in a bizarre purifying ritual. Duly covered, they return to the shrine to pray for a good harvest (see p. 97).

Mud fights are also an integral part of the Doronko Matsuri at Nagahama (see p. 97). Unusually, it is the women who are the main actors. They complete a solemn rice-planting ritual and then chase the men present and cover their faces in mud from the paddies. This mud is supposed to bring health and happiness, and the menfolk are obliged to thank the women for each application.

If celebrating without any clothes on seems incongruous, then some festivals take this even further, by invoking ancient fertility rites involving phalluses. Many cultures regard the phallus as a symbol of male fertility, but some of the Japanese festivals take this to extremes. At the Kawasaki Kanamara Matsuri the penis is undoubtedly king (see p. 98). Phalluses of all shapes and sizes – and dare I say it flavours – are everywhere.

The main element of the festival is a parade of penis-bedecked floats and a large steel phallus, which is helpfully painted a garish pink colour. For sale are penis-shaped boiled sweets called *o-chinko* as well as the female version, *o-manko*.

Many of the more outrageous Japanese festivals involve drinking of large amounts of *saké*, and at the Hounen Matsuri it's no wonder as the centrepiece of the festival is an eight-foot wooden phallus, this is no wonder. The culmination of the festivities is a scramble for lucky rice cakes in the main square.

Floats are a feature of many Japanese festivals, and are paraded around towns and cities. Some of these festivals take the ritual to extremes by including routes where the heavy floats have to be dragged uphill – a test of strength that is usually frenetic. The Chichibu Yomatsuri (see p. 97) has six massive floats called *dashi*, each weighing between ten and twenty tons each. They are covered in fire lanterns and the wild procession includes a mad dash up a steep hill, accompanied by much shouting and cheering.

In contrast the 1,200-year-old Onbashira Matsuri, held every six years at Lake Suwa, is about driving things downhill, with brave souls riding on them – in this case giant logs (see

TOP Reckless or daring, these men risk their lives manoeuvring, by ropes, four huge logs, slithering them down a mountainside. In a festival held every six years, the felled trees represent the 'honoured pillars' of the Suwa Grand Shrine in Nagano.

OPPOSITE Held high by sumo students and encouraged by the judge calling '*naki, naki*' (cry, cry), the first to cry of this pair of babies is the winner of the contest, and the louder it wails the more blessed it is with good health.

p. 99). There is genuine danger involved. The logs are virtually out of control as they career down the hill, and people are sometimes killed or injured. If the riders manage to survive, they try to cling to the logs as they are raised vertically to symbolize the foundations of Shinto shrines.

No matter how bizarre they might seem to outsiders, all these festivals are influenced by the Shinto religion, which is central to Japanese society. Arguably one of the strangest of all of the Japanese festivals, and one that features one of the most iconic Japanese traditions, is the Konaki Sumo festival. In an ancient ritual, said to be more than four hundred years old, students of sumo hold babies aloft in a mock contest to see which of them will cry first. The proceedings are overseen by a Shinto priest who adds to the cacophony with encouraging shouts. The festival is held all over Japan, but especially at the Sensoji Temple in Tokyo in April (see p. 99). The winning baby is the one who cries first or, in the case of a tie, the one who cries loudest. Rather than being thought of as child abuse, mothers queue up to take part, believing that crying makes a child healthy. Proof, it seems, that even if you don't always understand quite what is going on, or why, Japanese festivals are seldom dull.

> TAIWAN

PARADE OF THE GOD OF MEDICINE
Taipai and Hseuhchia

With up to 78 flamboyant theatrical troupes performing along a 3km procession, Hseuhchia's Parade of the God of Medicine is the largest and most frenetic in Taiwan. Up to 21 floral floats bear legendary figures that tell the story of the God of Medicine, who is honoured in more than 160 temples across Taiwan, especially in Taipei and Hseuhchia. Leading the parade of is a group of orange-clad priests, pilgrims and dancers, known as the Centipedes, who symbolically exorcize demons.

Where: Taipei and Hseuhchia, Taiwan
When: The 15th day of the 3rd lunar month (usually April)

> TIBET

CHUNGA CHOEPA
Lhasa

There's an art to sculpting butter – you mustn't let your fingers get too warm, which is why the monks who fashion lamps out of yak butter keep dipping their digits in cold water. Their imaginative sculptures of Buddhas, animals and plants symbolize the light of Buddhism. At night on the 15th day of the Tibetan New Year, the soft glow from myriad lamps, some placed on scaffolds three stories high, turns Barkhor Square in Lhasa into a dazzling arena where Tibetans meditate, dance, sing and indulge in local *chang* beer. The festival is said to mark the victory of the Buddha over cynics in theological debate, which perhaps accounts for the intense and noisy conversations as the party continues into the night.

Where: Barkhor Square, Lhasa, Tibet
When: The 15th day of the 1st Tibetan lunar month

LOSAR
Tibet

The most important festival in the Tibetan calendar, New Year, or Losar, is celebrated by Tibetans throughout Asia, but in Tibet itself it has become a controversial political event. Since 2009, scores of monks have immolated themselves in protest at the enforced exile of Tibet's spiritual ruler, the Dalai Lama, and Tibetan leaders have called for Losar to be a time of mourning rather than celebration. Even so, the three days of prayer rituals, masked dances and torch-lit processions that usually fall in January or February on Losar serve to re-affirm and reinforce Tibetan identity and culture.

Where: All over Tibet, especially Lhasa
When: Three days from the 1st day of 1st Tibetan lunar month. Some monasteries start events on 29th day of the 12th month.

Rural Kazakh women dressed in their traditional finery attend the festival of Nauryz in Astana, Kazakhstan.

NAGQU HORSE-RACING FESTIVAL
Nagqu

For the people of this remote area of northern Tibet, the horse-racing festival at Nagqu is even more important than New Year. Resplendent in their traditional costumes, herdsmen arrive from all directions, some from hundreds of miles away, to set up a chaotic and colourful tented camp. There are archery and tug-of-war competitions but the centrepiece of the festival is the series of equestrian events: target shooting from horseback and scooping up a ceremonial scarf at the gallop, as well as the breakneck horse races, the longest of which runs for 10km.

Where: Nagqu, Tibet
When: Five to 15 days in August

SAGA DAWA
Mount Kailash

Where better to celebrate the conception, enlightenment and death of the Buddha than at the centre of the universe? For that is how Buddhists, as well as followers of Hinduism, regard Mount Kailash in the far west of Tibet. On the full moon of the fourth month in the Tibetan lunar calendar

– May or June – pilgrims flock to the mountain in order to walk round it in a single day, a distance of more than 50km. Since prayers are thought to be particularly potent at this most holiest of months in the Buddhist calendar, pilgrims tie countless prayer flags to a giant flagpole, the Tarboche, which is then raised by hand, under the supervision of a *lama* (spiritual teacher), until it achieves perfect perpendicularity – a sign of good luck. For light relief, pilgrims visit the Dzongyab Lukhang Park at the foot of the Potala Palace to enjoy a late afternoon picnic.

Where: Mount Kailash, western Tibet
When: On the full moon of the 4th Tibetan lunar month
....

SHOTON FESTIVAL
Norbulingka, Lhasa
....

With an appetizing nickname like the Yoghurt Banquet Festival, it'll come as no surprise to learn that yoghurt is served up as a special treat during this annual celebration, held throughout Lhasa but notably at Norbulingka, the Dalai Lama's summer palace. The feast dates back to the 16th century when a meal of soured milk was prepared for the monks at the end of a long month's retreat, during which they had remained cloistered to avoid accidentally treading on any living creatures. As the monks emerge from their seclusion today, residents of the Tibetan capital gather in family groups in the palace gardens to watch performances of traditional opera and dancing, and to picnic – on yoghurt, of course.

Where: Norbulingka, Lhasa, Tibet
When: 7 days from 30th day of Tibetan lunar month (usually August)
....

>> CENTRAL ASIA
....

> AFGHANISTAN

NOWRUZ
Afghanistan
....

The spring equinox marks the beginning of Nowruz, the New Year for many countries in central Asia. The tradition was suppressed under the Islamic fundamentalist Taliban regime (1996–2001) because of its pagan roots, but is now widely celebrated again, especially in the northern city of Mazar-e-Sharif. To greet the New Year, people wear new clothes, clean and even refurbish their houses, then prepare festive picnics that are enjoyed out on the green plains of their homelands among springtime red cercis flowers. Nowruz is also the time for young women to attend shrines and pray for a good husband, while men play *buzkashi*, a type of polo using a headless goat carcass.

Where: All over Afghanistan, especially Mazar-e-Sharif
When: Two weeks culminating on 21 March
....

> TAJIKISTAN

AT CHABYSH
Murghab
....

In this remote outpost in the Pamir mountains, ethnic Kyrgyzs gather on a weekend in August to celebrate all things equine. The Kyrgyz horse, a particularly strong and hardy beast, symbolizes a self-sufficient, nomadic way of life that has remained essentially unchanged for millennia, and Kyrgyz horsemen congregate to express their love of their horses in dazzling feats of showmanship. There are endurance races, horseback wrestling and a game that requires riders to pluck scarfs from the ground at full gallop.

Where: Murghab, Tajikistan
When: A weekend in August
....

> KAZAKHSTAN

NAURYZ
Astana
....

A close relation to Nowruz ('new day') in Afghanistan and Iran, the age-old ritual bidding farewell to winter and ushering in spring was banned when Kazakhstan was part of the Soviet Union, and not properly revived till 1988. Now it is a national holiday, held on the spring equinox (late March) when the Kazakh capital comes alive after the long cold months of winter. Decorated *yurts* (tents) spring up in open spaces, and the people don colourful costumes to come out and celebrate – planting trees, feasting on *Nauryz kozhe*, a yoghurt delicacy, and competing in traditional sports, such as *kyz kuu*, a mounted game of kiss-chase.

Where: Astana, Kazakhstan
When: Spring equinox (around 20–22 March)
....

Afghanis see in the New Year during Nowruz, in Kabul, Afghanistan.

A Day at the Races

WHO CAN RESIST THE THRILL AND EXCITEMENT OF THE CHASE? THE QUEST FOR SPEED, THE DRIVE TO WIN, AND APPRECIATION OF STRENGTH, SKILL AND ENDURANCE ARE UNIVERSAL. HOWEVER LARGE OR SMALL THE OCCASION, OR WHETHER IT FEATURES HORSES, CAMELS OR BUFFALO, IN EVERY CULTURE RACES GRIP THE IMAGINATION AND QUICKEN THE PULSE. A DAY AT THE RACES IS AN UNMISSABLE SOCIAL EVENT.

ABOVE Buffalo racing, Indonesian style.

OPPOSITE L'Ardia di San Costantino, an ancient Sardinian
horse race in the town of Sedilo.

In rural communities people generally can't afford the luxury of keeping animals just for racing, and their everyday beasts of burden are transformed into prized 'racehorses' for festival occasions. In many parts of Asia, for example, the buffalo is king. Normally more sedate than the African buffalo, the Asian water buffalo is most often seen lounging around in paddy fields or mud wallows. Given the right encouragement, though, these animals have a surprising turn of speed, and buffalo racing is an exciting sport.

In Cambodia, buffalo races are held to mark the end of the Pchum Ben festival of the dead. The best known of these is at Preah Vihear Sour in Kandai Province (see p. 146). Competing buffalo wear ornate headdresses that cover their heads and horns, and the jockeys parade them around the course. After the races, the buffalo are auctioned off.

Khmer people living in the Vietnamese province of An Giang also have a version of this racing festival using cows (see p. 163). This is along a waterlogged course, with two cows linked by a yoke and a trailing harrow for the jockey to stand on. The jockey has to control the speed of the animals while not falling into the muddy water. The annual festival alternates between two different pagodas in the region, and is attended by a number of Buddhist monks who bless the beasts before the race begins. The winning pair of cows is believed to bring good luck to their village.

In Chonburi in nearby Thailand the buffalo are not decorated before the event, and are fed beer and raw eggs to get them in the mood. The jockeys ride bareback and often fall off. There is a long series of increasingly drunken races in which the numbers are whittled down to an overall winner (see p. 160).

OPPOSITE Chonburi buffalo races, Thailand.

ABOVE Horse race at the Nadaam, Ulan Bator, Mongolia.

In Indonesia, the buffalo race riderless through a waterlogged 100m course, and the 'jockeys' actually race after them amid sprays of mud and water. The Male'an Sampi festival on the island of Lombok is famous throughout the country (see p. 147). Its name means 'to run after a cow' in the local Sasak language. Buffalo are paraded and feted before the event with music played on wind instruments and gongs.

A number of communities pride themselves on their horsemanship. In Mongolia, the descendants of Genghis Khan compete in traditional tournaments called *Nadaam*, which include wrestling, archery and horse racing. The largest of these takes place in

ABOVE Visitors travel hundreds of miles to attend the two-week Nagqu Horse-Racing Festival. In addition to the equestrian events, there are a variety of cultural and sporting activities.

the capital, Ulan Bator (see p. 101). The race is a mass, long-distance event, in which the distance is determined by the age of the competing horses. Some of the races are 27km long and involve up to a thousand horses from all over the country. The jockeys can be as young as five years old.

The Kyrgyzstan festival of At Chabysh (see p. 111) is based around horse racing in various guises, reflecting the importance of the horse in Kyrgyz society. It features a range of equestrian events, such as endurance races and traditional horse games. One of the most popular games is the *kyz kuma* in which a horseman chases, at full gallop, a girl rider who is dressed as a bride. If he catches her he is rewarded with a kiss; if not he is derided and given a playful whipping by his erstwhile quarry. The horse games are a jovial distraction from the serious business of racing, which in the style of Central Asian horse racing is more of a marathon than a sprint, with the endurance of the horse and rider being more important than bursts of speed.

Horses are a central feature of the Nagqu Festival in Tibet (see p. 110). Attracting thousands of people to the grasslands outside Nagqu, the week-long festival features horse racing, as well as archery, wrestling, tug of war, rock carrying and even yak racing. It is a lively and colourful occasion, and much of the local *Chang* beer is drunk. Many horse traders come to the event and winning horses are greatly prized, commanding high prices.

ABOVE A rider scoops up the ceremonial scarf while at full gallop to demonstrate his horsemanship skills at the Shoton Festival at Norbulingka, Tibet.

ABOVE RIGHT Horse and jockey at the Palio of Siena.

The camel is, of course, the favoured mount in the Middle East, s and the annual Jenadriyah Festival in Saudi Arabia features camel racing (see p. 173). Up to two thousand camels start this race with a sprint, before settling down to trot the 19km course at a more sedate pace. Around the race there are a number of cultural, poetry and folkloric events, but it is the camel racing that brings in the crowds.

There is a tradition in Italy of *palios*. These are medieval horse races where the prize is a *palio*, or banner. The most famous is the Palio of Siena (see p. 207), which is run twice a year in the cobbled *campo*, or main square, of the city. It is a contest between Siena's competing *contrade* (districts). Lots are drawn to see which ten districts will compete and which horse and jockey they will be allocated. There then follows a week of intrigue and practice races, where representatives of each *contrada* try to nobble their competitors. Before the race itself, the *contrade* process to the *campo* in medieval costume, twirling their flags and banners.

The procession is an impressive sight, and somewhat like stepping back in time to the medieval heyday of the city. If, like me, you can't afford to pay the premium prices for the ticketed seats or balconies overlooking the *campo*, then you will have to make do with the sunny centre of the square, and a long, long wait (and the odd elbow battle) to protect a place by the barrier. After a wait of a number of hours, the actual race is generally so frenetic that it is hard to know what is happening and who has won.

All but one of the horses line up at the start, and the race begins when the final horse barges through them. There are a number of nervous false starts before the race gets underway. The race lasts only three short laps around the undulating and cobbled track, and riders and horses often fall at the tighter corners, skidding into large protective mattresses. Not infrequently a riderless horse will lead the race, and the fallen jockey

will beat a hasty retreat lest he be accused of throwing the race. When the first horse crosses the finish line, most of the crowd in the *campo* have virtually no idea who has won: the *contrade* in the banked seats on the outside of the campo have a better view and the winners will surge forward to claim the *palio*, or winners' pennant. Competing *contrade* will often try to get there first to spoil the party, and sometimes a sprawling punch-up will break out. It's a good idea not to wear any of the *contrade* colours,

OPPOSITE Sporting the colours of their *contrada*, these jockeys, riding in the Siena Palio, spur on their mounts around the treacherous corners of the *campo*.

OPPOSITE INSET Bird's eye view of the Siena Palio with the spectators corralled in the middle of the *campo*.

ABOVE A drummer in the *Corteo Storico* (historical costume parade) which precedes the Palio.

unless you know what you are doing; you may end up provoking a fight unwittingly.

A similar *palio* race is run at Asti, near Turin (see p. 206). Dating back to the thirteenth century, the period of the city's greatest splendour, this is older than the Siena race, and commemorates victory in a battle with the city of Alba.

Further south at Sedilo on the island of Sardinia, the annual L'Ardia di San Costantino is faster and more furious (see p. 206). On the evening before the race there is a re-enactment of the Emperor Constantine's victory charge at the battle of the Milvian Bridge in 312. The next morning the race is held in the grounds of the Santuario di San Costantino amid much dust, July heat and drunken crowds.

Part-way between a festival and a sporting event are the beach horse races of Sanlucar de Barrameda in southern Spain (see p. 225). These take place in August and are the oldest races in the country. There are no entrance fees: tourists and locals watch from the beach. A quaint characteristic of these events are the betting stands set up by local children. These are usually made of boxes, and the children compete to take bets on the results.

What all these disparate festivals have in common is that the racing, while spectacular, thrilling and often dangerous, is secondary to the celebration of local tradition and the people's relationship with their animals. Although at first glance these may appear to be simple sporting events, they are essentially displays of skill, courage and local culture.

>> SOUTH ASIA

> BHUTAN

DRAMETSE FESTIVAL
Mongar

The dramatic highlight of the Drametse Festival is the sacred Drametse Ngachan, a masked dance performed in honour of the Buddhist sage Padmasambhava. Sixteen masqueraders, clad in splendid monastic robes and vivid wooden masks, whirl to the rhythms of trumpets, drums and cymbals. The pace of the dance shifts from calm to agitated, depending on the nature of the deities represented, whether peaceful or wrathful. The dance and the atmosphere of the event are spiritually uplifting for the audience who come to receive blessings from the monks.

Where: Ogyen Tegchok Namdroel Choeling Monastery, Mongar, Bhutan
When: (movable) twice a year during the 5th and 10th months of the Bhutanese calendar

LOSAR ARCHERY FESTIVAL
Western Bhutan

The usually composed Bhutanese celebrate the Tibetan Buddhist New Year with a round of raucous and somewhat drunken archery matches. As the sport is a national passion, the event attracts leading marksmen to compete with traditional long bows trained on targets up to 140m away. On the eve of the match, rivals sleep away from home to aid their concentration. On the day itself, many consult shamans and chant mantras to stay calm. Once the event starts, though, contestants and spectators alike shout and heckle in an effort to unnerve the archers. Other New Year games played on the day include *degoer* (flat-stone hurling) and *khuru* (darts).

Where: Western Bhutan
When: The Buddhist New Year in late January or early February

PARO TSECHU
Paro Dzong

One of the biggest events in the mountain kingdom of Bhutan, this five-day dance festival is held in honour of Padmasambhava, the founder of Tibetan Buddhism. Thousands of pilgrims and camera-wielding tourists descend on the 16th-century monastic fortress of Paro Dzong, overlooking the lush Paro Valley, to witness a dazzling series of masked dances. Particularly splendid are the Black Hat Dance and the Dance of the Lords of the Cremation Grounds. On the final morning, monks ceremonially unfurl the monastery's silk *thangka,* which is used as a visual aid to meditation.

Where: Paro Dzong, Bhutan
When: Five days from 10th day of 2nd month of Bhutan lunar calendar

THIMPHU TSECHU
Thimphu

For three days towards the end of September, the Bhutanese capital of Thimphu reverberates to a cacophony of drums and cymbals as dancers celebrate the changing of the seasons, from autumn to winter. The centre of festivities is the courtyard of Tashichho Dzong, the most famous of the city's monasteries, where a series of ritual dances, such as the *tungam chham* (Dance of Terrifying Deities), are performed by monks and locals in elaborate masks, costumes and headdresses, watched by thousands of enraptured pilgrims and townspeople. First held in 1670, the festival has become a vigorous expression of Bhutanese culture and identity.

Where: Thimphu, Bhutan
When: Three days from the 10th day of the 8th lunar month

> INDIA

ALANGANALLUR JALLIKATTU
Alanganallur

If a charging bull is not your idea of light entertainment, stay indoors or at least on an upstairs balcony during Jallikattu, when bulls are released into the crowds as part of the Pongal harvest celebrations. The bulls head straight for the milling spectators. Whoever manages to hang on to the bull's horns or back for 50m is the winner. The bulls repeatedly charge the crowds and inevitably cause casualties. The nail-biting event was once a trial for prospective bridegrooms, but winners today get little more than bragging rights.

Where: Alanganallur, India (In 2014 the Indian Supreme Court banned Jallikattu; a decision that is currently being contested)
When: Mattu Pongal day, usually 15 or 16 January

BIKANER CAMEL FESTIVAL
Bikaner

The camel is king in the desert city of Bikaner, home to the only camel-breeding farm in India. With the citizens' long reliance on the local 'ships of the desert' – for both travel and survival – it's little wonder that they should throw a camel-themed party at the turn of the year. The popular event draws camel breeders from across Rajasthan, as well as tourists from around the world. The camels of the region are renowned for their strength and stamina – tested during World Wars I and II, when they served in the Ganga Risala, an elite camel corps. Camel races today show off the creatures' celebrated speed, while a lighter note is struck by a camel beauty pageant and a camel hair-cutting contest.

Where: Bikaner, India
When: Two days in January

Black Hat dancers wait in the wings to take to the floor and purify the ground with their steps, driving out evil spirits at Paro Dzong, Bhutan.

DEV DEEPAVALI
Varanasi

On Dev Deepavali, the gods descend to earth to bathe in the River Ganges. In their honour, the people of Varanasi light up the riverbank with more than a million *diyas* (clay lamps). Millions of visitors throng the sacred city to offer prayers. Many perform the ritual bath of *kartik snan* and set thousands of flickering *diyas* afloat. Predictably, the local tourist board has got in on the act with a five-day Ganga Mahotsav festival showcasing local culture, but the real beauty of Dev Deepavali lies in the eyes of the pilgrims huddled along the river, their faces lit up with the glow from their simple lamps.

Where: Varanasi, India
When: Kartik Poornima full moon, October or November

DIWALI
New Delhi

On rooftops and parapets, in houses and temples, little lights glow everywhere during Diwali. Traditionally people lit *diyas* (clay lamps) but now electric fairylights set the city aglow. It is a grand time for the whole family, when people exchange gifts and wear new clothes. The faithful flock to temples to make offerings, and everyone cleans their houses ready to welcome Lakshmi, goddess of wealth and prosperity. Although Diwali is celebrated across India, it is particularly evocative in the ancient, vibrant capital of New Delhi.

Where: All over India, especially New Delhi
When: October to November

DURGA PUJA
Kolkata, West Bengal and Assam

In the weeks leading up to Durga Puja, artisans model ornate statues depicting the goddess Durga's triumph over evil by defeating the demon king Mahishasura. The brightly painted clay figures, or *murti*, are placed in *pandals* – elaborate bamboo shrines erected in town squares, playgrounds and temples. During the six- to ten-day festival, the goddess is worshipped in her various forms, as Durga, Lakshmi and Saraswati. On the Vijaya Dashami (10th day of victory), the statues are paraded down to the rivers where they are bathed, symbolizing the deity's departure to her celestial home in the Himalayas.

Where: Kolkata, West Bengal and Assam, India
When: Beginning of the month of Kartik (End of September or October)

DUSSEHRA
Kullu Valley

The broad Kullu Valley, on the edge of the Himalayas, is known as the Valley of the Gods, as each village has its own god and, for a week every autumn up to 200 statues are brought together to celebrate the victory of Rama over the demon Ravana. Each village also has a shaman, who enters a trance during the festivities, enabling the deities to speak through him. On the final day animals, including a buffalo, are sacrificed on a sweet-smelling bonfire of wood grass.

Where: Kullu Valley, Himachal Pradesh, India
When: Seven days in October

GANGA SAGAR MELA
Sagar Island

This annual Hindu festival attracts up to half a million people for a day of ritual bathing in the waters of the Bay of Bengal. Ganga Sagar is an island about 100km south of Kolkata, auspiciously located at the mouth of the River Hooghly, a distributary of the sacred River Ganges. An awesome scrum of humanity descends upon it in the middle of January to cleanse their souls in the sea, lighting bonfires on the shore to keep warm before continuing their devotions at the Temple of Kapil Muni. The flowers, incense and vivid costumes, the nakedness of the *sadhus* – holy men – and the quiet fervour of the pilgrims create an extraordinary scene.

Where: Sagar Island, India
When: Makar Sankranti, 14 January or 15 January

GANGAUR
Jaipur

In this most colourful of states, there are no more colourful celebrations than those surrounding the 18 days of Gangaur, set among the rose-tinted buildings of the old 'Pink City' of Jaipur. Dressed in beautiful saris, jewellery and headdresses, women both married and unmarried pay homage to Parvati, the consort of Lord Shiva and supreme embodiment of marital love. During the festival, the women fast, confining themselves to one meal a day, and make statues of Parvati in clay or painted wood. For the grand finale on the last day, all the brightly painted Parvatis are paraded around the city on bullock carts and decorated palanquins, led by splendidly caparisoned elephants.

Where: Jaipur, India
When: 18 days from 1st day of the Hindu month of Chaitra (March or April)

GOUREESWARA TEMPLE FESTIVAL
Cherai

In a land of astonishing festivals, some of the most spectacular occur in the southern state of Kerala – and elephants inevitably figure largely. A memorable example is this temple festival near Kochi (formerly Cochin) where, over nine or ten days in January or February, up to 30 big beasts are decorated with gilded headdresses and paraded amid vast crowds in a large open courtyard in front of the temple. Sitting on top of the elephants, acolytes engage in a bizarre competitive show of paddle waving and parasol twirling.

Where: Cherai, India
When: End of January, beginning of February

High on the backs of caparisoned elephants, acolytes with twirling parasols and waving fans made of peacock feathers perform to the crowds at the Goureeswara Temple Festival in Cherai, Kochi.

HEMIS TSE CHU
Hemis

Ladakh, a former Buddhist kingdom in the high Himalayas, is renowned for its extraordinary clifftop monasteries, and Hemis has established itself as the most famous, thanks to its annual Tse Chu festival. Held over two days in June or July, the event commemorates the birth of Padmasambhava, the founder of Tibetan Buddhism. A huge crowd – of foreign tourists as well as locals – crams into the monastery courtyard to watch a dazzling pageant of masked dances and enactments of the stories of the divinities. Every 12 years, the monastery's most precious possession – a vast *thangka*, or religious tapestry, dedicated to Padmasambhava – is displayed. The next time will be 2016.

Where: Hemis, India
When: Two days in June or July

HOLI
Mathura

The 'Festival of Colours', Holi, is the wildest and literally the most colourful festival in India. It is reputed to date back almost 1,500 years in celebration of the triumph of good over evil and features the smearing of coloured powder and scented water on family, friends and random strangers. This ritual often gets completely out of hand. People are intoxicated with the moment, or perhaps with a little *bhang*, and vast crowds pelt and smear each other with abandon, leaving everyone completely covered. The festival is celebrated all over India, but especially in cities associated with Lord Krishna, most notably Mathura in Uttar Pradesh.

Where: All over India, especially Mathura
When: Phalgun Purnima (full moon), end of February to late March

HOLLA MOHALLA
Anandpur Sahib

This three-day festival, which begins the day after Holi, was established in 1701 by the Sikh guru Gobind Singh, who felt that the earlier festival had lost much of its original meaning. In order to remind people of the values of fraternity and valour in the battle with evil he arranged for demonstrations of the fighting prowess of the normally peaceful Sikhs, skills useful to the guru as he was fighting the Mughal Empire at the time. Today the festival features mock battles, displays of swordsmanship and horse riding. *Langars* (voluntary community kitchens) provide free vegetarian food.

Where: Anandpur Sahib, India
When: The 1st day of the lunar month of Chet (the day after Holi)

IGITUN CHALNE
Bicholim Taluq

This spectacular festival attracts devotees to the Sirigao Temple in Goa to prove their devotion to the goddess Lairaya by walking on a strip of burning coals in their bare feet in front of her effigy. Those preparing to walk wear brightly coloured sarongs and carry poles decorated with wisps of coloured yarn. The festival builds to a crescendo in the evening, when the coals can be seen glowing intensely. The secret is to make sure you have dry feet and to keep walking. So many people want to walk on the coals that they literally form a jostling queue. Religious sweets (*prasad*) are presented before the event, and prayers are offered to the goddess afterwards.

Where: Sirigao Temple, Bicholim Taluq, India
When: May

The air is thick with coloured powders thrown by joyful celebrants at the spring festival of Holi, popular throughout India.

INTERNATIONAL KITE FESTIVAL
Ahmedabad

Kite flying is hugely popular in Gujarat, and in the run-up to Makar Sankranti (or Uttarayan, as it is known there) – a festival that celebrates the movement of the sun into the northern hemisphere – the whole state is a frenzy of kite-making as people of all ages and backgrounds compete to make the best. Although predominantly a Hindu tradition used to wake the gods from their long winter sleep, kite flying is a popular pastime among the followers of several religions. On the big day the skies are crowded with kites of all shapes and sizes. Competition is fierce and strings are often dipped in glass powder to cut others in the battle for supremacy.

Where: All over India, especially Ahmedabad
When: Makar Sankranti, 14 January or 15 January

JAGANNATH RATH YATRA
Puri

This religious festival, held in Orissa on India's east coast, is massive. Full of drama and colour, it celebrates Lord Krishna's journey from Gokol to Mathura. Three vast wooden chariots – up to 14m high, decorated and pulled by thousands of pilgrims – are used to carry statues of Lord Jagannath, Lord Balabhadra and the goddess Subhadra in procession from the Jagannath Temple to the Gundicha Temple, a journey of around 3km. After nine days the statues are returned to the Temple and the chariots are dismantled and stored away for a year.. Linguists claim that the word juggernaut comes from Jagannath – one of Krishna's many names – and originates from the massive carts used here.

Where: Puri, India
When: 3rd month in the lunar calendar (June or July)

JHAPAN SNAKE FESTIVAL
Vishnupur

For a day in mid-August, thousands of celebrants and snake-charmers gather In the otherwise quiet town of Vishnupur (also known as Bishnupur) to honour Mansha, the goddess of snakes. They pray for good rains, fertile fields and safety from snakebites, and then settle down to a dazzling array of snake fights and snake shows, alongside breathtaking displays by fearless cobra-charmers.

Where: Vishnupur, India
When: Last day of the month of Shravan (mid August)

JAISALMER DESERT FESTIVAL
Jaisalmer

The Desert Festival is held in the Sam Dunes, near the fantastically atmospheric living fort at Jaisalmer in the Thar Desert of Rajasthan. The festival features three days of eclectic events that celebrate the area's rich local heritage, including singing, dancing, acrobatics, camel races, turban-tying contests and a longest moustache competition. For some the highlight is the annual Mr Desert competition for the most Rajputy-looking Rajput, although recent winners haven't been a patch on the original Mr Desert, who won the competition so many times he was awarded the title for life. Each day finishes off with folk music and dancing under the starry sky.

Where: Sam Dunes, near Jaisalmer, India
When: February

JANMASHTAMI
Mathura

Mathura is said to be the birthplace of Lord Krishna and although Janmashtami – the celebration of his birth – is observed all over India, it is held most enthusiastically in this city in Uttar Pradesh. Devotees flock to the Krishna Janma Bhoomi Mandir, the supposed place of his birth, now converted into a big temple, where they fast for the whole day. They chant and sing songs to Krishna, focusing on a statue kept in a small, unlit shrine called the Garbha Griha. At midnight it is bathed in milk and curd and rocked in a cradle. Prayers are followed by bell ringing and the blowing of conches before devotees break their fast.

Where: Mathura, India
When: August or September

KALI PUJA
Kolkata, West Bengal

At midnight on the first day of the new moon in the month of Kartik, while the rest of India is celebrating Diwali, the entrancing city of Kolkata pays homage to Kali, goddess of destruction. Kali symbolizes strength and Hindus believe she will protect them from evil. As darkness descends, people dress up, light candles, set off firecrackers and offer prayers to her. Consort of the Lord Shiva, Kali is also goddess of time and change and is regarded as a benevolent mother goddess. Celebrations are similar to the Durga Puja (see p .121), where the streets are full of *pandals* – temporary bamboo shrines – housing painted clay figures. At the Kali Ghat Temple, many thousands of devotees come to offer animal sacrifices, mostly goats, to the goddess, an unusual event in Hindu temples.

Where: Kolkata, India
When: New moon of Hindu month of Kartik (October/November)

KILA RAIPUR RURAL OLYMPICS
Ludhiana

A distinctly exotic echo of the Highland Games in Scotland, this annual showcase of rural sports attracts thousands of competitors and up to one million spectators over three days in February. Participants race practically anything on four legs, including camels and mules, but the biggest event, in which Punjabi men are said to demonstrate the full extent of their virility and bravery, is the bullock-cart race. Other shows of strength – if not stupidity – include lifting bicycles with your teeth and pulling cars with your ears.

Where: Ludhiana, India
When: Three days in February

KORZOK GUSTOR
Lake Tsomoriri, Korzok

This one will take your breath away – literally, for the village of Korzok, on the shore of Lake Tsomoriri, is nearly 5,000m above sea level. The Gustor festival, which takes place at Korzok Monastery over two days in July, attracts nomadic herders from the surrounding valleys to graze their herds of yak and Pashmina goats on the grasslands above the village. The festival features traditional *chams*, morality mystery dances performed by the monks. A highlight are the renowned Black Hat dancers, personifying Tantric adepts who subdue evil spirits. At a particularly noisy point, animals including goats, horses and a yak are are ceremonially 'blooded' and then released.

Where: Lake Tsomoriri, Korzok, Ladakh, India
When: Two days in July or August

KUMBH MELA, ALLAHABAD
Allahabad

Quite simply one of the great human gatherings of the world, the Hindu Kumbh Mela, commemorating the victory of gods over demons, is a mass bathing ritual. Millions of devout Hindus plunge into the Ganges to wash away their sins. It has a complex schedule involving different time cycles and four main venues (see p.133), but its biggest, most majestic manifestation occurs just once every 12 years at Allahabad, when many millions attend over a six-week period in January and February. The precise location is the Sangam, east of the city, where the Rivers Ganges and Yamuna are said to meet the mythical Sawasrati River. Here on the floodplain, a vast tented camp appears and endless ritual bathings, processions and devotions are carried out by a dazzling cast of holy men and devotees.

Where: The Sangam, near Allahabad, Uttar Pradesh, India
When: Full Kumbh, January to February, every 12 years from 2025. Next Ardh ('half') Kumbh in 2019

Har ki Pauri Ghat on the Ganges at Haridwar, one the four sites where a drop of the nectar of immortality was spilt. Haridwar has acquired a most holy significance for followers of Hinduism, which it shares with Allahabad, Ujjain and Nasi, the three other sites that were blessed with a bead of *amrit*.

KUMBH MELA, HARIDWAR
Haridwar

According to the legend behind the famous Kumbh Mela sacred bathing rituals, or 'holy dips', the Hindu god Vishnu was carrying a pot – *kumbh* – of the nectar of immortality when he spilled four drops. They landed at four different places, which are now the locations of the four main Kumbh Melas that take place every 12 years (see p. 138). At Haridwar, the mela is centered on the Har ki Pauri *ghat* which is both significant and dramatic, as it is said to be the precise spot where the River Ganges, the holiest of holy rivers, leaves the Himalayan mountains.

Where: Haridwar, India
When: Next Ardh ('half') Kumbh in 2016; next full Kumbh in 2022

KUMBH MELA, NASIK
Nasik

The Lord Rama, one of the great Hindu deities, made Nasik his home when he fled in exile from his birthplace. It is believed that he bathed in the Godavari River at a spot known as the Ramkund, which is now the focal point of the Nasik Kumbh Mela. The ritual 'holy dip' is thought to wash away sins and free people from the interminable cycle of birth and reincarnation. In 2003 it turned into a tragedy when 39 pilgrims died in a stampede.

Where: Nasik, India
When: August to September 2015; every twelve years thereafter

KUMBH MELA, UJJAIN
Ujjain

The final place where Vishnu's precious nectar fell to earth, Ujjain is built around the Shipra River, where pilgrims flock throughout the year for the Hindu bathing ritual, which is thought to free the faithful from the earth-bound cycle of reincarnation. A series of *ghats* and temples line the river banks and the river functions as a dividing line. On one side gather the naked holy men (*sadhus*) who follow Shiva; on the other side the followers of Vishnu congregate. This arrangement ensures that the Kumbh Mela, and the numerous other religious festivals at Ujjain are not blighted by the kind of arguments and scuffles that so often break out at other holy sites.

Where: Ujjain, India
When: April and May 2016 and every 12 years after

MADURAI FLOAT FESTIVAL
Madurai

This festival originated in the 17th century when King Nayak decided to build a new palace. A great excavation was dug to make the bricks and the king filled it with water to create a huge lake. He built a temple on an island in the middle of the lake and started the practice of taking statues from it on a boat ride in the waters on his birthday. Now, at dawn on the night of the full moon the statues of the goddess Meenakshi and her consort are brought from the temple on golden palanquin chairs, escorted by elephants and musicians. They are set afloat on a raft decked with flowers to the sound of music and chanting. Thousands of lights and a firework display illuminate a magical scene.

Where: Mariamman Teppakulam Tank, Madurai, India
When: Full moon of Tamil month of Thai (January/February)

MAHAMAHAM MELA
Kumbakonam

Devout Hindus believe that every 12 years the sacred waters of the River Ganges and India's other holy rivers will flow into Mahamaham, a vast temple tank in Kumbakonam. Devotees flock here in their millions to bathe in the holy tank, a pool of serenely still waters covering more than 2.5 hectares and surrounded by shrines. Within its watery depths, up to 20 wells allegedly feed India's holy rivers. With faith in the power of the sacred waters to wash away sin and restore sanctity, thousands plunge joyfully into the sea of humanity.

Where: Kumbakonam, India
When: Every 12 years; next in February to March 2016

MAHAMASTAKABHISHEKA
Shravanabelagola

This important festival of the Jain religion is held once every 12 years and involves the anointing of the head of an 18m-high statue of the Siddha Bahubali. Hundreds of thousands of pilgrims flock to the statue on top of a hill to watch as hundreds of vessels of consecrated water are poured onto the statue's head from a platform above. The statue is also bathed in milk and sugarcane juice, and sprinkled with sandalwood, turmeric and vermilion. Although the statue dates back to the 10th century, the festival has kept pace with the modern world. The last festival, in 2006, ended as masses of petals were dropped from a helicopter hovering above the statue.

Where: Shravanabelagola, India
When: Every 12 years (next time in 2018)

NANAK JAYANTI
Amritsar

This festival is held to honour the birthday of the founder of Sikhism, Guru Nanak. It is celebrated at *gurdwaras* all over the world, but the biggest and best is held at the Golden Temple in Amritsar, the spiritual centre of the Sikh religion. The day before Guru Nanak's birthday there are prayer meetings at the temple and a procession in which the holy book of the Sikhs, the Granth Sahib, is paraded around the town of Amritsar to much fanfare. Some of the devotees carry swords, displaying the martial prowess of the Sikhs. On the day itself, the Golden Temple is illuminated with lights and candles, which makes for a spectacular sight.

Where: Amritsar, India
When: Full moon of Sikh month of Kartik (October/November)

NAVARATRI (DASARA)
Gujarat

Navaratri, meaning 'nine nights', is a Hindu festival that celebrates the Mother Goddess in all her forms, including that of the many-armed goddess Durga. Although it is observed all over India, some of the most extravagant celebrations are held in Gujarat. Here, over the nine nights, people gather in open spaces to perform a *puja* to each of the manifestations of the feminine divinity. Accompanied by distinctive music they then perform a traditional local dance called *ras garba*, where people dance in a circle around a small goddess shrine. Sometimes dancers, often carrying swords or lit torches, enter a trance. The tenth day, known as Dasara, is a day of rest, representing the final victory of good over evil.

Where: All over India, especially Gujarat
When: Late September/early October

ONAM FESTIVAL
Kerala

Onam is the harvest festival of the people of Kerala, which can last up to ten days. Now the state's national festival, it is held to impress the spirit of King Mahabali on his annual visit, and sees everyone in a state of high excitement. The first and last days are considered the most important and are marked by feasts, traditional dances, visits to the temple and elephant parades. A highlight of the final day is a feast of nine courses called the Onasadya, which includes vegetarian curries, pickles, chutneys and fruits served on banana leaves. Another highlight is the spectacular Vallamkali Snake Boat race, in which up to 30 boats, each crewed by 150 chanting rowers, compete over a 40k course.

Where: All over Kerala, India
When: Ten days in Malayalam month of Chingam (August/September)

PHAYANG TSEDUP
Ladakh

Most monastery festivals in this former Himalayan kingdom, now part of India, take place in the depths of winter, when they provide a spiritual lift during the long snowbound months. But recently some monasteries have been switching their annual celebrations to the summer so that tourists can watch. Most follow a similar pattern, featuring masked *cham* dances in the monastery courtyards, enacting the history and precepts of Tibetan Buddhism, and the ceremonial unfurling of the sacred silk *thangka*, a visual aid to meditation. The festival at Phayang, in late July or early August, is one of the biggest in Ladakh.

Where: Phayang Gompa, Ladakh, India
When: July or August

PUSHKAR MELA
Pushkar Lake

Internationally famous for its camel fair, this festival is primarily a religious gathering to which pilgrims flock to bathe in the holy waters of Lake Pushkar at the auspicious time of Kartik Poormina, a Hindu holy day on the full moon in October or November. For five days leading up to the full moon, extended Rajasthani families gather here in their many thousands and are joined by camel traders – along with around 50,000 camels – who set up a market to the west of the lake. As well as the devotional activities, there are camel races, tug-of-war competitions, an ancient funfair – and much haggling over livestock.

Where: Pushkar Lake, Rajasthan, India
When: Five days leading up to the Kartik Poornima full Moon (October or November)

REPUBLIC DAY
New Delhi

India celebrates its independence with a national holiday and a massive Republic Day parade down the colonial Rajpath in New Delhi. This part of the capital was constructed during the swansong of British rule, and includes the India Gate and the formidable parliament buildings, the Lok Sabha and Rajya Sabha. The parade is a great source of national pride. There is a large military element to the day, including colourful cavalry parades, such as that of the Bengal Lancers and the camel-mounted Border Security Force. Floats representing each of the country's states and the city's schools also feature. A daredevil motorcycle display team and a flypast by the Indian Air Force ends a parade that is uniquely Indian.

Where: New Delhi, India
When: 26 January

Traders with their camels gather at the Pushkar Mela in Rajasthan, India, a livestock and camel fair that draws as many 50,000 camels to swell the crowds of pilgrims who come to bathe in the holy waters of Lake Pushkar.

SONEPUR MELA
Sonepur

If you're looking for a second-hand elephant, then this is the spot. This annual jamboree, like the Pushkar Mela, takes place on the Hindu holy day of Kartik Poormina. Billed as the largest livestock fair in Asia, its highlight is the *haathi*, or elephant bazaar, where these vast beasts of burden are bought and sold by the score. Plenty of other animals are also traded, including cattle, goats and horses, which are raced on a short course to attract buyers. While money changes hands at the fair, pilgrims rush to purify their souls where the Ganges and Gandak rivers meet.

Where: Sonepur, near Patna, India
When: One month from the Kartik Poornima full Moon (October or November)

'Holy Dip' – Indian Bathing Festivals

PILGRIMAGE TO A SACRED PLACE OR RELIGIOUS GATHERING IS AN IMPORTANT PART OF LIFE FOR MILLIONS OF DEVOUT HINDUS. THE NUMBER OF THESE OCCASIONS IS GROWING EVERY YEAR AND TODAY MORE PEOPLE THAN EVER ARE TAKING PART. MANY OF THESE HUGE GATHERINGS, OR *MELAS*, FEATURE RITUAL BATHING – THE DELIGHTFULLY NAMED 'HOLY DIP'.

ABOVE A devotee performs *Kartik Snan* (taking a holy dip in the Ganges during Kartika, November to December).

OPPOSITE Pilgrims bathing in the Ganges at Varanasi during the Dev Deepavali Festival.

The encampment of livestock traders around Lake Pushkar at the five-day festival of Pushkar Mela in Rajasthan, India.

Sadhu (Indian Holy Man) meditating by the holy Lake Pushkar with bathing pilgrims behind.

ABOVE Taking a 'holy dip' at the Ganga Sagar Mela.

The great Hindu bathing festivals of India are attended by vast numbers of people. Viewed from afar, the crowds, measured in the uniquely Indian denominations of *lakhs* (100,000) and *crores* (10 million), appear like teeming ants. Almost unimaginable numbers of people flock to points along one of India's seven sacred rivers to bathe and earn good *karma*.

Devout Hindus believe in reincarnation: that the soul is continuously reborn until it is freed from the cycle of *samsara* by the attainment of enlightenment, *moksha* or *nirvana*. There are a number of ways of doing this, involving good deeds and righteous living. A short cut is through pilgrimage and the 'holy dip'. The more auspicious the location and time of bathing, the more effective the spiritual cleansing.

Sometimes the bathing ritual is carried out according to the instructions of arcane and ancient texts, but more often it is a joyous bath, with pilgrims soaping themselves, laughing, splashing and ducking under the waters. It is an inclusive ritual, too: tourists and spectators will invariably be invited to partake in their own holy dip, irrespective of their religious beliefs.

Auspicious times are usually fixed by the lunar cycle and change in relation to the Gregorian solar calendar. Over the years, on particularly auspicious bathing dates, so many pilgrims have wanted to bathe that attendance at the great festivals has expanded, sometimes beyond counting. These large gatherings have each taken on their own life and character.

At the sacred Lake Pushkar, under the Kartik Poornima full moon (in October to November), tribal people from Rajasthan gather to bathe and trade camels. It is believed that Lake Pushkar was formed by a petal that dropped from the lotus flower used by Lord Brahma to slay the demon Vajranabha. The lake is considered one of the most holy places in India, and alcohol and all animal products are banned from the town.

Over the years tourists have made their own pilgrimage to the Pushkar Mela, which has been renamed the Pushkar Camel Fair (see p. 127), although for the locals the ritual bathing is more important than the camel trading, which is a secondary, commercial activity. The camel trading takes place in the days leading up to the full moon, at which point many of the traders and tourists drift away. The number of pilgrims peaks at the full moon and the steps, or *ghats*, that line the edge of the lake are thronged with people all night and well into the day.

ABOVE Crowds of pilgrims, traders and potential buyers gather to watch the elephants bathe on the banks of the Ganges at Sonepur, India, home to the largest livestock fair in Asia.

The Sonepur Mela in Bihar is the largest livestock fair in Asia (see p. 127). Here you can buy horses, goats, sheep, chickens, cattle and even buffalo, but the biggest draw is the *haathi*, or elephant bazaar, where scores of elephants are traded. The elephants are bathed and decorated to get the best price, and are kept in camps under ancient shady trees. Officially the buying and selling of elephants is not permitted, so they are traded with elaborate leases.

One of the oldest festivals in India, the Sonepur Mela dates back to a mythical struggle between two gods in the shape of a crocodile and an elephant. Pilgrims come to bathe under the full moon at the confluence of the holy Ganges and Gandak rivers. Around three *lakhs* of people can turn up on the main bathing day, swamping the village and prompting the police to set up a large one-way system for pedestrians. Most don't stay here, arriving early in the morning, bathing, then attempting to reach the small temple on the banks of the Ganges before fitting in a bit of shopping and heading home.

Not all Indian bathing festival dates are fixed by the moon. The Ganga Sagar Mela, which takes place on Sagar Island in the mouth of the Ganges River delta in West Bengal, is unique as it is set by the solar calendar (see p. 122). It is held on the same day every year, Makara Sankranti (14 January), when the sun begins its journey north, and the winter officially begins to turn to summer.

Up to five *lakhs* of pilgrims gather to bathe in the mouth of the Hooghly (a tributary of the Ganges) as it flows into the Bay of Bengal. It is a strange and atmospheric sight, as hordes of pilgrims head down to the beach to bathe in the dead of night. The ritual

132

ABOVE A Hindu devotee in prayer at Ganga Sagar, an annual festival of purification that takes place on Sagar Island in the Bay of Bengal.

ABOVE RIGHT Devotees flock to leave offerings and receive blessings in the form of sweets called *prasad* at the Kapil Muni Temple, during the Ganga Sagar Mela in West Bengal.

involves an element of suffering, too, as the nights are very cold and the water can be all but freezing. Many of the pilgrims camp out all night in makeshift shelters. To help them find their way in the dark, red, green and blue lights illuminate the main paths through the *mela* ground to the sea. Adding to the unworldly feel, there is often a deep fog swirling around the crowds.

After bathing, pilgrims head to the Kapilmuni temple, passing dozens of *sadhus*, holy men, who proffer blessings for a few rupees. These *sadhus* are often obscured in a haze of hashish smoke.

The holiest site in Hinduism is Varanasi, the ancient city on the banks of the Ganges in the state of Uttar Pradesh. Often referred to as the oldest living city in the world, it attracts vast numbers of pilgrims throughout the year who aim to bathe, and sometimes to die and be cremated, here. At auspicious times of the year, the number of pilgrims swells, but the festival that is most spectacularly associated with the city is Dev Deepavali (see p. 121). On this day, when the gods are thought to come to earth, countless tiny lamps are lit and placed on the ancient *ghats* leading down to the river as pilgrims bathe in the cold water.

The Kumbh Mela

The largest of all of the Hindu bathing festivals – in fact, the largest gathering of humans on the planet – is the Kumbh Mela (see p. 125). Dating back to ancient history, the Kumbh Mela is held in four different places over a complicated rotating twelve-

BELOW Women joyously give thanks to the gods for their victory over the demons at the mass bathing ritual at Allahabad in Uttar Pradesh, India.

BELOW RIGHT A bird's-eye view of the Har ki Pauri Ghat at night, aglow with the lights of the countless pilgrims who gather once every twelve years for the Haridwar Kumbh Mela.

year schedule. Its origins lie in Hindu mythology, in a battle between the gods and the demons over a pitcher (or *kumbh*) of *amrit* – the nectar of immortality. During a twelve-day titanic struggle four drops of nectar fell to earth at four different locations: Allahabad, Haridwar, Ujjain and Nasik. One god day is equivalent to a human year, which leads to the twelve-year schedule.

The most auspicious of the locations is Allahabad in Uttar Pradesh, where pilgrims bathe in the Sangam, the confluence of the holy Ganges, Yamuna and the mythical Saraswati rivers (see p. 124). Every twelveth Allahabad Kumbh Mela is designated as a Mahakumbh, or Great Kumbh, and the last Mahakumbh Mela in 2001 was the largest gathering of people with a single intent there has ever been. Over the six or seven weeks of the festival, some estimates put the number of pilgrims attending as high as 100 million. Certain days set by astronomical calculations, are designated as particularly

OPPOSITE *Akhara* of *sadhus* processing to Har ki Pauri Ghat during the Kumbh Mela, Haridwar.

OVERLEAF Elephant and pilgrims crossing the Ganges on one of the temporary pontoon bridges constructed by the *mela* authorities.

auspicious, and on these days the numbers of pilgrims peak. On the main bathing day in 2001 up to 35 million pilgrims are thought to have made their way to the water – making the temporary *mela* ground one of the largest cities in the world by population.

As well as pilgrims, the Kumbh Mela is noted for the legions of *sadhus* who turn up to bathe. Some of these are formed into great organizations, or *akharas*. The most fearsome of these are the *naga sadhus* who walk around covered only in the ash from fires, sport great dreadlocks, and smoke *charas* (cannabis resin) as an integral part of their veneration of Lord Shiva. The three or four most auspicious days of the Kumbh Mela are designated *shahi snans*, or royal bathing days. On these days, the *akharas* process to the Sangam to bathe. The largest is the Juna *akhara*, with thousands of members who carry tridents and swords and are an ancient and fearful sight. They have been known to attack people who inadvertently get in their way or somehow offend them, with virtual impunity.

ABOVE Followers of the Juna Akhara in procession on one of the main bathing days of the Maha Kumbh Mela 2001 at Allahabad.

OPPOSITE Hindu devotees and pilgrims practise their faith in a variety of ways to earn good *karma* at the one of the many bathing festivals that take place, at auspicious times, on one of India's seven sacred rivers.

Although the Kumbh Melas at the other holy sites are smaller, they still attract tens of millions of pilgrims (see pp. 124–5). In Haridwar, where the Ganges flows out of the Himalayas, the waters are cold and so fast-flowing that pilgrims have to hold on to chains fixed to the Har ki Pauri Ghat to avoid being washed away. At Ujjain in Madhya Pradesh pilgrims bathe in the slow-flowing Shipra River. Here there are *ghats* on either side of the river, which are used to separate the *sadhus* who follow Shiva from those who follow Vishnu. At Nasik in Maharashtra, the smallest of the Kumbhs, pilgrims bathe in the Ramkund, a holy tank, and also in the Godavari River.

The Joy of Bathing

Hinduism is essentially a very practical religion. If you need to appeal to a god for a particular reason, then there is likely to be one to suit you. If you can't afford to travel to one of the major bathing festivals such as the Kumbh Mela, or even if you live overseas, then there is likely to be another revered bathing place nearby. Combine this with the many auspicious times to bathe that are set by the stars or the lunar calendar, or by Hindu mythology, and you can find bathing festivals to suit you all over India. These include the Tarnetar Mela, which brings pilgrims to a tank in Gujarat, and the Mahamaham Mela, which happens at Kumbakonam in Tamil Nadu every twelve years (see pp. 126 and 142). There are even bathing festivals further afield, such as the

ABOVE Pilgrims bathing on one of the auspicious bathing days at the Maha Kumbh Mela at Allahabad.

INSET *Mela* ground constructed for the 2001 Maha Kumbh Mela at Allahabad, the largest ever gathering of humans on the planet.

annual Mahashivratri festival at the Ganga Talao, a crater lake in Mauritius (see p. 14).

One thing that has struck me at all of the many Hindu bathing festivals I have experienced is the sheer joy of those bathing. True, there are some pilgrims who take a more ritual and austere approach, such as the *kalpwasis*, who might spend as many as forty days at some of the bigger festivals, following an elaborate schedule of prayer and bathing, but many pilgrims laugh and smile in happy family groups. The important thing is for people to immerse themselves: how they do it seems to be up to them. Some jump into the water, others splash each other and giggle, while others laughingly duck hesitant family members. For many devout Hindus, travelling to one of the great bathing festivals is the culmination of a lot of planning, saving and expectation. This fulfilment brings a sense of euphoria that they want to share with family, friends and even the odd Western photographer.

I have taken a holy dip a number of times. Not because I am Hindu, or even because I am religious in any way. I have bathed simply because I would have felt bad not bathing. People have waved me over, included me and laughed with me. The question is always 'Have you bathed?' not 'Will you bathe?', and when I think of the hardships that so many of the pilgrims have endured for their holy dip, it would seem churlish not to join them. Even at the Sangam at the Mahakumbh Mela festival in 2001, said to be the holiest place in Hinduism at the most auspicious time in 144 years, I experienced nothing but smiles and entreaties to join pilgrims for a dip. I can't for the life of me imagine any other religion that would be so welcoming to a non-believer at such a special time.

Performers wearing oversized and elaborate masks tell the story, in dance, of the deities they represent at the Tak Thok monastery, Ladakh, India.

TAK THOK TSE CHU
Ladakh

A grotto, its walls blackened by centuries of smoke from butter lamps, lies at the heart of the Ladakhi monastery of Tak Thok. This cave is believed to have been the sheltering place of Padmasambhava, the guru who brought Tibetan Buddhism to this former mountain kingdom. It is this auspicious connection that is celebrated at the monastery's annual festival, which takes place in July or August. Two days of dancing and ritual in the monastery courtyard culminate in a masked dance in which figures with giant heads represent various deities – including Padmasambhava himself.

Where: Tak Thok, Ladakh, India
When: The 28th and 29th days of the 9th Tibetan month (July to August)

TARNETAR MELA
Tarnetar

If you're looking for a husband, wear a red skirt and head for this village near the town of Thangadh between the fourth and sixth days of the Hindu month of Bhadarva (August to September). The single men are the ones in the colourful *dhotis* and waistcoats, bashfully twirling umbrellas. The festival's matchmaking aspect is just one part of a glorious celebration of Gujarati folk traditions. As men and women in dazzling costumes perform traditional dances, children play at the funfair and a cast of magic men, tattoo artists and canny salesmen provide an entertaining sideshow.

Where: Tarnetar India
When: Fourth to the 6th day of the Hindu month of Bhadarva (August to September)

THRISSUR POORAM
Thrissur

Justly renowned for its fabulously decorated elephants and hypnotic drumming and percussion, Thrissur Pooram is the biggest and most dramatic temple pageant of its kind. It takes place over one day in April or May at the Vadakkunatha Temple in Thrissur, the largest temple complex in this south Indian state. Two processions converge on the temple, each with a contingent of 15 beautifully decorated elephants bearing sacred statues from the nearby temples and, as the music grows louder and faster, the holy men astride the elephants stand up to wave fans and parasols in frantic time. The climax of the evening is a firework display above the brightly lit temple.

Where: Thrissur, India
When: Maly month of Medam (around April)

> NEPAL

BISKET JATRA
Bhaktapur

Bhaktapur is one of the best-preserved towns in Nepal and over Nepali New Year – mid-April – its old cobblestones echo to the wheels of a huge chariot, hauled by scores of townspeople. The chariot is assembled for the occasion from pieces that for the rest of the year are kept next to the Bhairabnath Temple. Aboard the chariot is an image of Bhairab, a fearsome manifestation of Shiva. Smaller chariots, representing lesser deities, accompany the big one as it trundles its way through the town. At one point there is a tug of war between different neighbourhoods to determine who will have the honour of looking after the chariots and their precious cargo of gods. On the evening of the first day of the New Year, the images are returned to their temples and the chariots dismantled for another year.

Where: Bhaktapur, Kathmandu Valley, Nepal
When: Four days before and after the Nepali New Year

DASAIN
Kathmandu

Evil once reigned in the divine world, but the goddess Durga slayed the demon king Mahishasura and all was well again. Hindus all over Nepal give thanks to Durga over 15 days in the lunar month of Ashvin (September to October), the longest and biggest festival in Nepal. Durga is worshipped in all her manifestations but the centrepiece of the festivities is the mass sacrifice of animals, especially goats and buffalo – a spectacle that can be troubling to outsiders. The tradition of bloodletting is supposed to appease the darkest of Durga's manifestations, the goddess Kali.

Where: All over Nepal, especially Kathmandu
When: 15 days, finishing on the full moon of the Nepali month of Ashvin (September to October)

FAGU
Kathmandu Valley

An orgy of smearing and drenching characterizes this cheerful mess of a celebration that takes place over two days in February or March. This is the Nepali version of Holi, marked by Hindus all over the world, and represents a release from winter and a joyous embrace of the coming spring. People smear each other in coloured powder – especially red vermilion – throw water and generally run wild. In Kathmandu the action takes place on Durbar Square – wear old clothes and watch your back!

Where: Kathmandu Valley, Nepal
When: Two days around the full moon in the Nepali month of Falgun (February to March)

LOSAR
Kathmandu Valley

For more than two lively weeks in December to January, ethnic peoples of Tibetan origin – such as Sherpas, Tamangs and Gurungs – welcome in the Tibetan New Year. They dress in traditional costumes and attend monasteries where Buddhist monks offer prayers for an auspicious year to come. Families host feasts where gifts are exchanged and though practices vary according to locality and grouping, they all emphasize a sense of togetherness and identity.

Where: Kathmandu Valley, Nepal
When: Fifteen days in the Nepali month of Poush (December to January)

MANI RIMDU
Everest region

You couldn't get much nearer to the gods than this. In the shadow of the world's highest mountain, the Sherpa peoples of the Khumbu region celebrate the victory of Buddhism over the pagan gods of the ancient Bon religion. Over nine days, from the first day of the tenth Tibetan lunar month (October to November), the symbolic battle between order and chaos is ritualized in a series of dances in which monks assume the identities of various deities. An elaborate *mandala* – a sacred diagram of the cosmos – painstakingly constructed in coloured sand, serves as a focus for meditation.

Where: Tengboche Monastry, Everest region, Nepal
When: Full moon of the 10th Tibetan lunar month (October to November)

SHIVARATRI
Kathmandu Valley

An astonishing myth has been ritualized into one of the greatest of all Hindu festivals – Shiva saved the world by swallowing a poison that would have destroyed it, and Hindus have given thanks ever since during Shivaratri, the Great Night of Shiva. At Pashupatinath Temple on the banks of the holy River Bagmati, more than 100,000 pilgrims and *sadhus* (holy men) gather on a moonless night in February or March to pay homage to Lord Shiva with a night of prayers and chanting. The following morning, the faithful bathe in the river waters to wash the slate clean and start afresh. *Sadhus* and pilgrims alike smoke hashish liberally during Shivaratri as an aid to spiritual enlightenment.

Where: Pashupatinath Temple, Kathmandu Valley, Nepal
When: Chaturdashi (14th day) of Krishna Paksha (waning moon) of the Hindu month of Falgun (March)

A devotee of Lord Shiva draws on his pipe of hashish to help him on his spiritual path of enlightenment at the festival of Shivaratri in Kathmandu, Nepal.

> PAKISTAN

BASANT FESTIVAL
Lahore

Kites fill the sky – some as big as a light aircraft, others little bigger than pocket handkerchiefs. Their strings are embedded with sharp pieces of glass to sabotage rival kites. The winner is the last one flying. The action takes place during the beautiful kite festival, known as Basant, which occurs every spring (February or March) in the Punjab region of Pakistan. For days leading up to the festival – which is simply a way of ushering in spring – people are out practising, and on the day itself every open space and rooftop fills with kite flyers. In Lahore the celebrations are particularly intense and spectacular, with brass bands, firework displays and even acrobatic performances.

Where: All over Punjab, especially Lahore
When: At the start of spring, around February or March

CHAWMOS (WINTER) FESTIVAL
Kalash Valleys

When you live in as remote and inhospitable a place as this, you deserve to treat yourself with a winter knees-up. The Kalash minority people of north-west Pakistan inhabit three remote valleys near the border with Afghanistan. For two weeks around the winter solstice, they celebrate the end of the harvest by drinking mulberry wine, dancing and feasting on goats they have sacrificed. The Kalash are animists and believe that at this time of year their god Balimain comes to dwell among them. To show their strength and unity, they make model animals from pastry, which the children then 'hunt' by throwing stones at them.

Where: Kalash Valleys, Chitral, Pakistan
When: Two weeks at the winter solstice

JOSHI (SPRING) FESTIVAL
Kalash Valleys

As the days lengthen and the sun warms the hillsides, the Kalash people throw a springtime party, in which they give thanks to the god Goshidai for protecting their herds through the winter. For three days in May, at each of their three valleys in turn, men and women gather to dance to the rhythm of vigorous drumming, turning in spinning lines around the dancing ground or *charso*. At the height of the festival, bunches of herbs are waved around before being ceremonially into the valley. There is also a courting aspect to the festival, as it is traditionally a time where unmarried couples forge relationships by eloping!

Where: Kalash Valleys, Chitral, Pakistan
When: Three days in May

SEHWAN SHARIF FESTIVAL
Sehwan

The ancient city of Sehwan is a hugely significant site in Sufism – a mystical form of Islam – as this is the burial place of the Sufi patron saint, Lal Shahbaz Qalandar, who died in 1274. Pilgrims pay homage at his mausoleum throughout the year, but for three days and nights in September the devotions reach a crescendo as a more than half a million pilgrims, fakirs and devotees descend on the city from all over Pakistan. The celebrants dance and spin like Dervishes, whirling into an ecstasy of devotion as they press around Qalander's white tomb. It's an intense but happy occasion, enjoyed by women and men alike, with no underlying religious tensions.

Where: Sehwan, Pakistan
When: Three days in September

SHANDUR POLO FESTIVAL
Gilgit-Baltistan

Conducted at breakneck speed, practically on the roof of the planet, the polo matches of Shandur are one of the world's great sporting and cultural spectacles. At 3,734m, the polo field in this remote and mountainous part of northern Pakistan is the highest in the world. For two days in July, it hosts a tournament between teams from Chitral and Gilgit that attracts thousands of spectators and attendant entertainments, including music and dancing. This annual event was started in 1936 by a British political agent, a Major Cobb, but polo has been played by tribesmen for many centuries and the modern players who light up Shandur every year are highly skilled and brave.

Where: Shandur Polo Field, Gilgit-Baltistan, Pakistan
When: Two days in July

> SRI LANKA

DURUTHU PERAHERA
Colombo

One of the great elephant festivals of the Indian subcontinent, the Duruthu Perahera marks the visit of the Lord Buddha to Sri Lanka 2,500 years ago. First held in 1927, it takes place at the Kelaniya Raja Maha Vihara temple over three days in January and consists of three daily processions in which a casket holding a relic of the Buddha is carried through the streets. The most spectacular of these features gaily decorated elephants as well as whip-crackers, fire-jugglers and legions of monks and dancers.

Where: Colombo, Sri Lanka
When: Three days ending on the pre-full moon day in January

Polo at its highest! The Shandur Top in Gilgit-Baltistan, Pakistan provides a breathtakingly beautiful setting for a game played without rules or an umpire.

ESALA PERAHERA
Kandy

Magnificently caparisoned elephants are a feature of the Esala Perahera, which takes place over 10 days in July or August. At its heart is a tooth of the Buddha, or rather a replica of the tooth, the original of which remains in the Temple of the Tooth, Sri Lanka's most important Buddhist shrine. A golden casket, representing the Tooth Relic, is carried by an elephant whose path through the crowds is cleared by fire-jugglers and whip-crackers. In its wake trails a colourful and noisy parade of pilgrims, musicians, torch bearers, monks and more elephants. Various similar parades take place over successive days, each announced by the ceremonial firing of a cannon that booms out over the city.

Where: Kandy, Sri Lanka
When: Full moon of Buddhist month of Esala (July or August)

VEL FESTIVAL
Colombo

Vel, the mythic spear with which the Hindu god Murugan vanquished the evil deity Soorapadman, is worshipped throughout Sri Lanka as a symbol of Murugan's power and virtue. On the new moon in July or August, it becomes the focus of an elaborate festival in Colombo as an ornate silver chariot carrying a statue of Lord Murugan (or the war god Skanda) is processed through the streets accompanied by a retinue of decorated elephants, dancers and drummers. In keeping with the theme of Vel, some devotees perform acts of self-mutilation such as skewering their cheeks and suspending themselves on hooks piercing their bare backs.

Where: Colombo, Sri Lanka
When: Around the new moon of Ādi (July to August)

>> SOUTH-EAST ASIA

> MYANMAR (BURMA)

PHAUNG DAW U
Inle Lake

For more than 11 months of the year, the five golden Buddhas of Phaung Daw U Pagoda on Lake Inle remain in their temple shrine. Then, over a period of nearly three weeks in September and October, four of them are brought out and paraded around the lake, amid great celebrations (the fifth stays behind to guard the shrine). The Buddhas are displayed on a gilded barge which is towed in a clockwise direction round the shoreline by boats of leg-rowers, using oars controlled by their feet and calves. At each village the procession stops so that local people can honour the statues. Just as dramatic as the religious pageantry are the boat races between men's and women's teams of leg-rowers.

Where: Inle Lake, Myanmar
When: Around 18 days during the Burmese month of Thadingyut (September to October)

THINGYAN
Myanmar

For three or four days in mid-April the country is deluged with goodwill – and water – as it ushers in the New Year in a Burmese variant of the water celebrations that take place all over Southeast Asia. The first day starts soberly enough as people visit temples to lay offerings before monks and sacred images of the Buddha. As night falls, things loosen up with dancing and drinking and, on the next day, the mood intensifies with the drenchings – the heart of Thingyan proper. The signal is given by the firing of a cannon and then no one is safe. As people assail one another with hoses and water pistols, as well as bowls and buckets of cooling, cleansing water, it's sometimes easy to forget the symbolic origins of the festival – the washing away of sins and the hope for new life.

Where: All over Myanmar
When: Usually 13–16 April

> CAMBODIA

BON OM TUK
Phnom Penh

A natural phenomenon that was once regarded as miraculous is the focus of this ancient festival dating back to the reign of King Jayavarman II in the 9th century. The Tonlé Sap River, which converges with the Mekong River at Phnom Penh, feeds the enormous Tonlé Sap Lake. At the

Colourfully decorated Cambodian longboats with up to forty rowers prepare to outrace each other on the Tonlé Sap River for Bon Om Tuk celebrations at Phnom Penh, Cambodia.

end of the rainy season, in late November, it reverses its flow and drains into the Mekong, and the lake shrinks. The occasion is marked throughout the country but the capital is the main centre for festivities. Here residents and visitors take to the water for three days of boat races, concerts and ceremonial thanksgiving for the rains.

Where: Phnom Penh, Cambodia
When: Full moon on Buddhist month of Kadauk (November)

BUFFALO RACING CEREMONY
Preah Vihear Sour

The name is a slight misnomer, as horses as well as water buffalo are ridden through the narrow streets of this village to the north-east of Phnom Penh. The races mark the end of the Cambodian festival of Pchum Ban, when families honour the spirits of the dead over a 15-day period in September or October. Having discharged their obligations to their ancestors, Cambodians decorate the heads and horns of their water buffalo and take to the saddle. There are also Khmer wrestling bouts and, at the end of it, the buffalo are auctioned off, with the race winners receiving the best prices.

Where: Preah Vihear Sour, Cambodia
When: September or October

CHAUL CHNAM THMEY
Cambodia

New Year rituals can vary dramatically around the world. In the cold north, the Scots offer their hosts lumps of coal for the fire. In the tropical south, Cambodians throw purifying water instead. Chaul Chnam Thmey, Cambodian New Year, is marked by a countrywide water fight, after a more sober series of ceremonies. The festival, which falls in the middle of April, lasts three days, each of them distinct in character. The first day, Maha Songkran, is the last day of the old year and an opportunity to visit temples and monasteries and offer thanks to the Buddha. The second day, Virak Wanabat, is a time to make donations to the poor and remember ancestors, while on the final day, T'ngai Leang Saka, Cambodians traditionally bathe images of the Buddha with perfumed water – then go on to shower each other.

Where: All over Cambodia
When: Three days from 13 or 14 April

> INDONESIA

GALUNGAN
Bali

For ten festive days every 210 days, the tropical island of Bali is filled with the cheerful sounds and bright colours of Galungan. It is the sesason when the gods, including the supreme deity Sanghyang Widi, descend to earth – when *'dharma* (virtue) is winning'. To provide a fitting welcome for the immortals, the streets are dressed with *penjor* (decorated bamboo); the temples and shrines are showered with *banten,* or offerings of fruits, flowers and cakes; and everywhere *gamelan* orchestras fill the air with their shimmering rhythms. Across the island, shaggy, lion-like *barongs*, symbolizing guardian spirits, prance and pounce around the temples and villages. Many Balinese return to their home villages, or *kampung*, for the festivities. On the first day, men wake early to slaughter the pigs, which are turned into countless tasty dishes and served up with rice cakes and tropical fruits. Once sated, people sit back, chat and chill out over a glass of *arak*.

Where: Bali, Indonesia
When: Ten days around the 11th week of the Balinese calendar

MALE'AN SAMPI FESTIVAL
Lombok

Since *male'an* means 'chase' and *sampi* means 'cow', there are no prizes for guessing the focus of the Male'an Sampi Festival. Quite literally, it is a cattle race or, more exactly, a series of wild cattle races staged on a 100m waterlogged rice paddy. As the race is unique to the island of Lombok, it draws farmers, herdsmen and tourists from across Indonesia to place bets and marvel at the courage and skill of the riders. Before the race, the best cows are carefully selected, bedecked in trimmings and ceremonially paraded by their jockeys amid a fanfare of music and cheers. The chosen cows are paired and hooked up to a yoke that will be ridden by a brave and, as the race progresses, increasingly mud-bespattered jockey. The winning cattle gain star ratings and fetch the best prices at auction. As the event falls at the end of the harvest, it is an occasion to give thanks and celebrate with much dancing and feasting.

Where: Various villages, Lombok, Indonesia
When: April

NYEPI (BALINESE NEW YEAR)
Bali

Only the trill of insects and the barking of dogs can be heard across the island on Balinese New Year. The airport closes, cars stop running and even the famous beaches are deserted. The day is reserved for self-reflection, silence, fasting and meditation. The days leading up to Nyepi, though, are quite another matter. On Melasti, three days beforehand, temple statues are ceremonially processed downriver for ritual bathings. On Tawur Kesanga, the day before Nyepi, villages exorcize their demons by parading giant-fanged *ogoh-ogoh* effigies down to the village crossroads, where a lively carnival is held before the *ogoh-ogohs* are torched in a noisy, sunset finale.

Where: Bali, Indonesia
When: Start of the Balinese Year

PASOLA
Sumba

Much like a medieval joust, but with blunt lances, the Pasola is a ceremonial tournament between mounted riders who hurl wooden spears at their opponents in a dramatic display of prowess and courage. The popular pageant heralds the arrival of spring and pays homage to Nyale, goddess of fertility. She is represented by a remarkable natural coincidence – the arrival of thousands of multi-hued *nyale* (sea worms) along the shore. Although today the jousters' spears are blunt, injuries and even deaths still occur, but any blood spilled is regarded optimistically as the sign of a rich harvest.

Where: Sumba, Indonesia
When: February and March

PERANG TOPAT
West Lombok

This spirited food fight, in which Muslims and Hindus fling rice cakes at each other, is not what it seems – it is not an example of communal violence but rather a reflection of the harmony between the two communities, who unite to celebrate the harvest by showering each other with rice. In the run-up to the main event, each community prepares festive food, including the *ketupat* (leaf-wrapped parcels of rice) that will soon be hurled in the rice fight. Before then, both Muslims and Hindus proceed to the Pura Lingsar, a Hindu temple with a Muslim shrine, where they commemorate the temple's anniversary and thank the gods for the harvest with offerings of rice cakes, fruit and buffalo. When the first Waru flower wilts in the afternoon, it is a sign for everyone to start pelting each other with rice. Any leftovers are buried in the fields to ensure a fruitful harvest.

Where: Pura Lingsar Temple, west Lombok, Indonesia
When: The 6th full moon in the Sasak calendar (November to December)

PUKUL SAPU
Mamala and Morella

In a 400-year-old ritual, bare-chested men from the villages of Mamala and Morella beat each other in turn with homemade rattan or brushwood switches until they bleed. The wounds, inflicted on the back and chest, are swiftly treated with coconut Mamala oil, which is reputed to heal them within days. The puzzling custom stems from a bloody event in their shared history, when their ancestors were imprisoned for fighting the colonial Dutch in the Kapahala War (1643–6). On their release, the rebels held a farewell ceremony with dance and song, but also with broom-beating to mark the ground and the occasion with their common blood. The ceremony today seals the villagers' ancient friendship.

Where: Mamala and Morella villages, Bali, Indonesia
When: A week after the end of Ramadan

TANA TORAJA FUNERAL RITES
South Sulawesi

The Toraja are famed for their unique funeral customs and equally unusual burial grounds, carved out of sheer rock face. Although notionally Christian, the Toraja's traditionally animistic beliefs emerge in their elaborate funeral rites. When someone dies, they're not buried immediately but stored beneath the house, sometimes for years, until enough money has been raised for the funeral. When it comes, it is a jolly leaving affair. Buffalo and pigs are sacrificed to ferry the souls to the afterlife, after which a huge feast is thrown for the entire village. The week-long festival, known as a *tornate*, culminates in ritual dances and even bullfights. At the end the body is laid to rest, often in a small cave or tomb cut into the nearby cliffs, but sometimes in a bamboo casket suspended on a wooden ledge built into the rock face.

Where: Tana Toraja, south Sulawesi, Indonesia.
When: Variable

USABA SAMBAH
Tenganan Pegringsingan

Boys and girls take it in turns to display their respective attractions in the Usaba Sambah courtship ceremony of the Bali Aga mountain people. In massed duels, known as *makare-kare*, wiry young men clad only in sarongs whip each other with sharp-edged pandan leaves until blood is drawn. After the gladiatorial contests, it's the girls' turn to take centre-stage for the *maayunan* ritual. Dressed in their finest silks, seven at a time climb on to a giant wooden ferris wheel and rise serenely into the air, keenly watched by the embattled warriors below. At a deeper level, the wheel symbolizes the turning of fortune and the dynamic flux of nature.

Where: Tenganan Pegringsingan, Bali, Indonesia
When: The 5th month of the Tenganan calendar (May to June)

WAISAK DAY
Borobudur

Moonlight, lanterns, chanting – this annual pilgrimage of hundreds of monks is a breathtaking spectacle as well as being a profoundly spiritual event. Under a full moon in May, saffron-robed monks celebrate the Buddha's birthday by processing 3km from the Candi Mendut temple to the vast stone Borobudar monument, which represents the Buddhist cosmos. At its base are carvings of ordinary mortals, flawed and confused, and the path then winds up through representations of different levels of spiritual awareness till it reaches the enlightenment of Nirvana at the top. Here monks leave offerings and continue to meditate and chant into the night before releasing a thousand lanterns into the sky.

Where: Borobudur, Java, Indonesia
When: Full moon in 4th Lunar month (usually May)

>LAOS

BUN BANG FAI
Laos

One by one, the giant fire rockets fizz and roar and shoot for the stars, leaving a trail of cloudy white smoke streaking across the spring sky. The Laotian fire rocket festival is an age-old ritual to encourage the gods to send abundant rain. Noisy rockets might seem an odd way to petition the gods but the custom apparently harks back to a rain god who was partial to fire, prompting his devotees to send him a trial *bun bang fai* (fire rocket). This seemed to do the trick and the habit stuck. Many rockets today can be 6m long and most are homemade, but the Buddhist monks build the best to an age-old formula, stuffed with black gunpowder and decorated with ribbons and a dragon's head. As the rains herald the planting season, Bun Bang Fai is also an occasion for gathering and bonding before the toil of planting starts.

Where: All over Laos
When: Mid-May

LAI HEUA FAI
Luang Prabang

Like no other boats, the boats of Lai Heua Fai are built not to float but to burn in a pyrotechnic show of amber light. Fashioned from bamboo and tissue paper and filled with tiers of candles, they are ceremonially launched into the river and set alight as an offering to the *nagas* (water spirits). In the run-up to the festival, homemade boats of every size, shape and colour are paraded through the town in a candlelit procession with much chanting and drumming. Once safely lined up at Wat Xieng Thong, the boats are judged, then lit and set adrift on the Mekong River, where they blaze alight. Along the bank, people make their wishes

Young Buddhist monks receive a rather wet blessing from New Year well-wishers in Luang Prabang, Laos.

as they scatter a myriad little fire boats and flowers on to the river to thank the *naga* and honour the Buddha.

Where: All over Laos, especially Luang Prabang
When: One day after the full moon of the 11th lunar month.
....

PI MAI LAO (LAO NEW YEAR)
Luang Prabang

In Laos the theme of renewal inherent in New Year festivities is expressed through the liberal throwing about of water – and, if it's a really good soaking you're after, then head to the beautiful old capital, Luang Prabang, in mid-April, when the New Year celebrations are in full swing. On a sandbar in the middle of the Mekong River, people make sandcastles. The city's principal image of the Buddha is processed through the streets and lesser images are ritually cleansed. And then there is no hiding place as the buckets of water begin to fly.

Where: Luang Prabang, Laos
When: Events last a week, but the main days are 14–16 April
....

PHA THAT LUANG
Vientiane

Celebrated all over the country, but especially at That Luang – the Golden Stupa in the capital of Vientiane – Pha That Luang draws in tens of thousands of pilgrims to honour the Buddha. On the first and final mornings, people gather to give alms to the monks and receive blessings in return.

Throughout the festival, but especially on the final night, many circle the *stupa* three times in honour of the Buddha, Buddhist *dharma* (virtue), and the Buddhist community. After the spiritual ceremonies of the first three days, a lively carnival unfolds on the parade ground outside the *stupa*, with music troupes and beer tents and even a Miss Lao beauty pageant.

Where: All over Laos, especially Vientiane
When: Full moon of the 12th Lunar month (beginning of November)
....

WAT PHU CHAMPASSAK
Wat Phu Champassak

The ancient temple complex of Wat Phu, built on a hill during the Chenla kingdom (5th–8th century), is dedicated to the Hindu god Shiva. With multiple unexcavated ruins, it is the largest archaeological site in Laos and one of only two UNESCO World Heritage Sites in the country. A series of steep steps leads up to a shallow cave that drips with sacred water. Buddhist monks and pilgrims flock to Wat Phu from all over Laos and make their way up the steps to the temple where they pray, leave offerings and collect precious holy water. Alongside the spiritual ceremonies, more worldly festivities take place, as the ringing sounds of Thai boxing and cockfights compete with concerts of traditional and contemporary music.

Where: Wat Phu Champassak, Laos
When: Full moon of the 3rd lunar month
....

> MALAYSIA

FESTIVAL OF GODDESS AMMAN (MARIAMMAN)
Kuala Lumpur

In ancient Tamil, *mari* means rain and *amman* means mother, making Mariamman, or Amman for short, a very popular mother goddess for Hindus in Malaysia. The rural poor, especially, pray to her for bountiful harvests, healthy children and relief from diseases, such as pox, measles and rashes. Mariamman draws thousands to her annual festival at the Sri Nageswary Amman Temple at Bangsar. Many come bearing urns of milk in her honour. A more extreme side of her cult is the fire-walking ceremony where devotees stagger across a pit of burning coals to show their devotion, ask for help or give thanks for blessings granted. A similar festival also occurs at the Sri Maha Samundeeswari Kaliamman Temple at Ipoh.

Where: Sri Nageswary Amman Temple, Kuala Lumpur, Malaysia
When: Tamil month of Adi (July to August)

GAWAI DAYAK
Sarawak

Gawai Dyak literally means the festival of the Dayak, who are the native people of Sarawak. Conceived in 1957 by the radio producer Ian Kingsley, it has since become an important social and cultural event. The festival opens at the chief's ancestral longhouse with the *Muai Antu Rua* ceremony to cast out the spirit of greed. As the sun sets, the chief conducts a ritual offering to the gods with a sacrificial cockerel, after which people enjoy a communal feast and torchlit procession welcoming the gods. At midnight, the gong calls everyone to listen to the chief's toast to long life, health and prosperity, after which things loosen up, with traditional dance and epic songs. People open their longhouses to each other, enjoy a chat over a glass of *tuak* (strong rice wine), and take part in cultural events such as dancing, blowpipe competitions and cockfights.

Where: Sarawak, Malaysian Borneo
When: 1 June

THAIPUSAM
Kuala Lumpur

During this most intense of penitential pilgrimages, devotees demonstrate their sincerity by carrying burdens and sporting all manner of spikes and hooks in their flesh. The Hindu festival commemorates Parvati's gift of the Vel (spear) to the hero Lord Murugan and many participants pay their respects to Murugan by piercing their tongues with a small spear. At midnight, devotees start the 13km walk from downtown Kuala Lumpur to the base of the sacred Batu cave complex. Here, the devout will have priests insert hooks and spikes into their flesh before they climb the 272 steps to the main Temple Cave. To endure their self-imposed penances, most devotees will have prepared themselves with fasting and meditation, enabling them to enter a trance-like state.

Where: Batu Caves, Kuala Lumpur, Malaysia
When: Full moon of 10th Tamil lunar month (January to February)

> PHILIPPINES

ATI-ATIHAN
Kalibo

With all the spirit and verve of a South American Mardi Gras, Ati-Atihan is a vibrant carnival fiesta combining both pagan and Christian elements. At one level, Ati-Atihan honours Kalibo's patron saint, Santo Niño, the Christ Child. As its name implies, though, Ati-Atihan also celebrates the local Ati (aboriginal) heritage, particularly their age-old friendship with the people of Kalibo. It all started in the early 13th century, when Malay chieftains fleeing Borneo were granted rights to settle in Panay by the mountain Ati. In return, the Malay helped feed the Ati when freak rainfall destroyed their crops. The Ati's dance of gratitude is performed during the festival. Masqueraders with soot-blackened bodies, clad in fabulous battle regalia, dance to a cacophony of riotous drumming, whistles and percussive pots and pans. On the second day, the townsfolk take up the Christian theme with a religious procession of Santo Niño. The festival climaxes with a mass torchlit procession in tribal costume, after which the dancers bathe in the river to remove their soot.

Where: Kalibo, Panay Island, Philippines
When: Three days ending on the 3rd Sunday in January

Celebrating their heritage at Gawai Dyak, the people of Sarawak picnic in front of the chief's longhouse before the evening's ceremonies begin.

BLACK NAZARENE PROCESSION
Manila

In an awesome show of faith, more than 100,000 penitential pilgrims swarm around the venerated statue of the suffering Christ, or the Black Nazarene, as it is paraded through the packed streets of the small parish of Quiapo in the heart of Manila. The life-size wooden statue of Christ shouldering his monumental cross is borne on a carriage pulled by devotees clad in penitential purple and walking barefoot as a sign of humility. Exactly how the statue acquired its unusual black colour remains unknown. One legend has it that the wood was charred by a fire aboard a Spanish ship in the 17th century. The statue was first brought from Mexico to Manila by Augustinian friars some 150 years ago on 9 January, a day marked ever since by the largest procession in the Philippines.

Where: Manila, Philippines
When: 9 January (also Good Friday and New Year's Day)

DINAGYANG
Iloilo City

Dinagyang is nothing if not merry, as implied by its native Llonggo name meaning 'merrymaking'. At the heart of the festivity, a noisy street parade celebrates the Llonggos' conversion to Christianity and pays homage to the city's patron saint, Santo Niño, the Christ Child, who is cheered with joyful shouts of '*Viva Señor Santo Niño*' amid excited drumming. Set in Iloilo City, the festival reflects the cultural heritage of the Llonggo with street dances and processions of the local tribes, such as the Ati and Kasadyahan, clad in splendid battle regalia with huge feathered and beaded masks. The costumes are, indeed, so imaginative that Westerners sometimes wonder if they are parodies of the real thing – the answer is that truth really is stranger than fiction.

Where: Iloilo City, South Panay Island, Philippines
When: Fourth weekend of January

PARADE OF ROASTED SUCKLING PIGS
Balayan

The pigs in question are paraded through the streets of this small town south of Manila while onlookers throw water – a bizarre event that has evolved over 100 years or more to celebrate the feast day of St John the Baptist on 24 June. Some of the pigs – *lechon* – will be dressed up as St John, who baptized Jesus in the river Jordan, while others might be decked in flowers and skirts. After receiving a blessing at the church, the roasted pigs are paraded through the streets, while celebrants douse themselves in water – a symbolic baptism. The succulent pigs are then taken home for a communal feast.

Where: Balayan, Philippines
When: 24 June

SAN ISIDRO LABRADOR (CARABAO FESTIVAL)
Pulilan

The water buffalo is much prized in the rural Philippines – it ploughs the fields that produce the food for the table and puts money in pockets – and every year the people give thanks for these unwieldy beasts of burden. For the Festival of San Isidro Labrador (St Isidro the Labourer), which happens over two days in the middle of May, farmers deck their *carabao* (water buffalo) in ribbons and parade them through the streets to the church of San Isidro, where the animals have been trained to kneel in supplication and to receive blessings. On the second day, the buffalo compete in a friendly race through the town, after which the people take to the streets for a day of dancing and processions.

Where: Pulilan, Philippines
When: 14 and 15 May

SAN PEDRO CUTUD LENTEN RITES
San Fernando

In one of the most extreme displays of faith that you are likely to witness, penitents volunteer to be nailed to a cross during the San Pedro Cutud Lenten Rites. Nails of stainless steel, some 5cm long, are disinfected in alcohol before being hammered into the palms of the *penitentes*, who are left hanging for about five minutes before being rushed off to a medical tent. They endure the ordeal for varied reasons – by way of a petition, in thanksgiving for wishes granted or as penance for sins committed. The real-time crucifixions attract thousands to marvel at the penitents' devotion or to perform alternative acts of penance, such as flagellation and cross-bearing. The main act is preceded by a dramatic passion play enacted by the locals.

Where: San Fernando, Philippines
When: Good Friday

SINULOG
Cebu City

Sinulog is a dance ritual that commemorates the conversion to Christianity of the local Bisayan people. It was a traditional dance form that was performed in honour of the idols of their native religion, but when Magellan landed in 1521 he gave the local king a statue of Santo Niño, or the baby Jesus, and the Sinulog was subsequently performed as a Christian ritual. The dance itself is colourful and fluid, likened to the movement of water. It is performed to drums, trumpets and gongs. Since 1980 the Sinulog has been more formalized, with a parade to the Basilica to re-enact the conversion of the locals to Catholicism.

Where: Cebu City, Philippines
When: Nine days ending on 3rd Sunday in January

Transcending Pain

TO THE FAITHFUL OF MANY RELIGIONS, PRIVATION, ASCETICISM OR
MORTIFICATION OF THE FLESH IS A WAY OF SHOWING THEIR DEVOTION.
SOME RISK LIFE AND LIMB ON A DANGEROUS PILGRIMAGE. OTHERS FIND
IMAGINATIVELY PAINFUL WAYS OF DOING PENANCE OR IDENTIFYING WITH THE
SUFFERING OF MARTYRS, OR UNDERGO AN EXTREME PHYSICAL ORDEAL TO
DEMONSTRATE THE ILLUSORY NATURE OF THE MATERIAL WORLD. FOR BOTH
PARTICIPANTS AND ONLOOKERS THESE PUBLIC ACTS OF SELF-INFLICTED PAIN
ARE LIVING PROOF OF THE POWER OF FAITH TO TRANSCEND SUFFERING.

ABOVE Procession at the Vegetarian Festival, Phuket.

OPPOSITE A penitent and devotee of Lord Murugan, Hindu god
of war and victory, endures a spear through the tongue during
Thaipusam festivities in Kuala Lumpur, Malaysia.

As we have seen, the largest religious gatherings are the vast Hindu bathing festivals, which can attract tens of millions of pilgrims. The largest yearly pilgrimage is the Hajj to Mecca, the performance of which is one of the main tenets of the Muslim faith. Attending these festivals requires devotion, effort and endurance, but for some believers pilgrimage is not enough.

In many cultures there is a tradition of suffering pain for religious reasons. For some it is born out of a desire to emulate the pain of their religious founding figure; for others, it is a way to atone for their sins, or simply to demonstrate their faith. I have noticed that many of the more extreme observances happen in areas where people's lives are hard and painful. Perhaps in poor rural Christian communities the time spent sitting in church might be seen as too easy after six days of unrelenting toil with little return. The practice of repeated prostration – up to 108 times – performed by Vajrayana Buddhists is possibly a way in which physically harsh devotions can challenge the complacency of daily life and alter one's state of consciousness.

Examples of the self-infliction of pain can be found in many religions. Some strict Christian doctrines encourage mortification of the flesh – the wearing of hair shirts, flagellation, fasting or carrying heavy weights – to emulate the suffering of Christ. In Shi'a Islam some penitents will whip themselves with flails in memory of the suffering of Imam Hussein, grandson of the Prophet Muhammad. Some Hindu monks and ascetics subject

themselves to extreme ordeals in order to transcend the temporal realm and reach a higher level of spiritual enlightenment.

In some of the festivals in this book pilgrims deliberately inflict suffering on themselves in order to make their pilgrimage more challenging and poignant. At the Procession de San Lazaro in Cuba and the Black Christ Festival in Panama many penitents walk barefoot and some crawl on their hands and knees, leaving themselves bruised and bloodied (see pp. 45 and 57). In Ireland on Garland Sunday, many pilgrims climb the holy Croagh Patrick mountain wearing few clothes and barefoot, despite rough stones and the often cold and wet weather (see p. 210).

A number of festivals involve rituals where self-harm is deliberately intended. The spectacular Parade of the God of Medicine in the Taiwanese capital of Taipei (see p. 110) sees a long procession of floats and statues of gods carried on litters. The procession is led by a group of priests, dancers and pilgrims called the Centipedes, and

ABOVE With fishhooks pierced through their skin and flesh and attached to ropes, penitents drag a heavy chariot through the streets of Phuket at the annual Vegetarian Festival.

OPPOSITE Running over hot coals is a test of faith for some celebrants at the Vegetarian Festival held in October in Thailand.

OPPOSITE INSET Orthodox Greek Christians participate in the ancient fire-walking ritual known as Anastenaria.

somewhat incongruously, members of the crowd will deliberately throw themselves in front of these characters to be trampled on as a way to bring themselves good health.

Often celebrants will enter a trance in order to overcome the fear and pain of a particular ritual. A number of festivals involve fire-walking. Although this is something of a trick, and many people with hard, dry feet can walk briskly over hot coals without harm, it still takes a degree of faith, whether in science or in religion, to perform it. Fire-walking features at the Festival of Goddess Amman, the South Indian goddess of rain, in Kuala Lumpur, Malaysia (see p. 150) and at the Igitun Chalne at the Lairaya Temple in Goa (see p. 123), where there are so many participants that they virtually have to fight to get a place in the queue. Fire-walking doesn't just appear in the developing world – celebrants walk across hot coals as part of their devotions at the Anastenaria, which is held at various locations in Greece (see pp. 202–3).

The annual pilgrimage to the Batu Caves in Kuala Lumpur, during the Hindu festival of Thaipusam, is one of the most shocking orgies of pain in the world. For anyone into body piercing, this festival – and the very similar Vegetarian Festival at Phuket in Thailand – could well change your mind (see pp. 150 and 162). Devotees at both festivals skewer themselves extravagantly with an arsenal of sharp implements. Thaipusam, held by Tamils in South India and elsewhere to commemorate the giving of a divine lance to Lord Murugan, the Tamil god of war, in order to vanquish the demon

Soorapadman, sees people tow heavy chariots using chains attached to their skins with scores of fishhooks, or carry heavy ornamental structures (*kavadi*) that pierce their skin with all manner of spikes and blades. In the weeks leading up to the festival, devotees undergo lengthy purification rituals, often entering into a trance state to help them through the pain. Surprisingly, there is little blood or scarring in evidence.

Many of the Christian Easter penances are intended to recreate the ordeal and suffering of Christ's crucifixion. The San Pedro Cutud Lenten Rites (see p. 151) take this literally as the faithful allow themselves to be hammered to a cross using stainless

steel nails soaked in alcohol. This takes place at San Fernando in the devoutly Catholic Philippines on Good Friday. Others flagellate themselves until they bleed, in a re-enactment of the whipping that Jesus endured before he was put up on the cross. This ritual started as recently as 1955, since when a carpenter called Ruben Enage has been nailed up over twenty times.

Sometimes a penance can be so extreme that performing it will leave the penitent physically disabled. The vast Kumbh Mela festival in India attracts legions of

ABOVE In a re-enactment of Christ's suffering on the cross that takes place on Good Friday in the Philippines, a stainless steel nail is driven through the hand of a penitent at the San Pedro Cutud Lenten Rites.

OPPOSITE A crucified devotee at the San Pedro Cutud Lenten Rites endures the pain in the belief that such extreme sacrifices are a way to atone for his sins, attain miracle cures for illnesses, or give thanks to God.

sadhus, Hindu holy men. Some of these are the extreme *naga* (naked) *sadhu*s, who eschew all material possessions, including clothes, preferring to walk around covered only in the ash from fires. The most austere and devout of all the *sadhu*s belong to the Juna Akhara sect, who are noted for being fiercely trained in martial arts, and often carry tridents and swords. The *naga sadhu*s have a tradition of performing extreme penances – often lasting for twelve years, starting and finishing at the Kumbh Mela at Allahabad (see p. 124). Standing penances, for which *sadhu*s will remain standing for years at a time, their weight supported by slings as they sleep, are common, as are the penis tricks – supporting weights or even other *sadhu*s with this most delicate of human body parts. The most extreme penance, though, has to be that of Amar Bharti Baba, who over forty years ago decided that he would hold his right hand in the air. His arm is now withered and locked in place. Sacrificing the use of a limb for spiritual reasons is surely the ultimate renunciation of material attachments!

> THAILAND

AKHA NEW YEAR
Northern Thailand

The Akha are one of the numerous hill tribes that live in and around the so-called Golden Triangle, where Thailand, Burma, China and Vietnam meet in a confusion of mountains and valleys. Each has its own traditions, language and costume. The Akha mark New Year with a series of parties and festivals throughout December, spread among the villages and often staggered so each can visit the others' celebrations. Ancestor worship and animism – belief in the spiritual worth of living things – feature in the proceedings and there are plenty of games, including spinning tops, as well as feasting, singing and dancing.

Where: Various Akha villages in northern Thailand
When: Around December; varies by village

AKHA SWING FESTIVAL
Northern Thailand

The Akha New Year (see p .167) is regarded as a predominantly male event, sometimes being referred to as the Men's New Year, whereas the Akha Swing Festival, which takes place over four days at the end of the rainy season, usually in August, is the female equivalent. Each village builds a large swing, often overlooking a steep hillside, which villagers swing on in an expression of freedom and celebration and a general release from hard work in the fields. Meanwhile the women dress up in traditional clothes and jewellery, denoting their age and status, and draw much appreciation and admiration from the menfolk.

Where: Various Akha villages in northern Thailand
When: End of August, beginning of September

BUN BANG FAI
Yasothon Province

Watch your back – and other parts of your anatomy – if you're in north-east Thailand, or neighbouring Laos, in the middle of May. That's when hundreds of homemade rockets are fired into the night sky to celebrate the coming rainy season, and people let their hair down for three days before the hard work starts in the fields. The rockets, which are launched from oxcarts or ceremonial floats, are judged by height, by distance travelled and by the beauty of their vapour trails. Spectacular they may be, but they can also be dangerous, especially when the people launching them have been on the local grain spirit, and errant missiles have caused fatalities.

Where: Yasothon, Thailand
When: Mid-May, Friday to Sunday

CHIANG MAI FLOWER FESTIVAL
Chiang Mai

This charming festival has been going for over 33 years, and has become a true part of the psyche of Chang Mai. The flowerbeds in this town's public gardens and other places are especially beautiful at this time of year and a heady fragrance fills the air. The highlight is a large procession in which ornate sculptures made entirely of flowers are paraded through the streets. Many of these have a distinctly Thai theme, with monasteries, Buddhist teachings and elephants rendered in bud and petal. The parade ends at the Suan Buak Haad park in the centre of town, which is turned into a market with a variety of stalls and displays of some of the world's most beautiful blooms.

Where: Chiang Mai, Thailand
When: First weekend in February

CHONBURI BUFFALO RACES
Chonburi

The provincial capital Chonburi plays host to a festival of buffalo races that dates back centuries. The streets are filled with costumed dancers who move to the music of traditional Thai songs amidst flags and banners. A parade of buffalo carts leads the competing animals and their riders to the stadium, where they are fed a questionable diet of eggs and beer to improve their performance. They race bareback around a dirt track in front of a large and wildly enthusiastic crowd, the riders struggling to hold on to their rampaging mounts. The winner is feted with garlands. There is also a competition for the best-decorated buffalo and local beauties vie for the title of 'Miss Farm Maiden'.

Where: Chonburi, Thailand
When: Full moon of 11th lunar month (usually October)

FULL MOON PARTY
Koh Phangan

The full moon parties at Had Rin resort on Koh Phangan are legendary, attracting backpackers, gap-year adventurers and hippies old and new from all over the world. More than a dozen times a year – when the moon is full – the resort rocks and raves through the day and night. Beach bars pump out dance music, the dancing spills out on to the beach, and the hardcore are still going strong as the first rays of sun hit the sand the next morning. From small beginnings in the 1980s, the parties have grown and can now attract up to 30,000 revellers in high season – as well as police on the lookout for illegal drugs.

Where: Kho Phangan Island, Thailand
When: Every full moon

Villagers circling a tree decorated with rice cakes and gifts on the final day of the three-day festivities for Lisu New Year in northern Thailand, a ritual performed in front of each house in the village.

HMONG NEW YEAR
Northern Thailand

The Hmong are part of the patchwork of hill tribes and minority peoples inhabiting Laos, Burma, Thailand, Vietnam and southern China. From November to January, on different days according to local tradition, they mark New Year with celebrations that place an emphasis on courtship. Young unmarried men and women are encouraged to meet and play games under supervision, and there is much feasting and merriment. As well as looking to the future, the Hmong are careful to pay homage to their ancestors, who are honoured with a shrine in every house.

Where: Villages in northern Thailand
When: From November to January

LISU NEW YEAR
Northern Thailand

Originally from northern China and Tibet, the Lisu people have migrated south over the centuries and now occupy mountain villages in northern Thailand. Befitting their heritage, their New Year coincides with the Chinese New Year and the two celebrations bear some similarities, but with a distinctive Lisu spin. On the first of three days of festivities, the family makes rice cakes and goes out into the forest to choose a small tree, which is placed in front of their house. On the final day, they attach the rice cakes to the tree, along with other small gifts, and sacrifice chickens, and the whole village dances round each tree in turn – with a grand finale of dancing and singing at the shaman's house.

Where: Various Lisu villages in northern Thailand
When: Three days coinciding with Chinese New Year

LOPBURI BANQUET
Lopburi

This monkey banquet was started in the 1980s by a local businessman as a way of expressing his gratitude to the many crab-eating macaques whose presence in the Khmer ruins in the centre of town brought in welcome tourist revenue. There is an official opening ceremony before a banquet of fruit is laid out on tables for the monkeys. There are food stalls for the humans too, but watch out for those pesky monkeys, who regard any food as theirs for the taking.

Where: Lopburi, Thailand
When: Last Sunday in November

MAGH PUJA
Bangkok

A candlelit festival full of promise, Magh Puja is marked with mass meditations and celebrations all over Buddhist Southeast Asia – but nowhere more spectacularly than at the Wat Phra Dhammakaya, north of the Thai capital. On the full moon of the third lunar month, which usually falls in February, many thousands of monks and devotees gather in the temple courtyard to celebrate the occasion when the recently enlightened Buddha preached a sermon to 1,250 monks who had turned up spontaneously. They heard the three basic precepts of his teaching that inspire the faithful today – to do no evil, to do only good and to purify the mind. On Magh Puja, Buddhists everywhere bear these spiritual aims in mind. As night falls, candlelit processions circle the temple courtyard three times in recollection of the Three Jewels in the Lotus – the Buddha, his teaching and the community of Buddhists.

Where: All over Thailand; especially Wat Phra Dhammakaya, Bangkok
When: Full moon of 3rd lunar month (February)

SONGKRAN
Chiang Mai

It cools you down in the gathering heat of mid-April, it washes away bad luck – above all, it's just great fun to throw around. Water is what the Thai New Year is all about, and the various religious ablutions and cleansings that lie at this festival's heart are a great excuse to have fun. Songkran is celebrated all over South-east Asia and Thailand but in the city of Chiang Mai they do it with particular élan. Over three days of festivities, revellers in open vehicles drive around the city centre throwing water at the crowds, who respond in kind. To cap it all, there's a Miss Songkran contest.

Where: Chiang Mai, Thailand
When: 13–15 April

SUKHOTHAI ELEPHANT ORDINATION
Sukhothai

Living as a monk is a rite of passage for most men in Thailand. At the monastery of Wat Hat Siao in Sukhothai, northern Thailand, they make sure the new monks will never forget the experience by bringing them to the ordination ceremony on the backs of elephants. On the mornings of 7 and 8 April, novices are the guests of honour at parties in family homes where their heads are shaved and they are dressed in Buddhist robes. Sometimes they also put on make-up, representing the profane world they are leaving behind, before taking to elephants for the procession to the monastery.

Where: Sukhothai, Thailand
When: 7 April

SURIN ELEPHANT ROUND-UP
Surin

The annual elephant round-up harks back to the days when the people of Surin were experts in the capture and training of wild elephants from nearby Cambodia. The weekend's events begin on Friday morning when a procession of around 300 elephants marches through town accompanied by local schoolchildren and teachers in traditional dress, dancing and playing music. The procession stops at tables piled high with fruit for the elephants to feast on. On Saturday and Sunday the action moves to the stadium for a series of games displaying the strength and skills of the animals, including football, tug of war and log pulling. The show culminates in the re-enactment of a medieval battle with the elephants in full battle dress.

Where: Surin, Thailand
When: Third week of November

Buddhist novices ride high on the backs of elephants to their ordination ceremony at the monastery of Wat Hat Siao in Sukhothai, northern Thailand.

VEGETARIAN FESTIVAL
Phuket

If you thought that vegetarians were weak and pasty-faced then a visit to Phuket's Vegetarian Festival will certainly change your mind. This is not a celebration of tofu – rather it's a traditional period of self-purification marked with gruesome processions where penitents from the local Chinese community pierce themselves with all manner of spiky objects. The faithful believe that abstinence from meat and other stimulants will help them obtain good health and peace of mind and that they will be protected from pain and scarring by the gods. The tradition is believed to date back over 150 years when a troupe of wandering Chinese minstrels was struck down by malaria, but made a full recovery after a period of self-purification.

Where: Phuket, Thailand
When: Nine days in October

YI PENG AND LOI KRATHONG
Chiang Mai

These two festivals of light take place simultaneously, usually towards the end of November. Yi Peng is an ancient local tradition and involves the release of thousands of tissue paper lanterns called *khom loi*. Each has a candle or fuel cell at its base and acts like a mini hot-air balloon ascending slowly into the night sky. Other lanterns are carried in procession and hung from buildings and temples. Although held throughout Thailand, celebrations of Loi Krathong, which have their roots in Hindu Brahmanic ceremonies, are particularly beautiful in Chiang Mai. As well as offering prayers locals float banana leaves, adorned with candles, incense and money, down the rivers. The lights floating away symbolize the drifting away of bad luck and misfortune.

Where: Chiang Mai, Thailand
When: Full moon of 12th month of Thai lunar calendar

> VIETNAM

COW-RACING FESTIVAL
An Giang

This annual cattle-racing fiesta is held by ethnic Cambodians living in the Mekong Delta province of An Giang as part of a festival in which people pay respects to their ancestors. A day of celebration with prayers and food precedes the main event. The venue, a muddy rice field dotted with Buddhist pagodas, is meticulously prepared – and the going is very heavy for the contestants. Before the race riders select a pair of cows, which are then blessed by monks and harnessed to a harrow. The drivers stand on the harrow and try to control the beasts without falling off as they stampede along the 120m track. In recent years the racing has been televised, earning even more prestige for the winners.

Where: An Giang, Vietnam
When: End of 8th to start of 9th Lunar months (September/October)

LE MAT SNAKE FESTIVAL
Le Mat

Predictably, snakes are at the centre of this celebration. Unfortunately for them, they are more likely to appear on the menu than anything else. The festival commemorates the relocation of the village to more fertile land near Hanoi almost 1,000 years ago after a local snake catcher was credited with fighting off a giant snake to rescue the king's daughter. The festival also celebrates the village's subsequent dominance of the snake trade – both in catching and rearing venomous species and producing all manner of associated products. A day of events begins with dancing and prayers and ends with a recreation of the legend of the princess's rescue. There are also snake beauty competitions and much consumption of snake wine and snake meat.

Where: Le Mat, Vietnam
When: (movable) 23rd day of the 3rd lunar month (April/May)

PERFUME PAGODA FESTIVAL
Huong Tich

Known as the largest and longest religious celebration in Vietnam, this festival takes place amongst a complex of temples and shrines. The first structures here are believed to date from the 15th century, and a pilgrimage to make offerings in return for good health, good luck and prosperity is popular throughout the country. It is seen by some as an opportunity to find romance. There are a number of events, but the most spectacular is a journey by boat past stunning limestone formations and statues to the Perfume Temple in the cave of Huong Tich. Although the festival lasts for almost three months, peak times are from the 15th to 20th days of the second lunar month.

Where: Huong Tich, Vietnam
When: Sixth day of 1st to end of 3rd lunar months

TET NHUYEN DAN
Hanoi

Tet, which marks the start of a new year, is the most important festival in Vietnam. For many the aim of the three-day festival, which also marks the arrival of spring, is to start the year correctly by cleaning the house, paying off debts, giving gifts and resolving conflict. In Hanoi, Da Nang and Ho Chi Minh there are massive firework displays, but Tet is celebrated all over the country with many regional activities such as boat races, dragon dances, parades of floats and swinging contests, some dating back 2,500 years. It is also a time to be at home with the family and to make offerings to your ancestors for good luck in the coming months.

Where: Events all over Vietnam; particularly Hanoi
When: First day of 1st lunar month

An impressive dragon float joins the parade in Hanoi to celebrate Tet Nhuyen Dan (New Year).

Happy New Year!

THE START OF THE NEW YEAR VARIES AROUND THE WORLD ACCORDING TO CALENDAR, FAITH AND CULTURE. ALL THE MAIN RELIGIONS HAVE THEIR OWN DATES FOR MARKING IT, AND DIFFERENT COUNTRIES AND SOCIETIES EACH HAVE THEIR OWN WAY OF THROWING A PARTY TO USHER OUT THE OLD AND WELCOME IN THE NEW. IF YOU TIME THINGS RIGHT, YOU CAN CELEBRATE THE NEW YEAR A DOZEN TIMES IN A DOZEN FESTIVE WAYS.

ABOVE Nobody is spared some form of 'water treatment' in the festivities celebrating the New Year in Laos.

OPPOSITE Spectacular dragon dances mark Chinese New Year throughout the Chinese diaspora.

OPPOSITE TOP Extravagant displays of fireworks over the skyline of Hong Kong herald the New Year.

OPPOSITE BOTTOM Partying in the streets of Hong Kong at New Year.

BELOW A generous 'blessing' pours forth from a watering can as celebrants enjoy the fun of New Year festivities.

I once spent a glorious few months of New Year celebrations in South-east Asia. Between November and April I managed to see in the year five times: the Akha, Lisu and Hmong New Years, the Western New Year and the chaos of Songkran, the Thai New Year. Unfortunately, it didn't make it any easier for me to keep my New Year resolutions, but it did give me a few extra chances at making a new start.

South-east Asia is noted for its minority peoples, the so-called hill tribes. Many of these originated in south-west China and Myanmar and migrated to other countries in the region, taking with them a rich culture of language, customs and dress. Two of the best known of these are the Akha and the Hmong peoples, who are found all over the region. Both these minorities have their own New Year celebrations, for which the precise date is fixed by each village, sometimes to make sure that neighbouring villages can join in, or to coincide with local events or village history. Traditional dances are performed, and various games are played, allowing young people to meet prospective partners from other villages (see pp. 160–1).

Officially defined as the first day of the first lunar month, Chinese New Year is observed wherever there are significant Chinese populations and is marked by fireworks displays and dragon dances, where dancers carry traditional paper dragons to bring good luck to households and businesses (see p. 94). A number of other religions and cultures use the same calendar. The Vietnamese Tet Nhuyen Dan and the Tibetan New Year of Losar are both held around the first day of the first lunar month.

The Lisu minority, who live in south-west China, the mountain region of Myanmar, Thailand and the Indian state of Arunachal Pradesh, hold their celebrations at the same time with three days of festivities. Starting with the collection of a tree from the forest and the preparation of special foods, this is a communal time, with the whole village turning out to dance and drink through the night. Lisu women wear brightly coloured clothes, ornate silver jewellery and headdresses with tassels that obscure their faces. Drinking and feasting goes on through the nights, and from personal experience it is hard to keep up with the number of drinks of potent rice wine that people want to toast with you (see p. 161).

The last celebration on my Asian odyssey was the Thai New Year of Songkran (see p. 162). This is the Theravada Buddhist New Year and is celebrated in many countries in South-east Asia. In Cambodia it is known as Chaul Chnam Thmey, Thingyan in Burma, Po Shui Jie in parts of south-west China and Pi Mai Lao in Laos. All these celebrations involve water, originally used by monks to bless the laity and clean statues of the Buddha, but recently, the ritual has escalated into crazy water

fights that stretch over a number of days. Some of the best celebrations are in the Laotian town of Luang Prabang, where the water fights are interspersed with processions of hundreds of saffron-robed monks (see p. 149). No one is spared a drenching, including the monks and also the police in what is one of the last Communist states, although the monks receive a delicate, respectful sprinkling whereas the police receive slightly more robust treatment.

In India, there are a number of New Year celebrations in various states, but many consider Diwali, the festival of lights, to be the closest thing to a Hindu New Year as it marks the start of the Vikrama lunar calendar (see p. 121). A common custom across India is to welcome in the New Year by lighting tiny lamps, which represents the transition from the dark to the light months. Nepali New Year is called Bisket Jatra, and is held on the first day of the month of Baisakh, which usually falls in April. The entire festival lasts over a week, and is marked by religious processions, feasting and visits to the temple (see pp. 142–3).

The Western New Year marks the beginning of the Gregorian calendar, which falls on 1 January. However, many religions follow different calendars and do not have the year starting on the same day. Some of these have fewer or more days than the Gregorian calendar; others follow the lunar calendar and so fall on a different Gregorian date each year. The Jewish New Year, known as Rosh Hashanah, falls around September–October; the Islamic New Year, Al-Hijra, falls on the first day of the Muslim month of Muharram (mid-October in 2015, moving forwards eleven days each year relative to the Western calendar).

Some followers of the Gregorian calendar celebrate the New Year in unfamiliar ways. Villagers from Comanesti in Romania mark it by dressing up in bearskins and parading around the village (see p. 175). Having a bear visit your home is considered good luck, and many of the skins have been handed down over the generations. In the Bahamas, thousands of people in brightly coloured carnival costumes take part in the Junkanoo processions (see p. 44). These originated on the sugar plantations, when New Year's Day was one of two days in the year that slaves on the plantations were allowed to spend with their families.

A number of celebrations also involve ways to see out the old year. In Rio de Janeiro, followers of Lemanjá, the goddess of the sea, congregate on the famous Copacabana

ABOVE For those waking up with a hangover on New Year's Day, a traditional cure in Scotland is the Loony Dook – 'dooking' yourself in the freezing River Forth.

OPPOSITE TOP Lisu hill-tribe women in northern Thailand dressed in all their finery enjoy traditional dancing at New Year.

OPPOSITE A stilt-walker, followed by admiring horsemen, at the New Year celebrations of Nowruz in Afghanistan.

Beach to carry out a purification ritual that was brought from Africa in the days of slavery. Dressed in white, adherents throw white flowers into the sea and send offerings to Lemanjá in tiny boats (see p. 89). Owru Yari in Suriname mixes traditions from Africa with the Chinese custom of setting off firecrackers to get rid of the baggage from the old year, ready for a fresh start (see p. 93).

Arguably one the most famous of these celebrations is Hogmanay, 'the last day of the year' in Scottish English. The old year is seen out in flaming style in Stonehaven near Aberdeen as a band of locals (the number varies each year) parades through the town swinging burning fireballs above their heads. However, the main celebrations take place over at least two days in Edinburgh. A torchlight parade sees out the old year before a giant party is thrown in the shadow of the famous Edinburgh Castle (see pp. 250–1). The whole country sees much 'first footing'– being the first visitor of the year – which starts immediately after midnight and involves visiting neighbours and taking gifts such as coal, cake and whisky to bring various kinds of luck to the householder.

In Iran, Nowruz – the old Persian New Year, which dates back over 5,000 years and marks the exact astronomical beginning of the spring equinox – is the main holiday for most people (see p. 172). A jovial character called Haji Firuz and his troupe of musicians spread news of good cheer for the coming year. A similar festival marks the start of the Afghan New Year. These festivals predate Islam, and in Afghanistan it was banned by the Taliban because of its pagan roots.

Another odd tradition follows the old Julian calendar (which predates the Gregorian calendar). The Rite of the Kalyady Tsars in Semezhava in Belarus takes place on 13 January and sees seven local 'Tsars' dress up in white shirts and trousers along with traditional decorated belts and bands and tall hats. Each one represents a typical local character and they march around, visiting houses, singing songs, telling jokes and dispensing good luck to the people of the village (see p. 174).

Of course, despite the differences caused by calendar, custom, culture and even climate, all New Year celebrations have a common theme in that they mark the passage of time. In the spirit of looking both back and forward, with hope for the future, many people use this celebration as an opportunity for making resolutions – viewing life from a fresh angle, and correcting past mistakes in order to become a better person. That, perhaps, is what unites us all, however we decide to party.

>> WESTERN ASIA AND THE LEVANT

> IRAN

NOWRUZ
Iran

At the time of the spring equinox in March Iranians mark Persian New Year with an ancient tradition redolent with the region's Zoroastrian roots. It is the biggest and most significant holiday of the year, for which people prepare by spring-cleaning their houses, symbolically and literally ridding themselves of the last year's debris. Some people blacken their faces and dress in red to masquerade as Haji Firuz, the character who ushers in the New Year. Families then embark on a round of visiting friends and relatives, exchanging good cheer for the coming year.

Where: All over Iran
When: The spring equinox in March

SADEH
Yazd

In the depth of winter – usually around the end of January – the followers of Zoroastrianism hold a fire-burning festival to ward off the forces of cold and darkness. The Province of Yazd, in the centre of Iran, is a stronghold of the ancient religion, attracting pilgrims from far and wide to gather around the flames at the Chak Chak Fire Temple, an atmospheric cave temple in the mountains. Elsewhere in Iran, the tradition is observed with the lighting of bonfires.

Where: All over Iran, especially Yazd
When: The 10th day of the Iranian month of Bahman (28, 29 or 30 January)

> ISRAEL

EASTER
Jerusalem

Jerusalem is a spiritual magnet throughout the year for people of many persuasions, but never more so than in Holy Week, when pilgrims from all over the world come to celebrate the Christ's Resurrection on Easter Sunday. The week is filled with ceremonies marking spiritual rites of passage. Maundy Thursday commemorates the Last Supper, when Christ instituted the sacrament of the Eucharist. On Good Friday, pilgrims line the Via Dolorosa in the Old City for a re-enactment of the 14 Stations of the Cross. Easter Sunday is a time of rejoicing on the Mount of Olives, where Christ ascended to heaven.

Where: Jerusalem, Israel
When: Weeks leading up to Christian and Orthodox Easters

Easter celebrations in Jerusalem attract pilgrims from all over the world. Here they participate in the Good Friday re-enactment of the fourteen Stations of the Cross.

LAG B'OMER
Israel

Dancing around bonfires, haircuts and parties are the order of the day on Lag b'Omer, when Jewish communities across the world enjoy a day's respite from the solemn period of the 'Counting of the Omer', which lasts from Passover to Shavuot, the Festival of Weeks. Bonfires symbolize the light of the Torah. People plan outings and even weddings on Lag b'Omer, while young boys receive their first haircuts and play with toy bows and arrows, re-enacting the historical revolt against the Romans. Some believe that manna first fell from heaven on this, the 33rd day of the 'Omer'.

Where: All over Israel
When: The 18th day of the Hebrew month of Iyar (April to May)

PURIM
Israel

The spirit of carnival reigns on Purim, a joyous Jewish holiday when norms are reversed to commemorate a lucky reversal of fortune in Jewish history. The story is recounted in the biblical Book of Esther. More than 2,500 years ago, in the time of King Xerxes of Persia, the evil court official Haman plotted to exterminate the Jews, but his scheme was foiled by the king's brave wife, Esther, and her cousin, Mordecai. Today, their lucky escape is celebrated in Mardi Gras fashion, with drinking, cross-dressing, masquerading and parodies. When the story is read out in synagogues, people boo and hiss at the mention of Haman's name. The same lighthearted and generous tone continues as friends swap gifts, make donations to charity and gather for celebratory treats, including *hamantaschen* – fruit-filled pastries representing Haman's three-cornered hat.

Where: All over the Jewish world, especially Jerusalem
When: The 14th day of Adar, usually in March

> PALESTINE

CHRISTMAS
West Bank, Palestinian Territories

These days the Christmas period may seem to go on too long in the West but that's nothing compared to the place where it all started. In the little town of Bethlehem, the celebrations last till 18 January. Manger Square, outside the Byzantine Church of the Nativity, is packed with thousands of pilgrims and tourists awaiting their turn to vist the Grotto beneath, where it is believed Jesus of Nazareth was born.

Where: Bethlehem, West Bank, Palestine
When: 25 December–18 January

> SAUDI ARABIA

JENADRIYAH NATIONAL FESTIVAL
Al Jenadriyah

Although a relatively recent festival – first established in 1985 – the Jenadriyah National Festival has become an important way of preserving the culture and traditional crafts of Saudi Arabia. The two-week festival kicks off with a spectacular mass camel race in which some 2,000 animals compete across 19km of desert track. There are also horse races and demonstrations of falconry as well as performances of traditional singing, dancing and poetry. A large artisan market sells traditional pottery, jewellery, metalwork, woodwork and weaving. There is a heritage village that illustrates the traditional life and culture of the Kingdom.

Where: Al Jenadriyah, Saudi Arabia
When: End of February/beginning of March

> TURKEY

DEVI GURESI
Selçuk

Selçuk, near ancient Ephesus, plays host to the colourful festival of Devi Guresi – an all-day event at which specially bred male Tulu camels 'wrestle' others in their same category. Camel fighting is traditional in Turkey, probably dating back to the time when camel trains passed this way on the Silk Route to the Far East. There are about 30 competitions a year, but the highlight is the Selçuk championship. The day beforehand the gorgeously bedecked fighting camels are paraded through town followed by musicians. On the day itself, pairs of camels, stirred to action by the presence of a female, 'wrestle' each other using the power of their necks, and butting and shoving until one falls to its knees and the one standing is proclaimed the winner.

Where: Selçuk, Turkey
When: The 3rd weekend in January

KIRKPINAR OIL WRESTLING FESTIVAL
Edirne

Not for the squeamish, or prudish, this – muscle-bound men squeeze into heavy leather shorts, cover themselves in olive oil and grapple like octopuses in a Middle Eastern tradition that goes back millennia. The annual tournament at Edirne in Turkey, which lasts for the best part of a week from the end of June or beginning of July, has been taking place for 650 years. Thousands flock to watch the *pehlivans* – wrestlers – compete in a variety of categories, to the accompaniment of drum rolls and traditional bands, the ultimate prize being the Golden Belt.

Where: Edirne, Turkey
When: End of June or beginning of July

WHIRLING DERVISHES FESTIVAL
Konya

This most Islamic of Turkish cities is home to the spell-binding Whirling Dervishes of the Sufi Mevlevi Order, founded in the 13th century by followers of the Sufi mystic Mevlana, also known as Rumi. The order became famous for their ritual prayer – performed spinning on one foot – during which they enter an ecstatic trance. Although the fraternity perform throughout the year, they gather for a week in December in the city's sports stadium to dance in celebration of their founder. The climax of the festival is the final night, on 17 December, when the dancers celebrate the anniversary of Mevlana's wedding night – a mesmerizing spectacle of perfectly coordinated movement, with the dancers' white skirts lifting to form spinning discs.

Where: Konya, Turkey
When: Week leading up to 17 December

These Dervish dancers, wearing traditional white dress and belted white coats, spin into a trance. In symbolic imitation of the planets orbiting the sun, their circular dance is an expression of cosmic love.

EUROPE >> EASTERN EUROPE

> BELARUS

RITE OF THE KALYADY TSARS
Semezheva

The night of the Julian calendar's New Year sees the unique procession of the Kalyady 'Christmas' Tsars around the village of Semezheva in Belarus. The tradition is believed to date back to the 18th century when the Tsar's army was stationed nearby. On the last night of the year, the soldiers travelled around the village entertaining the locals, for which they were rewarded with food and drink. The tradition has persisted and today over 500 people take part in the festival, of whom seven are chosen to represent the Tsars. Dressed in red and white, wielding wooden sabres, each one plays a particular character from local stories and mock fights are re-enacted in houses around the village. Once it gets dark, the procession continues by flaming torchlight.

Where: Semezheva, Belarus
When: 13 January

> BOSNIA AND HERZEGOVINA

IKARI BRIDGE JUMPING
Mostar

The oldest diving competition in the world, dating back to 1566, sees up to 70 divers plunge 21m from Stari Most (Old Bridge) into the Neretva River below in front of 30,000 spectators. Leaping from twice as high as the highest Olympic diving board, divers can plunge in head or feet first, and there is no competition as such, the tradition is simply a daring male rite of passage. The bridge's intentional destruction in 1993 during the vicious war in the Balkans was a national tragedy for Bosnians. The opening of the reconstructed bridge in 2004 and the subsequent revival of this age-old custom have seen the festival develop into a symbol of resilience as well as daring.

Where: Mostar, Bosnia and Herzegovina
When: Last week in July

> CROATIA

DUBROVNIK CARNIVAL
Dubrovnik

First established in the 14th century and almost as old as the city itself, Dubrovnik's carnival has been an integral part of the history of this walled coastal city. The tradition began when the authorities permitted its citizens to wear masks and dress up as whoever they pleased. Today's five-week extravaganza sees a wide variety of events taking place in

The 21-metre plunge from the Stari Most into the Neretva River below is a rite of passage for many young Bosnian men.

the city's many historic locations. The streets and squares are filled with costumed performers – soldiers, fortune-tellers, nannies, priests and devils – who sing, dance, recite poetry and perform astonishing acrobatic displays to the music of trumpets and other traditional instruments. Masked parades, parties and music festivals are held each weekend. Festivities end with a masked ball at the Revelin Fortress.

Where: Dubrovnik, Croatia
When: Leading up to Ash Wednesday (February or March)

RIJEKA CARNIVAL
Rijeka

Hairy, lairy and scary, the Rijeka Carnival features folkloric *Zvončari* characters. Dressed in sheepskins and wearing fearsome masks of stylized animals, they are similar to characters seen at festivals all around Eastern Europe, notably the *Kurents* of Slovenia and the *Busójárás* of Hungary. Like the Busójárás they are reputed to have chased off Turkish invaders, but now are used to chase away evil spirits. The city has been known for its carnival since the Middle Ages, but the tradition fell out of favour until it was revived in the 1980s. Today's Lenten extravaganza begins when the Mayor hands over the keys of the city to the carnival's Master of Ceremonies. There are costumed parades, a masked vintage car rally and the burning of Pust, a puppet, who carries the blame for all the bad things that happened the previous year. Legend has it that the boisterous activities of the masqueraders will drive away the forces of evil, while celebrating the arrival of spring and the creation of new life.

Where: Rijeka, Croatia
When: Leading up to Ash Wednesday (February or March)

> CZECH REPUBLIC

INTERNATIONAL BAGPIPE FESTIVAL
Strakonice

If you thought that the Scots had a monopoly on bagpipes then you might be surprised to hear that the International Bagpipe Festival is actually held in South Bohemia in the Czech Republic. The country has a long tradition of bagpipes, which are known locally as *dudy* or Bohemian-style *bock* (the German word for goat – their skins are used to make the bagpipes). Essentially a folklore festival, this five-day event was conceived in 1967. It attracts pipers and enthusiasts from the 15 countries in Europe with a tradition of piping for concerts, presentations, seminars and workshops in the setting of a 16th-century castle. If bagpipes aren't completely your thing, then you might be interested to know that the festival has its own signature beer: Dudák, 'the piper'.

Where: Strakonice, Czech Republic
When: Every two (even) years, usually late August

STRÁŽNICE FOLKLORE FESTIVAL
Strážnice

The small picturesque town of Strážnice, near the border between the Czech Republic and Slovakia, hosts one of the most significant folklore festivals of the region. The annual weekend event features music, singing, costume dancing and the consumption of much of the local wine. The 'official' festival takes place in the daytime and features more traditional elements such as a costumed parade and a *verbunk* (dancing competition), while the more 'unofficial' events, comprising freer pick-up bands and dancers, take place into the small hours of the morning. Whichever events you choose, if your taste is for *cimbalom* (fiddle) bands playing Moravian songs and dances, including a few polkas and waltzes for good measure, then this festival, held in the grounds of the local *zámek* (castle), will allow you to indulge your guilty pleasures in full.

Where: Strážnice, Czech Republic
When: Last weekend in June

> HUNGARY

BUSÓJÁRÁS FESTIVAL
Mohács

Devilish horned characters called *Busós* take over the town of Mohács in a riot of noise and mischief-making that both sees off the winter and heralds the beginning of Lent. They are a scary sight, sporting horned wooden masks and dressed in hairy sheepskin cloaks, as more than 500 of them arrive by boat down the River Danube. They tease passers-by and carry all sorts of noisemakers to create a racket. The main parade of the Busójárás (*Busó*-walking) takes place on Sunday. On the final evening, Shrove Tuesday, the *Busós* light a massive bonfire and burn a coffin, signifying the death of winter. The tradition reputedly dates back to the days of the Turkish occupation of Hungary, when the outnumbered villagers of Mohács dressed up in fearsome wooden masks to intimidate the advancing Turkish army. Believing the villagers to be devils, the Turkish army is said to have retreated.

Where: Mohács, Hungary
When: Thursday to Tuesday before Ash Wednesday (February or March)

> POLAND

LAJKONIK FESTIVAL
Krakow

Few places get to celebrate victory against the hordes of Genghis Khan. Krakow has been attacked and destroyed many times, but managed to score one victory in 1241. Legend has it that a group of raftsmen came across Tartar raiders sleeping in the forest nearby and attacked them. One of the raftsmen, dressed in the clothes of a Tartar then paraded around town to announce their victory. This parade is re-enacted every year at the festival when a Lajkonik, an eccentric rider wearing a pointed hat and a parody of oriental silk clothes, rides a wooden hobby horse into town to announce the victory to the mayor. Accompanied by musicians and riders, he hits people he meets with a comedy mace to bring them good luck. When the ensemble reaches the mayor in the Market Square, they drink a toast and make victory speeches.

Where: Krakow, Poland
When: Thursday after Corpus Christi (June)

> ROMANIA

NEW YEAR CELEBRATION
Comanesti

If you go down to the woods in Comanesti, you really are sure of a big surprise! This is no teddy bears' picnic; in this new-year ritual villagers don bearskins and dance around to chase off evil spirits ready for the year ahead. In Romania the brown bear is said to signify strength and courage. If a bear enters a house it is said to bring good health and good luck. Hunting bears is now illegal in Romania, so people either use old family bearskins or make bear costumes. Real skins are very valuable and are treated as heirlooms. Hundreds of people dress up and go round the houses in the village accompanied by drummers and musicians.

Where: Comanesti, Romania
When: New Year's Eve

PAGEANT OF THE JUNI
Brasov

The origins of this colourful pageant, held in Brasov, an atmospheric medieval town in deepest Transylvania, are lost in the mists of time. The Pageant of Juni (young men) is a horseback parade that celebrates the only day of the year – the first Sunday after Easter – on which, traditionally, Romanians could freely enter the Saxon city of Brasov. Dressing up in elaborate costumes, some of which are 150 years old, young townsfolk ride through the streets of the historic quarter – with the married men, or 'Old Juni', trailing behind. That procession then heads into a gorge in the surrounding hills, where they break off into groups to perform the *cateaua* (dog's dance) and rhythmic *horas* (round dances) in a stamina-sapping danceathon that's almost as tiring to watch as it is to perform.

Where: Brasov, Romania
When: First Sunday after Easter (Usually April)

> RUSSIA

ALKHALALALAJ (ITEL'MEN TRIBAL HARVEST FESTIVAL)
Kovran

For years the indigenous Itel'men, Koriak and Sunda tribesmen from the snowy wastes of the Kamchatka Peninsula were discriminated against, even being displaced from their traditional fishing and reindeer herding grounds. Now they are undergoing a cultural revival as they try to reclaim their heritage. The harvest festival of Alkhalalalaj is a time for cleansing, and the week-long celebration sees fire dances, drumming, chanting, singing and totem carving. One totem pole is erected on the top of the revered Mount Elvel, some 70km away. Once it is in place, offerings of food are left for the spirits of the mountain. In the evening people gather around a fire and compete in a dance marathon, which only permits breaks for drinking water and… kissing.

Where: Kovran, Russia
When: Second to third week in September (corresponding to the full moon)

FESTIVAL OF THE NORTH (PRAZNIK CEVERA)
Murmansk

During December and January Murmansk is in the grip of the 'Polar Night': two months of perpetual darkness. No wonder that the Festival of the North, held at Murmansk on the Kola Peninsula 210km north of the Arctic Circle at the end of March in celebration of the 'lights of spring', is such a joyful occasion. This ten-day festival, nicknamed the Polar Olympics, features a host of sporting contests including ice hockey, reindeer racing, cross-country and downhill skiing and underwater swimming in the icy waters of Lake Semyonovskaya. It's also the only time that the traditional Sami people come to the city to show off their reindeer

and celebrate a culture that has survived in the harshest conditions for thousands of years.

Where: Murmansk, Russia
When: Ten days at end of March to the beginning of April

MASLENITSA
Moscow

As if trying to live up to all of the clichés of Russian-ness, thick pancakes, drunken bears and vodka-fuelled fights are all important elements of the Maslenitsa. True, the punch-ups are in good humour and the dancing bears are now rare, but this festival is a wild and exuberant affair. Although its origins lie in a pagan festival marking the end of winter, the Maslenitsa has been incorporated into the pre-Lenten celebrations of the Eastern Orthodox Church. Suppressed during the Communist era, it has recently undergone a resurgence. The name itself is a derivation of the Russian word for butter (*maslo*) and people feast on blini pancakes smothered in butter to symbolize the sun of spring. Celebrations culminate with the burning of a 'winter' scarecrow and Forgiveness Day, on which people traditionally say sorry to their family and friends for wrongdoings in the past year.

Where: Moscow, Russia
When: Week before Orthodox Lent

> SERBIA

GUČA TRUMPET FESTIVAL
Guča

Trumpets are big in Serbia. That is not to say that they are larger than in other places, but the brass band is an integral part of rural life there. Trumpets are played at births, weddings, funerals and just about every significant life event in between. Trumpet playing in the region has been popular for over 200 years, popularized by the indigenous Roma, and the first Dragacevo Assembly of Trumpet Players was held in 1961. Now also known as the Guča Trumpet Festival, the largest brass band festival in the world, it attracts players and aficionados from all over the globe as well as gypsy bands. Friday sees the opening ceremony, Saturday a major celebration of trumpet and brass band music, and Sunday a competition for the best trumpet player. The festival is also a major celebration of local culture, a wild event, featuring traditional folk dancing.

Where: Western Serbia
When: August

Costumed straw effigies and dolls on parade before their ritual burning to mark the passing of winter during the festival of Maslenitsa in Russia.

TESTICLE FESTIVAL
Ozrem

The biggest celebration of balls in the world takes place in the remote Serbian mountain village of Ozrem. In the World Testicle Cooking Championship, chefs serve up delicious/ disgusting dishes (depending on your taste) with bull, boar, camel, ostrich and kangaroo testicles, usually battered or fried. Politely called 'white kidneys' in Serbian, they are believed to be rich in testosterone and to help men's libido. 'This festival is all about fun, food and bravery,' says Ljubomir Erovic, the Serbian chef and testicle gourmand who organizes this bizarre event. Prizes are also awarded to people who have demonstrated their 'ballsyness' in the previous year. Recent winners have included Barack Obama, Julian Assange and Felix Baumgartner, who skydived from 40km above the earth in 2012.

Where: Ozrem, Serbia
When: September

> SLOVENIA

DORMOUSE FESTIVAL
Snežnik Castle near Kozarišče

Unless you are a starving cat, you might imagine that there isn't a great deal of meat on the humble dormouse, but it has been feasted upon in the Gorski kotar region of Slovenia since the Middle Ages. Granted the edible dormouse, or

polh as it is known in Slovenia, is larger than its non-edible cousin, but it still takes a number of them to make a meal. This festival celebrates the start of the official dormouse hunting season. A series of events takes place over a long weekend, including local folklore presentations and the consumption of a range of dormouse-related dishes. Saturday sees a competition to see who can trap the most dormice: an able hunter can catch 100 in a night, and apparently it only takes 20 to make a good hat.

Where: Snežnik Castle, Kozarišče, Slovenia
When: Late September/October

KRAVJI BAL (COW BALL)
Ukanc

All summer long the cowherds of Ukanc graze their cattle on the high pastures of the Slovenian Alps, returning to lower levels at the end of September before the cold winter sets in. To mark the return of both the herders and their cows, the locals hold a series of other cow-related events. They start with a parade that sees the best cattle decorated with garlands and bells and processing to the town's famous Govin waterfall, accompanied by most of the villagers. There is a market of milky delicacies such as cheese, as well as contests where those who have spent the summer entirely in the company of cows reassert their *machismo* by sawing logs or hurling horseshoes. In the evening the actual Cow Ball takes place, as the locals let down their hair and pick up their heels with traditional folk dancing to the strains of accordions and fiddles.

Where: Ukanc, Slovenia
When: Third Sunday in September

KURENTOVANJE FESTIVAL
Ptuj

Kurentovanje in its current form dates back to 1961, but draws on the older folk traditions of the region. The central characters of the festival are the hairy *Kurents*. Dressed in sheepskins with chains and bells around their waists to frighten off winter, and wearing leather masks with long noses and long red tongues, they are said to be able to chase off the winter and welcome in the spring. The making of their masks is considered a major folk art, and only two master mask-makers remain. The actual festival is a lively mix of concerts, balls and traditional folk processions, commencing at midnight on the first Saturday with Kurents dancing around a bonfire and the ceremonial crowning of the Prince of Carnival, who will rule the town for the duration of the festival. A major masked parade is held on the second Saturday, and on Shrove Tuesday Carnival is ritually buried.

Where: Ptuj, Slovenia
When: 10 days leading to Shrove Tuesday

Fire and Light

COMPELLING, PRIMEVAL, MYSTERIOUS AND DANGEROUS, FIRE IS A FEATURE
OF MANY FESTIVALS AROUND THE WORLD. IT INVOKES THE SUPERNATURAL
AND IS USED FOR PRAYER, PURIFICATION, ORDEAL, COMMEMORATION AND
CELEBRATION. IT CAN BRING DEATH AND DESTRUCTION – YET OFFERS
HOPE AND RENEWAL, LIGHT IN THE DARKNESS AND A WELCOMING HEARTH.
WHATEVER THE SYMBOLISM OF THE OCCASION, THIS POWERFUL AND DRAMATIC
ELEMENT PUTS US DIRECTLY IN TOUCH WITH THE FORCES OF NATURE.

ABOVE To commemorate their Viking heritage, celebrants carry flaming
torches at Up Helly Aa Festival in the Shetland Islands, Scotland.

OPPOSITE A *ninot* comes to a fiery end in the bonfires celebrating the
festival of Las Fallas in Spain.

Since our earliest ancestors, over a million years ago, discovered how to control fire, it has been central to human life, and its magical properties are associated with religion. Fire enabled early man to change his diet by cooking and eating meat, to keep himself warm and to protect himself from dangerous animals. In later years it was fire that allowed the creation of iron and then steel, developments that led to technological development in warfare and agriculture, and underpinned the entire Industrial Revolution. It is therefore no surprise that over the years a great mythology and symbolism has been built around this vital element.

ABOVE Fires frighten off Satan at the Sadeh Festival in Iran.

ABOVE RIGHT A straw effigy of winter is symbolically burnt at the Russian festival of Maslenitsa.

Much of the symbolism associated with fire is pagan in origin, sometimes representing the transition of darkness to light in the passing of the seasons or the battle between good and evil or its destructive powers. Some of this has found its way into the observances of more established religions.

Although many fire festivals have a religious element, there is only one that centres on the apparent worship of fire, that fairest form of Ahura Mazda, the Wise Lord on high. The religion of ancient Persia, Zoroastrianism, reveres fire and, as a part of the Sadeh Festival at Yazd in Iran (see p. 172), the faithful still visit a fire temple in a cave and also light bonfires to keep Satan, in the form of Ahriman, at bay.

Rural and tribal communities have often lived around bonfires. Representing protection and warmth, fires are therefore the backdrop to many rituals and ceremonies. At the Alkhalalalaj (see p. 176), the harvest festival of the tribal Itel'men of the Kamchatka Peninsula in the Russian Far East, traditional dances take place around a bonfire.

Fire often marks the passing of the seasons, particularly the transition from winter to spring and the coming of light into the world. The Russian Maslenitsa Festival (see p. 176) incorporates pagan elements to herald the beginning of spring, including the burning of a straw effigy that represents winter. Beltane is the Gaelic celebration of the end of winter and is a time for lighting fires that symbolize the beginning of new life. The Beltane Fire Festival in Edinburgh (see p. 250) is a recent interpretation of this Celtic tradition, and is celebrated with a torchlight procession and a bonfire. The Marsden Imbolc Festival in Yorkshire (see p. 238) recalls another pagan festival: the midpoint between the winter solstice and the spring equinox. Torch processions, fire sculptures, jugglers and fire-eaters are the backdrop to a symbolic fight between Jack Frost and the Green Man of Spring.

ABOVE Fires are lit to celebrate the coming of summer at the Celtic festival of Beltane, when celebrants walk around bonfires, leap over the flames and the brave run through the embers. In the past the practice was performed to encourage good crops and healthy livestock.

ABOVE RIGHT Participants at the Easter ritual of Holy Light at the Church of the Holy Sepulchre in Jerusalem.

Further afield, fire features in the torch festivals of minority peoples in China. The Bai people honour their god of fire at the Bai Torch Festival (see p. 94) by lighting a giant torch in the centre of the village and carrying flaming torches in procession. This act is believed to drive away evil spirits and also to bring luck to anyone who catches an ember falling from the torch.

The pagan symbolism of bringing light into the darkness is also reflected in Christianity. This is especially prominent at Easter, the celebration of the Resurrection of Christ and his triumph over death. At the Easter service in Jerusalem, the tomb of Christ in the Church of the Holy Sepulchre is flooded with candlelight in a ritual called Holy Light (see p. 172). In Florence, Italy, at the Scoppio del Carro (see p. 208). 'Holy Fire' is carried through the city and used to light a dove-shaped rocket that in turns sets off a number of fireworks, symbolizing the Resurrection.

At Riosucio in Colombia, the Carnaval del Diablo (see p. 90) sees the ceremonial burning of the Devil. This battle against the forces of darkness is symbolically commemorated in a number of religions. The Torch Festival of the Yi people in China (see p. 96) celebrates the victory of their ancestors over a demon king. At the Hindu

OPPOSITE TOP LEFT A celebrant carries a flaming pine torch at the Nachi Fire Festival in the Kumano Mountains, at one of Japan's largest fire festivals.

OPPOSITE TOP RIGHT A spectacular fireworks display over the 30-minute ritual burning of Mt Wakakusayama at New Year in Nara City, Japan.

OPPOSITE BELOW The small coastal town of Lewis, England, celebrates the burning of Guy Fawkes on 5 November with great gusto.

RIGHT A flaming tar barrel is shouldered by a celebrant at the Festival of Ottery St Mary held on 5 November in Devon, England.

festival of Diwali (the Festival of Lights, see p. 121) tiny lamps, and more recently, electric fairy lights, light up the night skies to signify the triumph of good over evil, and at Dev Deepavali in the Holy city of Varanasi (see p. 121) pilgrims leave lamps on the *ghats* (steps) lining the Ganges to welcome gods who are said to come to Earth that day.

Sometimes fire is used simply to commemorate or celebrate significant events. A large bonfire is the centre of the celebrations atthe Ethiopian Maskal in the capital Addis Ababa (see p. 14). It honours the finding of the True Cross by the Empress Helena, mother of Constantine the Great, in AD 326. To remember the triumph of the Shakyamuni Buddha in a theological debate, at the Tibetan Chunga Choepa (Butter Lamp Festival, see p. 110) butter and *tsampa* are sculpted into colourful figures and then set alight.

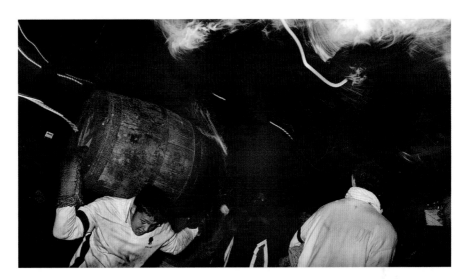

In Great Britain, fires light up the country on the night of 5 November to celebrate the foiling of the Gunpowder Plot to blow up the Houses of Parliament, and King James I to boot, in 1605. Shortly after the event, an act was put through parliament decreeing that people should mark the occasion each year, and the tradition continues to this day, with fireworks and effigies of the lead plotter, Guy Fawkes, being burnt on bonfires. The most famous of the Bonfire Night celebrations takes place at Lewes in East Sussex (see p. 236), where a number of Bonfire Societies hold impressive themed torchlight processions and their own bonfire parties.

The practice of carrying flaming tar barrels through the streets of Ottery St Mary in Devon (see p. 239) is derived from Bonfire Night. The crazy Bolas de Fuego in El Salvador (see p. 56), where people hurl great fireballs at each other, remembers the deliverance of the town from a volcano in 1658. At Las Luminarias de San Anton in Spain (see p. 224), where daring riders jump horses across huge bonfires, they celebrate the feast day of St Anthony, the patron saint of animals, and re-enact a pagan purification right for the horses which are said to be blessed by the smoke for the following year.

ABOVE Against a backdrop of fire, a Beltane festival-goer dressed as Flora celebrates the arrival of spring.

Fire forms part of many purification rituals, particularly in Japan. At the Nachi Fire Festival in the Kumano Mountains (see p. 99), massive flaming torches are used to purify several shrines for the deities that live there; and at the Omizutori Festival at the Todai-ji Temple (see p. 99), flaming embers from the torches used to purify the shrines are dropped on to crowds in the courtyard to bring them good luck. More worldly explanations suggest that the origins of the Yamayaki Festival (see p. 100), which sees the slopes of Mount Wakakusayama at Nara City being torched, arose from a boundary dispute, or an attempt to drive away wild boar and nasty creepy-crawlies.

With its pagan roots, the old English custom of Wassailing (see p. 236) sees the 'purification' of apple trees. Bonfires are lit and the trees are beaten with sticks by Morris Dancers to drive out evil spirits and thereby ensure a good harvest. At the Quema del Diablo in Guatemala City (see p. 56) people clean their houses and make pyres in the streets in order to burn their old, unwanted possessions. People believe that the Devil lives in dirty houses and sometimes effigies of the Devil are burnt on the pyres, which are torched just before dark, sending a pall of thick, acrid smoke across the city.

The destructive power of fire is harnessed in a number of festivals – most spectacularly in Las Fallas in Valencia, Spain, and Up Helly Aa in the Shetland Islands of Scotland.

At Las Fallas (see p. 223) effigies called *ninots* are constructed and paraded through the town. Often having a contemporary or political theme, these are ceremonially burned on vast pyres, amidst a cacophony of fireworks. Although it has elements of the pagan celebration marking the end of the Yule season, Up Helly Aa (see p. 251) is predominantly a re-enactment of a Viking funeral, reflecting the Norse influences in the islands off the north coast of Scotland. A traditional longboat is constructed, then up to a thousand 'Vikings' carrying torches parade through the town before throwing the torches on board, sending the whole thing up in flames.

The very danger of fire presents another opportunity to challenge the frailty of human flesh. Even when there is a greater symbolism or meaning to the appearance of fire in a festival, people like to test themselves against it, happily leaping over bonfires, carrying fire, throwing fire or riding horses through the flames. Underlaying this defiance of danger in a spirit of enjoyment and bravado, there is always the awareness of our own mortality. Some of the most spectacular festivals involve an ordeal by fire. Some commemorate a significant event in the history of a culture, but others, such as those that include fire-walking, are simple tests of faith and bravery. Fire-walking barefoot over hot coals is a part of a number of festivals, including the Festival of the Goddess Amman in Kuala Lumpur (see p. 150) and the Vegetarian Festival in Phuket in Thailand (see p. 162).

>> SCANDINAVIA

> DENMARK

AALBORG CARNIVAL
Aalborg

Adopting many of the festive aspects of Carnival, but decidedly secular in nature, the Aalborg Carnival was dreamt up in 1982 as a celebration of spring and the coming of summer. It has since grown into the largest carnival in Northern Europe. The undoubted highlight is the Carnival Parade, or rather parades, as four different routes converge on the Kildeparken where four stages host music and dance performances. The parade is led by the symbolic *Carrus Navalis*: a carnival boat that signifies the change of the seasons. Walking in front of the boat, shadow men carry brooms to sweep away winter; behind the boat are a pair of oxen and the farmer, who plants seeds. Before the parade, the Battle of Carnival Bands is staged, where groups from all over the world compete against each other.

Where: Aalborg, Denmark
When: 22nd Saturday of the year (usually last week of May)

> FINLAND

HELSINKI HERRING FESTIVAL
Helsinki

Although it sounds like something dreamt up by a committee of the Finnish Herring Marketing Council, this festival is actually the city's oldest traditional event, dating as far back as 1743. Essentially a week-long seafood festival, this is not a place for ichthyophobes. Countless stalls try to tempt you with their favourite herring recipes, and fishermen moor their boats at the edge of the harbour and sell Baltic herring dishes directly to the public. There is a host of other stalls selling other fish-related items too. In case this all sounds too fishy, the Herring Market Jury meets to decide on who has produced the top marinated fish and the best herring surprise.

Where: Market Square, Helsinki, Finland
When: Usually a week in October

VAPPU
Helsinki

It might be something to do with the lack of sunlight in the long northern winter, but May Day is celebrated with wild abandon by the citizens of Helsinki in a traditional festival called Vappu (Walpurgis Night). The party starts at 6.00 p.m. the day before May Day with a mass scrubbing-down of the naked statue of Havis Amanda in the Market Square, and carries on through the night. On May Day itself everyone heads to one of two parks for a picnic of traditional Finnish foods, washed down with copious amounts of booze. Many bring tablecloths and candelabra to lend a civilized air to the proceedings before the hard partying starts. As befits the day when workers of the world are supposed to unite, unions and political parties stage a march with speeches, but most people simply use the occasion as an excuse for an enormous party.

Where: All over Finland, especially Helsinki
When: May Day (Begins 30 April at 6.00 p.m.)

WIFE CARRYING WORLD CHAMPIONSHIPS
Sonkajarvi

Believe it or not, the 'sport' of wife carrying (*eukonkanto*) is very popular in Finland. One theory is that it dates back to a gang of robbers from the 1800s who used to 'steal' women by slinging them over their shoulders. Wife carrying was first designated a sport in the Finnish town of Sonkajarvi, which has been holding the World Championships since 1992. The idea is that a man carries a 'wife' (not necessarily his own) over a 253.5m obstacle course that includes a number of water features. The winner wins the 'wife's' weight in beer – throwing up the interesting conundrum as to whether it is worth going for the bigger prize or the easiest carry. Although the competition is taken seriously, the atmosphere among the spectators is considerably less sober.

Where: Sonkajarvi, Finland
When: July

> ICELAND

JÓ HÁTÍ (PEOPLE'S FEAST)
Heimaey Island

The problem with throwing a party in your own house is that it can get trashed. The people of Heimaey Island have come up with the ideal solution: they decamp to the Herjólfsdalur Valley near the main town of Vestmannaeyjar and hold their party there. Legend has it that in 1874 bad weather prevented the islanders travelling to the mainland to join in the celebrations for the ratification of Iceland's constitution. Undeterred, they organized their own festival and have been doing so ever since. People stay in rows of white tents, picnic and feast on such local delicacies as smoked puffin, while listening to music and watching comedy acts, many of which are native to the islands. On the Sunday evening they all sit on a hillside in front of a large bonfire to watch fireworks and hold a 'hillside singalong'.

Where: Heimaey Island, Westman Islands, Iceland
When: Weekend before 1st Monday in August

Husbands sweat it out carrying wives, not necessarily their own, at speed around a track in a bid for beer.

> NORWAY

SAMI EASTER FESTIVAL
Karasjok and Kautokeino

The Sami peoples have always celebrated the end of the harsh Arctic winters with gatherings to strengthen cultural and social bonds, and it is a good time for weddings. The Sami were traditionally nomadic reindeer herders. Their homeland is known as Sápmi (often erroneously referred to as Lapland) and covers the northern areas of Norway, Sweden, Finland and Russia. Traditionally shamanist, most were converted to Christianity in the 18th century and the gatherings are now referred to as Easter festivals. The two main Sami towns in Norway hold Easter festivals with traditional theatre and dance performances, films and exhibitions of Sami culture. Kautokeino (seat of Sami learning) is noted for the Sami Grand Prix – a sort of Samivision Song Contest – and Karasjok (home of the Sami Parliament) for the Reindeer Racing World Cup.

Where: Kautokeino and Karasjok, Norway
When: One week over Easter

> SWEDEN

MEDELTIDSVECKAN (MEDIEVAL WEEK)
Visby

Most places throw a big celebration to commemorate great victories; the town of Visby on the Swedish island of Gotland holds Medeltidsveckan to commemorate the royal thumping that the town received at the hands of Danish King Valdemar in 1361. Some 1,800 peasants were killed by Valdemar's soldiers, who then set up three giant barrels outside the city wall and demanded they be filled with treasure in return for sparing the town from further destruction. Visby is a medieval town with cobbled streets and many historic buildings. During Medeltidsveckan many of the local people dress up in period costume, put on a traditional market and entertain visitors with jesters, street entertainers and musicians playing lutes and flutes. The highlight is a knights' jousting tournament, complete with archers and fighting men-at-arms.

Where: Visby, Sweden
When: 32nd week of the year, Sunday to Sunday (August)

MIDSOMMAR
Stockholm

If you live in a country where the winters are long and cold and there are just six hours of daylight in the capital and 24 hours of darkness further north, then summers are a big deal. Many consider that the Swedish midsummer festival dates back to the days of the Vikings. Although celebrating the summer solstice (the day with the longest period of daylight), Midsommar is traditionally held on the third Saturday of June. Many people go to the countryside, but one of the best parties is held at the Skansen open-air museum in Stockholm. The party starts on Midsummer Eve with singing and dancing around a midsummer pole with celebrants dressed in traditional costume. This is a fertility rite and the pole is decorated with greenery and flowers. Traditional foods such as pickled herring and potatoes with soured cream and chives are consumed, washed down with Schnapps and spiced vodka.

Where: Skansen open-air museum, Stockholm, Sweden
When: Third Friday and Saturday in June

>> WESTERN EUROPE

> AUSTRIA

NARZISSENFEST
Altaussee

Tthe Austrian Narzissenfest is a celebration of the humble daffodil. While Welsh people might worry that the citizens of Altaussee are trying to hijack their national flower, the daffodil at the centre of this festival is a local white variety. Over four days a Daffodil Queen is elected, and there are parades of large intricate flower displays by road and by boat on the Grundisee or Altausseer lakes. As well as celebrating the Pheasant's Eye daffodil, the Narzissenfest is a perfect opportunity to join in an Austrian festival. Locals dance and play music wearing traditional clothes, including the legendary *Lederhosen* (leather shorts) for men and the Heidi-chic *Dirndl* for the women, so that everyone looks like an extra from *The Sound of Music* (not the ones in uniform).

Where: Altaussee, Austria
When: Thursday to Sunday, end of May or June

> BELGIUM

AALST CARNIVAL
Aalst

Cross-dressing, satire and a willingness to offend characterize this 600-year-old carnival. The madness begins with the election of Prince Carnaval, who takes the keys of the city from the ridiculed civic authorities and becomes the *de facto* mayor. For the next three days the lunatics really do take over the asylum. On Sunday and Monday a parade of satirical floats takes to the streets parodying local and world events. Locals refer to themselves as 'onions', and on Monday Prince Carnaval lobs onions into the crowd from City Hall. Shrove Tuesday is marked by the appearance of *Voil Jeanetten* (Dirty Jennies). They run riot in the streets,

One of the many extravagantly costumed troupes that join the grand parade at carnival time in Aalst.

camping it up and insulting people before the traditional burning of the carnival effigy, which means it is time for the Prince to hand back the keys and end the madness for another year.

Where: Aalst, Belgium
When: Carnival Sunday to Shrove Tuesday

ATH PROCESSION OF GIANTS
Ath

Way back in 15th-century Europe, someone decided that the best way to educate the peasantry about religious matters was to parade a whole bunch of giant statues around the town. The idea took off and the tradition persists in a number of towns in Belgium and France. The giants, some weighing as much as 350kg, vary depending on the history of the town and the religious message they are trying to convey. Some feature animals and dragons, but the Ath procession retells the biblical story of David and Goliath. Saturday is the more religious day, with a secular procession on Sunday including a range of floats. Other cities to head for in Belgium for some giant action are Brussels, Dendermonde, Mechelen and Mons.

Where: Certain towns in France and Belgium, especially in Ath, Belgium
When: Fourth weekend in August

BOMMEL FESTIVAL
Ronse

Before you start poring over Google Maps looking for a town in Belgium called Bommel, the name of this festival comes from the giant characters who parade through the town barging into each other and generally tussling and trying to knock each other over. These *Bommels* (corks) wear extravagant costumes – making the wearers appear much taller than they are – and huge masks. Although the festival is held on the first Saturday after Epiphany, the day is termed 'Crazy Monday'. The tradition dates back to the parades of masked characters known as *Bonmohs* from the Middle Ages. These include a king, a jester, minstrels and characters called *Longue-langue* (long-tongues) and *Lèche-assiettes* (licking-plates). The parade was resurrected in the 1950s, when the current festival was reborn.

Where: Ronse, Belgium
When: First Saturday after Epiphany (6 January)

CARNAVAL DE BINCHE
Binche

Most people would say that oranges are good for your health, but not when they are hurled at your head from the middle of a carnival procession. This is what is likely to happen if you watch the show-stopping Shrove Tuesday procession of the Carnaval de Binche. Up to a thousand masked characters called *Gilles* form the procession. Reputed to have originated from Inca characters created by local journalist Adolphe Delmée at the end of the 18th century, they wear bright costumes, wooden clogs, distinctive wax masks and hats with sweeping ostrich feathers. The *Gilles* throw out oranges as they dance through the streets to the rhythms of loud drumming. If you catch one it is supposed to bring good luck. On Sunday and Monday there are processions through the town with music, dancing and firework displays.

Where: Binche, Belgium
When: Week before Lent
....

GOLDEN STILT COMPETITION
Namur
....

Since 1411 the citizens of Namur have battled it out on metre-high stilts in a unique jousting tournament. The 'gladiators' dress in red and white costumes and mount what resemble old-fashioned barbers' poles. The dog-eat-dog competition features 50 jousters in two teams – both men and women – who battle it out with long jousting poles, aiming to knock each other over. When one team is victorious the surviving jousters fight each other until only one is left standing. He or she is the winner of the Golden Stilt; the runner-up is rewarded with a silver version. The origins of stilt-walking in Namur date from the Middle Ages, when the local rivers regularly burst their banks and flooded the town. If you miss this tournament, stilt fights are staged at many local festivals all over the Wallonia region.

Where: Namur, Belgium
When: Third Sunday in September
....

HANSWIJK PROCESSION
Mechelen
....

There are many old traditions in Europe, but the procession of Our Lady of Hanswijk is one of the very oldest. First held in 1273, it commemorates the town of Mechelen surviving the plague. Locals believed that they were saved by a statue of the Virgin, and have staged the procession ever since. The parade features hundreds of people in various costumes, supported by musicians, choirs and dance troupes. The procession is split into three parts representing the history of the town, the life of the Virgin Mary and the life of Jesus. The statue of the Virgin Mary is carried through the streets as a part of the procession. Every 25 years there is another event, the Hanswijk Cavalcade. Similar to the annual procession, it also includes horses, sheep and floats. It was last held in October 2013.

Where: Mechelen, Belgium
When: One Sunday in May
....

HOLY BLOOD PROCESSION
Bruges
....

The celebration of *Brugges Schoonste Dag* (the Most Beautiful Day in Bruges) sees a sacred relic of the blood of Christ carried through the town. Legend has it that the coagulated blood turns to liquid on this day. Brought back from the Crusades by Derrick of Alsace, Count of Flanders, the relic has been processed in a great pageant since 1291. Almost 2,000 participants act out scenes from the life of Christ and the history of the town. Escorted by members of the Brotherhood of the Holy Blood, brass bands and a carillon of bells, the relic brings up the rear of the procession and, as it passes, the crowd falls silent in a moving show of respect.

Where: Bruges, Belgium
When: Ascension Day (30 days after Easter Sunday, April or May)
....

KATTENSTOET
Ypres
....

Although on the face of it the Ypres Cat Festival celebrates the humble moggy, at its heart is a re-enactment of the cruel medieval custom of throwing cats from the belfry of the Cloth Hall into the town square. The most likely explanation for this tradition lies in the implied connection between cats and witchcraft, and that the throwing of cats represents the killing of evil spirits. The Kattenstoet began in 1938 with a parade of nine altar boys who carried toy cats to the belfry, which were ceremonially thrown from the top. In subsequent years the parade has grown into a fully cat-themed procession with floats, cat costumes and theatre groups. People try to catch the thrown toy cats, believing it to be good luck. After the parade, there is a ceremonial mock burning of a witch.

Where: Ypres, Belgium
When: Every three years, in May (Next in 2018)
....

LA DUCASSE FESTIVAL
Mons
....

Known locally as 'La Doudou', the centrepiece of this festival is a ritual battle between St George and the dragon, representing the eternal struggle between good and evil. This battle is called the *Lumeçon* and features George on a black horse and a wicker dragon almost 10m long. The dragon is wielded by a cohort of devils and St George is aided by an army of soldiers called *chinchins*. As the battle is ritually enacted to the sound of 'Doudou' music, members of the crowd rush forwards to try to snatch bits from the dragon's tail. On the morning of Trinity Sunday there is a procession with the relics of St Waltrude, the city's patron saint.

Where: Grand Palace, Mons, Belgium
When: Trinity Sunday (57 days after Easter, usually May or June)
....

Medieval Europe

THE COUNTRIES OF EUROPE ARE A TREASURE TROVE OF DIFFERENT CUSTOMS
AND TRADITIONS, MANY OF WHICH ARE ROOTED IN A REAL OR IMAGINED
MEDIEVAL PAST. TAKE A JAUNT AROUND THE MYRIAD COLOURFUL FESTIVALS OF
EUROPE AND YOU CAN IMAGINE THAT YOU'VE TRAVELLED BACK IN TIME TO A
WORLD OF MEDIEVAL COSTUMES, PAGEANTRY, GAMES AND
JOUSTING TOURNAMENTS.

ABOVE A larger-than-life Crusader participates in the
Procession of the Giants in Ath in Belgium.

OPPOSITE A masked rider demonstrates her equestrian
skills by trying to plunge her sword into a hanging star at full gallop,
at the Sa Sartiglia Festival in Sardinia.

ABOVE Costumed knights will engage in mock battle with Moors at the Fiesta de Moros y Christianos to commemorate the Christian victory over the Moors.

ABOVE RIGHT A festival participant is dressed up as a defeated Tartar general at the Festival of Lajkonik in Krakow, which celebrates the city's brief victory over Genghis Khan in the 13th century.

European festivals, both national and local, reflect the richness, complexity and distinctive quirks of their national cultures and traditions. Very many are a living link with the past, and in particular with the great formative period of European history known as the Middle Ages.

The Middle Ages are generally defined as the period between the fifth and the fifteenth centuries, running from the decline of the Western Roman Empire to the discovery of the New World. It was a time before nation states, when social structures were largely feudal and the Church wielded enormous influence and power. There were invasions by Goths, Vikings, Magyars, Moors, Saracens and Huns, culminating in the fall of the Byzantine Empire to the Ottoman Turks, and all of these groups left their mark on the collective European memory. There were heresy and schism within the Church, peasants' revolts and brutal civil wars. Between 1347 and 1350 over a third of the population of Europe died from the Black Death, and famine was never far away.

Yet in the medieval courts of Provence and Burgundy the arts of war were tamed and transmuted into the ideals of courtly love and Christian chivalry. Intellectual life, kept alive by the Church, broke the bounds of the monasteries with the founding of the great universities, and prosperous trading cities developed civic life, and pride, independently of their feudal overlords. No surprise, then, that so many European festivals have their roots in this tumultuous age.

Some of the medieval-themed festivals commemorate actual historical battles and plagues. The Fiesta de Moros y Cristianos at Alicante in Spain (see p. 222) re-enacts a victory for the Spanish forces over the occupying Moors from North Africa. Over 5,000 people dress up with painstaking observance of the period, with the officially sanctioned exception of watches and glasses, and take part in mock battles to eventually liberate the castle with the help of St Jorge.

Genghis Khan's armies repeatedly sacked many cities in Eastern Europe in the thirteenth century. The Lajkonik Festival (see p. 175) re-enacts a rare victory by the city of Krakow over the invading Mongol horsemen. Granted, the enemy was killed while sleeping in a forest nearby, but it was a victory nonetheless and has been celebrated ever since with an eclectic parade led by a character dressed in the clothes of the vanquished Tartar general, who announces the city's triumph.

Perhaps the most bizarre medieval battle is the Battaglia delle Arance at Ivrea in Italy (see p. 204), where a people's revolt against an oppressive feudal lord is played out with citrus fruit. Hundreds of people dress up in medieval costume and hurl oranges at each other for three days. Those on foot represent the townspeople, those on horse-carts the soldiers of the feudal lord.

BELOW The heroine Jeanne faces charges of heresy in a re-enactment of her trial and execution at the annual Festival Jeanne d'Arc, which takes place in several French cities to commemorate her death on 30 May 1431.

Not all of the battle re-enactments celebrate great victories. Medeltidsveckan (Medieval Week) in Sweden (see p. 187) commemorates the massacre of some 1,800 peasant soldiers by the invading Danish King Valdemar. The whole town turns medieval for the week and holds a jousting tournament that sees knights in armour do battle.

Themed festivals celebrate other important events in the lives of our medieval forebears. The Procession of Our Lady of Hanswijk at Mechelen in Belgium (see p. 189)

OPPOSITE TOP A magnificent gilded gondola replete with costumed characters takes part in the water pageant on the Grand Canal at the Regata Storica to celebrate Venice's glorious past.

OPPOSITE BELOW Performers wearing oversized masks entertain the crowds at the Corpus procession of La Patum in Berga, Spain.

is a parade that dates back to 1273, celebrating the deliverance of the town from an outbreak of the plague. Slightly more gruesome, the Festival Jeanne d'Arc (see p. 199) marks the burning at the stake of *La Pucelle* for heresy by the invading English forces.

Although not commemorating any particular event, some places like to turn back the clock to their heyday of power and glory. The Regata Storica in Venice harks back to the city's past as a great maritime republic ruled by the Doges (see p. 207). It features a costumed water pageant of gondolas on the Grand Canal, followed by a series of gondola races. In the tiny Republic of San Marino during the San Marino Medieval Days (see p. 220) a number of historical societies, such as the fabulously named San Marino Federation of Crossbowmen, dress up in costume and recreate a medieval village in the centre of town.

The Middle Ages was a period of aggressive proselytizing and repression of other religions. It was the age of the Crusades and the Spanish Inquisition, when people were tortured and executed for heresy, and when Islam swept into Southern and Eastern Europe at the point of a sword. In Western Europe a tradition of large religious parades grew up in order to carry the Christian message to an often illiterate populace. Prime examples of this are the Procession of Giants in Ath and Brussels and the Bommel Festival at Ronse (see p. 188).

La Patum de Berga, in Spain (see pp. 222–3), has its origins in the celebration of the summer solstice; however, like many other pre-Christian festivities, the Catholic Church repurposed it with a new symbolism and assimilated it into the celebration of the Feast of Corpus Christi. An early reference to a Corpus procession in Berga dates back to 1454, during which short farces were performed. Drawing on its medieval past, La Patum has evolved into an event of popular theatre with a colourful cast of giants, demons, angels, dwarves, knights, Turks and Moors in a battle between good and evil.

ABOVE A participant at the Holy Blood Procession, which has taken place in Bruges every year on Ascension Day since 1291.

At La Ducasse (see p. 189) in Mons, Belgium, good is represented by St George and evil by a dragon. As the two engage in a mock battle (called the *Lumeçon*) in the central square of Mons, people in the crowd attempt to grab parts of the dragon's thrashing tail to bring themselves good luck. The Holy Blood Procession in Bruges, Belgium (see p. 189), parades a relic, said to be the Blood of Christ that was brought back from the Crusades, through the city. Accompanied by almost 2,000 participants acting out scenes from the life of Christ, the coagulated blood is supposed to become liquid on this day.

Of course, the Middle Ages were not all doom and gloom, and there are a number of festivals that celebrate the sporting life of the period. In the early years, some of the most prominent sporting events were the tournaments, where knights in armour competed in martial combat. The Giostra del Saracino (see p. 206) in Arezzo, Italy, recreates such a contest from the days of the Crusades. Knights from different districts gallop at a metal figure representing a Saracen. They hit it with their lances, and then try to avoid a ball that swings around when the target is hit. Jousting is also a feature of the Sa Sartiglia on the island of Sardinia (see p. 207). As part of a larger display of equestrian skills, masked figures try to spear a hanging star with their swords: the more holes they make in it, the luckier the subsequent year will be.

The Palio of Siena (see p. 207) is a medieval bareback horse race which is run twice a year in the city's undulating cobbled main square. Lots are drawn between the city districts, (contrade) to see which ten compete and what horses and riders they get. After a series of practice races, the horses are processed to the campo by their contrade in full medieval dress. This includes knights in armour and traditional flag twirlers. It is a race full of intrigue and skulduggery, in which people try to bribe competing jockeys or nobble their horses. The actual race lasts for three frenetic laps of the campo and a number of the horses and jockeys fall at the tight corners. A similar race takes place each year at Asti in Piedmont (see p. 206).

Two medieval sporting events are recreated in the city of Pisa: the Gioco del Ponte and the Regata di San Ranieri (see pp. 205 and 207). Dating back to 1290, the Regata di St Ranieri is a rowing race down the River Arno. Each boat carries a montatore whose job is to climb a ten-metre cable and snatch a coloured pennant at the end of the race. The Gioco del Ponte (Game of the Bridge) is a test of strength where men in medieval costume from different districts compete in a trial of strength to push a giant cart across a bridge. The two teams push against each other and the winner is the team that drives the other backwards.

Although not officially a sporting event, the Corsa dei Ceri at Gubbio, Italy has a race at its heart. This twelfth-century ritual sees three statues of saints paraded at speed through the town and uphill to the Basilica di Sant' Ubaldo (see p. 205).

One of the most bizarre medieval sports that you will find anywhere in Europe is the Golden Stilt Competition at Namur in Belgium (see p. 189) which dates back to the fifteenth century. Jousters on metre-high stilts, dressed in red and white, duel it out to knock each other over. The fight starts off as team against team, but then the surviving members of the winning team battle each other until one emerges victorious.

ABOVE Musicians and flag twirlers dressed in medieval costume perform ahead of the *palio*, the bareback horse race around the *campo*, Siena's central square.

OPPOSITE Thousands of locals and visitors gather in the main square of Gubbio to witness the Corsa dei Ceri, the race of the saints. Statues of Saints Ubaldo, George and Anthony are ferried by three competing teams to the Basilica di Sant' Ubaldo.

LA RÉGATE INTERNATIONALE DES BAIGNOIRES
Dinant

The owl and the pussycat may have gone to sea in a beautiful pea-green boat, but the craft of choice on the River Meuse is the humble bathtub. The rules are simple: competitors have to pilot a floating bathtub up the river, and although it is a straight race – with the first over the finishing line being declared the winner – contestants are also required to make an effort when decorating their bathtub. There is a theme chosen for each year. Contestants aren't allowed to try to try to sink other bathtubs, but they often have water fights – hurling buckets of water at opponents to put them off.

Where: River Meuse, Dinant, Belgium
When: Mid-August

OMMEGANG
Brussels

Ommegang is a generic term for a type of pageant celebrated in Belgium, Holland and northern France. Perhaps the best known is held in the iconic Grand Place in Brussels and re-enacts the triumphant entry into the city of Emperor Charles V in 1549, when the city wanted to show off its grandeur and prosperity. Today's version is a parade of some 1,500 people dressed in authentic costumes, with horses and coaches, which makes its way through the city streets. A medieval village is reconstructed, which hosts performances of equestrian jousting, falconry, stilt-walking and archery. The pageant was first mentioned in 1359, when it was a major religious procession. The name is Dutch for 'go around [the church]', although the event has since become a more secular celebration.

Where: Brussels, Belgium
When: Usually three days in July

STAVELOT CARNIVAL
Stavelot

Inflated pigs' bladders seem an odd choice of weapon, especially when wielded by people dressed in white robes, wearing masks with long, red carrot-noses. But then the *Blancs Moussis* (meaning 'clad in white') are distinctly odd carnival characters, as they move through the crowds, grunting and laughing and hitting people with dried fish and pigs' bladders date back to a rather eclectic protest by the townsfolk after the local monks were banned from joining the carnival by their abbot over 500 years ago. This is a three-day mid-Lenten festival, but the *Blancs Moussis* only come out to play on Carnival Sunday, which is also the day of the big parade of floats and marching bands. Everyone in town wears fancy dress.

Where: Stavelot, Belgium
When: Fourth weekend of Lent (March or April)

> FRANCE

BASTILLE DAY
Paris

The French celebrate Bastille Day with great pride. On 14 July in 1789 the people of Paris stormed the medieval fortress-prison. Although only seven prisoners were actually in the Bastille at the time, the act marked the beginning of the French Revolution and the formation of the Republic. Official celebrations in Paris kick off with a strangely triumphant military parade down the Champs-Elysées. Planes from the Patrouille de France aerobatics team fly overhead. The official end of the celebration is a massive fireworks display at the Eiffel Tower, although there are concerts, balls and parties held all over the city.

Where: All over France, especially Paris
When: 14 July

CARNAVAL DES SOUFFLETS
Nontron

You might think that the Carnaval des Soufflets is some sort of refined food festival, but *soufflets* are bellows and this strange tradition sees villagers blowing air from bellows up each other's nightshirts to blow away evil spirits. Villagers walk in single file and blow the bellows while singing a song in the ancient Occitan language of southern France which starts with the lines 'We are all children; Our father was a bellows maker'. The festival begins on Saturday night with a banquet. On Sunday there is the Parade of the Soufflaculs, to which anyone sporting a long nightshirt and toting a set of bellows is welcome. The tradition is thought to have been originated by local monks who would perform it on Ash Wednesday to purify themselves for Lent.

Where: Nontron, France
When: First weekend in April

FERIA DE NÎMES
Nîmes

For five days over the Pentecost weekend, Nîmes is transformed into Spain, with paella, sangria and bullfights in the ancient Roman Arena. The citizens of this part of southern France are completely bull-mad, but the *feria* retains a number of uniquely French touches. There are French-style *abrivado* bull-runs through the town, where feisty local black bulls are galloped through the streets by the *gardian* cowboys of the Camargue. These are smaller than Spanish fighting bulls, and locals often run towards them, sometimes bundling them into a bar, so the *gardians* have to ride in to recover them.

Where: Nîmes, France
When: Pentecost weekend, 10 weeks after Easter (May or June)

FERIA DE PAQUES
Arles

Some 30km south-east of Nîmes is the city of Arles, the citizens of which seem even keener on bullfighting than their neighbours. Not content with one *feria* they have two, beginning at Easter with the Feria de Paques and ending in September with a similar event called the Feria de Riz. All the essential ingredients are included, such as bull-runs and marching *peñas* (bands) through the streets, bull games and bullfights in the Roman Arena. Festival-goers are served huge portions of paella washed down with sangria, of course, at the open-air *bodegas* that spring up for the events.

Where: Arles, France
When: Easter weekend. Feria de Riz is mid September
....

FESTIVAL JEANNE D'ARC
Rouen

The good citizens of Rouen get seriously medieval to commemorate their town's most famous resident and folk heroine: Jeanne d'Arc, the Maid of Orleans. Known in these parts as *La Pucelle*, Jeanne d'Arc was tried for heresy by the invading English and burned at the stake in 1431. To commemorate her grisly end, the entire town is decorated in blue and white, and stages a medieval fair with a series of contemporary tournaments and performances. Jesters, puppeteers, tumblers and fortune-tellers entertain the crowds, and there are fencing, skittles and crossbow-shooting competitions. On the Sunday, there is a solemn costumed procession to the Boieldieu Bridge, and flowers are cast into the River Seine at the point where Jeanne D'Arcs ashes were scattered.

Where: Rouen, France
When: Last weekend in May
....

FESTIVAL OF THE GIANTS
Douai

There are a lot of giants in Belgium and France. Not vicious ogres that terrorize villagers, but traditional characters brought out at festival time. The figures here are called *Gayants*. The largest is Monsieur Gayant, weighing in at 350kg and soaring to an impressive 8.5m. He is paraded with his 'wife' and three children. Mr and Mme Gayant started their processions in 1530, but didn't have any children until 1720. Giants from other towns are brought to join in the festival and there can be up to 100 of them in the parade. Special sweets called *Gayantines* are handed out to everyone. Other towns in France that hold parades of giant folk characters are Tarascon, Cassel and Pézenas.

Where: Douai, France
When: July
....

FÊTE DU CITRON
Menton

Visit the town of Menton during the Fête du Citron, and you will, probably, never see more citrus fruit in one place. For two weeks every year this Riviera town devotes itself to the humble lemon and other locally grown citrus fruits. The festival dates back to the 1930s and was the idea of a local hotel which wanted to celebrate the town's lemon production. There are processions with lemon floats, which pass lemon statues and lemon displays. Every year there is a different theme, such as Spain or Disney, and various tableaux and figures are constructed – almost entirely from lemons. On Sundays there is the Parade of the Golden Fruit, and on Thursdays, the Moonlit Parade.

Where: Menton, France
When: Mid-February for two weeks
....

Floats fashioned from lemons at the Parade of the Golden Fruit during the two-week Fête du Citron at Menton, France.

FÊTES DE BAYONNE
Bayonne

If imitation is the sincerest form of flattery, then the town of Bayonne has a serious crush on nearby Pamplona, just over the border in Spain, as its festival is a copy of the far more famous San Fermin fiesta popularized by Ernest Hemingway in *The Sun Also Rises*. The locals dress in the same white tunic and trousers with a red sash and scarf and there is a programme of bullfights in the arena. This is Basque country, and your ability to drink, eat and party around the clock will be seriously examined. The fêtes start with a ceremony in front of the town hall, at which a symbolic set of keys to the city is thrown into the crowd. The person who catches them gets a free run of the 80 bars in the city for the duration of the festival.

Where: Bayonne, France
When: Five days from the Wednesday before the 1st Sunday in August

FÊTE DES GARDIANS (JOURNÉE BARONCELLIENNE)
Saintes Maries de la Mer

The *gardians* of the Camargue delight in their reputation as the cowboys of France. They ride the famous white horses and raise the black Camargue bulls. This annual fête commemorates their hero: the Marquis de Baroncelli, a fierce advocate of *gardian* rights and friend of Wild Bill Hickok. Starting with a round-up and the branding of calves, the *gardians* then ride to a commemoration at the Marquis's graveside. In the afternoon there is an *abrivado*, where bulls are stampeded through the streets, followed by a display of local folklore, horsemanship and bull games in the arena. I speak from bitter personal experience when I say that anyone brave or indeed stupid enough is welcome to jump into the arena with a bull, where he or she will be chased around – much to the amusement of the locals.

Where: Saintes Maries de la Mer, France
When: 26 May

MONACO GRAND PRIX
Monte Carlo

You don't need to buy a ticket to soak up the atmosphere of the Monaco Grand Prix or to hear the throaty roar of the Formula One cars racing round this twisty street circuit. First held in 1929, this is now one of the most famous and prestigious motor-racing events in the world, and uniquely, you can be a part of the action just by being in town. Granted, you might not see much of it, unless you turn up in a super-yacht, or stump up for one of the expensive grandstands. But there are parties all over town or you can just sit at a pavement cafe and watch the international stars and former racers who flock to this iconic sporting event. Qualifying takes place on Saturday, and the big event on Sunday afternoon. As it is a street race, you can even drive the circuit yourself once the whole show moves on.

Where: Monte Carlo, Monaco, France
When: Last weekend in May

PÈLERINAGE DES GITANS
Saintes Maries de la Mer

Roma gypsies from all over Europe congregate in the tiny village of Saintes Maries de la Mer for a colourful two-day pilgrimage in honour of St Marie-Jacobé and St Marie-Salomé (who were said to have fled here following the Crucifixion), as well as Sara, their patron saint. Each day at a fervent mass, statues of the saints are lowered from the church loft, then processed around the town and out into the sea by hundreds of gypsies, and an honour guard of *gardians* on their white horses. These are the cowboys of the Camargue who farm the local bulls. On the first day St Sara is processed and the statues of the two St Maries are taken to the sea on the following day. At night the square around the fortified church comes alive with music and dancing, sometimes by famous gypsy musicians.

Where: Saintes Maries de la Mer, France
When: 24–25 May

POURCAILHADE
Trie-sur-Baïse

Once home to France's largest pig market, Trie-sur-Baïse celebrates its porcine obsession with this annual pigfest. Predictably, being a French festival, there are plenty of chances to tuck into pork in all its many guises. The town is decorated with piggy kitsch, and there are a whole series of pig-related competitions. The black pudding eating competition sees who can eat a 1m blood sausage in the fastest time and the *Cri do Cochon* (pig-squealing) competition is for pig-impersonators, who aim to imitate the noises a pig makes over its lifetime: from piglet to old boar, with a bit of pig-love in between. First held in 1975, the festival is organized by the rather shady-sounding La Confrérie du Cochon (Brotherhood of the Pig).

Where: Trie-sur-Baïse, France
When: Second Sunday in August

TOUR DE FRANCE
France

Although in recent years the Tour de France has been more awash with drugs than the Ibiza closing parties, it is a national institution in France. It is also far more than a simple bicycle race. All along the route, people come out to cheer, and witness the spectacle. Le Tour is noted for its mountain stages, and these attract particularly large

The equestrian skills of a Camargue *gardian* (cowboy) in the bullring win the admiration of a spectator at the Fête des Gardians at Saintes Maries de la Mer, France.

crowds. As the roads are closed, people often arrive in advance and camp by the side of the road, picnicking, drinking and partying. The atmosphere is lively, raucous and unashamedly partisan. Large crowds also gather to witness the exciting sprint finishes of each stage. The route of Le Tour varies every year and is usually announced each January.

Where: All over France
When: Three weeks in July

> GERMANY

COLOGNE CARNIVAL
Cologne

Large areas of Germany are predominantly Catholic, and many cities celebrate Carnival, the period leading up to Lent, in a very big way. One of the biggest and most exuberant celebrations takes place in the streets of Cologne in the traditionally Catholic Rhineland region. Carnival in most parts of Germany hinges on the number 11, with preparations starting at 11 minutes past 11 on 11 November. The number symbolizes foolishness, and represents the 11th commandment that turns all the others on their heads. Local parades start on Carnival Sunday, but the main event is on Rose Monday, with a procession representing the Cologne *Dreigestirn* (Triumvirate) of the Prince, Peasant and the Maiden, who collectively personify the carnival. There are parties in the city's many squares and bars stay open late as the whole city celebrates.

Where: Cologne, Germany
When: Carnival Sunday to Ash Wednesday

FASNACHT KARNEVAL
Konstanz

The Schwäbisch-Alemannische Fasnacht (Southern German Carnival) has its own Carnoval traditions and heritage. This is epitomized by the pre-Lenten Fasnacht celebrations in the beautiful lakeside town of Konstanz on the Swiss border. Carnival events start on 6 January, but the climax of the 'crazy' season kicks off on the Thursday before Ash Wednesday with a party in the town, followed by a procession of schoolchildren in white nightclothes. The main parade takes place on Sunday, when masked characters take to the streets. Tuesday evening is the official Fasnacht, the night before the fast of Lent, when the locals light fires to signify the end of carnival.

Where: Konstanz, Germany
When: From preceding Thursday to Ash Wednesday

GÄUBODENVOLKSFEST
Straubing

This big folk festival celebrates all things Bavarian and that being Bavaria that obviously includes beer. All the beer for the festival is brewed specially, and must come from the local area. On the first day there is the *Bierprobe* ceremony (trying of the beer), followed by a parade of 2,000 people in traditional Bavarian costume – some in horse-drawn carriages. The Gäubodenvolksfest was founded as an agricultural festival by King Maximilian Joseph of Bavaria in 1812, and is a perfect blend of the traditional and the modern. Beer tents, oompah bands and Bavarian costume contrast with carousels, roller coasters and rock concerts. This mix seems to work, attracting over a million people at the last count.

Where: Straubing, Germany
When: Eleven days in mid-August

OBERAMMERGAU PASSION PLAY
Oberammergau

The Oberammergau Passion Play is performed every ten years. It involves up to half the townsfolk, over 2,000 people, acting out the trial, suffering and death of Jesus of Nazareth. The actual play lasts some seven hours, but it is performed over a hundred times, attracting audiences from all over the world. To qualify for a part, you have to have lived in the town for at least 20 years. All the 'actors' are locals, and have to juggle the play with their day-to-day lives. The devotion of the town stems from an outbreak of the plague in 1633. The inhabitants of Oberammergau promised God that if they survived they would perform a passion play every decade. Their descendants have kept this promise ever since.

Where: Oberammergau, Germany
When: Every 10 years; next in 2020

OKTOBERFEST
Munich

Somewhat incongruously, Oktoberfest – the largest beer festival in the world – kicks off in September. Most of the drinking takes place in vast corporate beer tents run by the breweries. Packed with lines of tables and benches, the rules state that you need to have a seat in order to get a drink. The beer is served in litres in glass mugs called *Maß krüge*, which are brought to the table by buxom waitresses who manage to carry a number in each hand. Visitors are encouraged to dress the part, which unfortunately means *Lederhosen* (leather shorts) for the men, and *Dirndl* dresses for the women. Background music is provided by seemingly endless Bavarian oompah bands. If you manage the boozing without throwing up then there is a large funfair and roller coaster to finish you off.

Where: Munich, Germany
When: 16 days; September to the 1st weekend in October

STARKBIERZEIT
Munich

If you think that Oktoberfest is too big, too crowded and serves weak beer meant for softies, then Starkbierzeit is the one for you. Translated as 'Strong Beer Time', this is for lovers of strong beer or *doppelbock*. Although the beers are strong in alcohol (more than 7 per cent), the name actually refers to the *stammwürze*, or the high amount of solids in the beer, an important characteristic as *doppelbocks* were originally brewed by Paulaner monks in the 17th century to cheat their way through the fasting period of Lent.

Where: Munich, Germany
When: Two weeks around St Joseph's Day (19 March)

WALPURGISNACHT
The Brocken, Harz

The night before May Day is supposed to be the final chance for witches and evil spirits to do their evil deeds before the coming of spring warms the earth and drives them away. Borrowing the location from Goethe's *Faust*, and encompassing elements of Viking pre-May Day pagan fertility rites, Walpurgisnacht is celebrated all over Northern and Central Europe. One of the most authentic events sees hordes of people dressed as witches dancing around bonfires that are lit at the top of the Brocken, the highest peak of the Harz mountains, a point that marks the end of the Harz Witches' Trail. Ironically Walpurgis was an 8th-century nun who spoke out against witchcraft, and would probably not appreciate her name being associated with all of this witchiness.

Where: The Brocken, Harz, Germany
When: 30 April

The rule of the Oktoberfest – 'Be seated and be served' – is being adhered to by the participants in one of the vast tents at the world's biggest beer festival in Munich, Germany.

WASSERSCHLACHT
Berlin

Young, brash and often quite intentionally disgusting, the Wasserschlacht started off in 2001 as a water fight between the rival East and West Berlin districts of Friedrichshain and Kreuzberg, who converged on the Oberbaumbrücke bridge to do battle with each other. The winning district is the one who forces the other to retreat from the bridge. Definitely a festival of the counter-culture, the intention is to intimidate and offend. Weaponry has escalated, and the arsenal now includes foam-rubber clubs and all manner of slimy, smelly and stomach-churning missiles. Eggs, flour, rotten fruit and vegetables, salted herring and even dirty nappies have all been hurled at the opposition. The festival is also called Gemüseschlacht (Vegetable Battle), and 'combat groups' are formed by each district, with names like the Friedrichshain Feminist Women's Front and the Kreuzberg Patriotic Democrats.

Where: Oberbaumbrücke, Berlin, Germany
When: One Sunday in the summer (very variable)

> GREECE

ANASTENARIA
Agia Eleni and Langada

You might imagine that to see animal sacrifices and fire-walking you would have to head to North Africa, or a remote village in Asia, but in villages in Greece men and women also enter trances before walking on red-hot coals. A number of villages hold the Anastenaria fire-walking ceremony, including Agia Eleni and Langada in Central Macedonia on the Greek mainland. Although the tradition has pagan roots, celebrants carry icons of St Helen and St Constantine as they walk or dance barefoot on the coals to ensure a good harvest. Goats are led to the church in procession, sprinkled with holy water and then dispatched in honour of the saints. It is thought that the custom came here with refugees from the Balkan Wars of 1911–12.

Where: Agia Eleni and Langada, Greece
When: 21–23 May

APOKREAS
Galaxidi

Apokreas, the Greek manifestation of Carnival, is celebrated all over the country. Many of the local festivities are similar, but over the years certain towns have developed their own unique and somewhat bizarre style of celebrating. At Galaxidi, north-east of Athens, people see in the start of Lent on the Monday (ironically known here as Clean Monday) with a colossal flour fight known locally as *alevromoutzouroma* (flour smudging). In a ritual that goes back over 200 years, cowbells mark the start of the action, and then the mayhem begins. Much of the flour is coloured and the whole thing ends up in an exuberant mess. Some people decide that the only way to clean themselves up is to jump into the sea before carrying on the partying on what is traditionally a big night out.

Where: Galaxidi, Greece
When: Clean Monday (start of Orthodox Lent)

APOKREAS
Messini

In stark contrast, the Apokreas celebrations in the town of Messini in the Peloponnese take on a rather ghoulish turn with a series of ritual hangings. The mock executions date back to 1825 or 1826 when an elderly woman was hanged here on the orders of Ibrahim Pasha, who had been sent to Greece to crush the Greek revolt against the Ottomans. Mother Sykou dared to interpret one of Ibrahim's dreams as foretelling the defeat of his armies. On the morning of Clean Monday, gallows are built in the town and the execution is re-enacted. Afterwards, everyone is welcome to be 'hanged' by Ibrahim's hooded executioners. That is not to say that the good people of Messini are completely sombre. In the afternoon following the executions there is a lively masked parade with floats, bands and dancing.

Where: Messini, Greece
When: Clean Monday (start of Orthodox Lent)

APOKREAS
Patras

The city of Patras in the Peloponnese celebrates Apokreas in a way that is arguably more energetic than anywhere else in Greece. The carnival officially lasts for three weeks, but climaxes on the final weekend. In the first week, people slaughter fattened pigs; in the second, everyone gorges on meat and in the final week, they eat as much cheese as they can stomach. On the Saturday there is a parade for children and a night parade, followed by the *Bourboulia*. This carnival ball features women dressed in black 'domino' robes and wearing masks who are allowed to flirt with men with anonymity. A Grand Parade is held on Sunday when up to 50,000 masked participants take to the streets. The carnival is closed with the ceremonial burning of the float of the Carnival King.

Where: Patras, Greece
When: Three weeks leading up to Clean Monday (start of Orthodox Lent)

FEAST OF ST GEORGE
Skyros

Although many English people think that St George is English through and through, he was actually a Greek from Asia Minor, and is the patron saint of a number of places from Beirut to Ethiopia. Various towns in Greece also claim his patronage, and his feast day is a major celebration all over the country. In addition to his other roles, St George is the patron saint of shepherds, so the Feast of St George is a major event in rural communities. He is also the patron saint of Skyros and so celebrations on this small island in the Sporades are particularly exuberant. Following a mass, there is traditional dancing, eating, drinking and merrymaking until early the next morning, when another mass ends the party.

Where: Skyros, Greece
When: 23 April

MIAOULIA
Hydra

In 1821, Admiral Miaoulis set fire to much of the Turkish navy by ramming it with boats filled with explosives. He is regarded as one of the heroes of the Greek Revolution against the Ottomans, but the respectful Greeks believe in forgiving and forgetting, and they don't like to mention it very often. However, they do like an annual celebration on the Saronic Island of Hydra where the Admiral was born. They throw a three-day celebration that culminates in the ceremonial burning of a ship which represents the flagship of the Turkish fleet under a massive fireworks display. Held as a part of 'Navy Week' celebrations, Miaoulia is a time for patriotism and merrymaking, with traditional Greek dances and sports being performed.

Where: Hydra, Greece
When: Long weekend closest to 21 June

ROUKETOPOLEMOS
Vrontados

It might seem strange, but the inhabitants of the town of Vrontados on the Greek island of Chios celebrate Easter with a rocket war that sees some 60,000 rockets being fired between rival churches. The two churches, St Mark's and the Virgin Mary Erethianis, are on hills some 400m apart. Along with the surrounding buildings they are boarded up to protect them from damage. Parishioners gather in the churchyards to fire rockets at each other, aiming to get the most hits on the opposing belfry. In the meantime the priest in each church is intent on holding midnight mass. The origins of this tradition seem to lie in the Ottoman occupation of Greece. Locals were forbidden to celebrate Easter and so used the noise of the rocket war as cover while services continued.

Where: Vrontados, Chios, Greece
When: Greek Orthodox Easter Saturday night

TIRNAVOS CARNIVAL
Tirnavos

Dionysian, hedonistic and sybaritic are all Greek words, and all of them could have been coined to describe this 100-year-old carnival. One of the biggest and best in Greece, celebrations last around a month, but the most important – and wild – days are Carnival Sunday and Clean Monday. Sunday sees a Grand Parade through the city with a number of floats accompanied by people in carnival costume. The ironically named Clean Monday is when the more controversial events of the carnival occur. Called *Bourani* (which is a kind of spinach soup), it is said to be a celebration of fertility and reproduction. In practice it is a time when people have a large party, drink too much and wave large painted phalluses around to general hilarity, and generally indulge in lewd comments and licentious behaviour.

Where: Tirnavos, Greece
When: Greek Orthodox Carnival Sunday and Clean Monday

> ITALY

BATTAGLIA DELLE ARANCE
Ivrea

Those with a citrus allergy should avoid Ivrea during the Battaglia delle Arance, when the entire town turns out to pelt each other with oranges. Dating back to the 12th century, there is a medieval theme to festivities, with 3,000 townsfolk dressing up in period costumes for the three-day battle. The tradition arose when the people of the town threw away an unwanted gift of beans from an oppressive feudal lord. At first beans were used in a re-enactment of the event, then oranges, which girls would throw at boys they fancied from balconies. If the boys were interested they returned the compliment, and now the whole town uses oranges as weapons – bizarrely, as they are not grown in Piedmont and have to be imported for the festival each year at considerable expense.

Where: Ivrea, Italy
When: Sunday, Monday and Shrove Tuesday

CARNEVALE DI PUTIGNANO
Putignano

The citizens of Putignano in Puglia love their carnivals. The town's first recorded celebration came in 1394 and today's events begin the day after Christmas and continue with a masked ball every Thursday in the run-up to a three-week-long extravaganza that ends on Shrove Tuesday. The celebrations have several purposes: to welcome in the spring, to indulge before Lent and to atone for the sins people will probably commit during carnival. The last three Sundays see the famous processions when dozens of huge, lavishly decorated floats of towering figures up to 12m tall take to the streets amidst a riot of music, entertainers and locals in costume. The biggest parade takes place on Shrove Tuesday and is followed by a number of masked priests carrying a papier-mâché pig, which is ritually cremated in the main piazza.

Where: Putignano, Italy
When: Three weeks leading up to Shrove Tuesday

CARNEVALE DI SAMUGHEO
Samugheo

Take a stroll through the Sardinian village of Samugheo during carnival and you will probably think that you have stepped into the middle of some ancient pagan fertility ritual rather than a Catholic pre-Lenten celebration. The truth lies part-way between the two as carnival in this rural part of the world involves a wild dance with costumed dancers representing a shepherd and a herd of goats acting out the eternal cycle of nature. In the dance, S'Urtzu, half goat and half man-god, is sacrificed. He flails around the streets surrounded by masked *Mamutzones* who dance wildly around him, simulating the fighting of goats on heat. The shepherd, S'Omadore, repeatedly strikes S'Urtzu, who falls again and again, only to be revived by wine, until he eventually bleeds to death. His blood replenishes the earth and so the cycle begins again.

Where: Samugheo, Italy
When: Thursday to Shrove Tuesday

CARNEVALE DI VENEZIA
Venice

No other festival defines a place as completely as the Carnevale does for Venice. Officially launched with a religious procession through St Mark's Square in the period costume of the Doges and the launching of a giant white dove on a wire from the Campanile, the carnival is really about posing – at least in public. Most famous for its masks, which are made of leather, porcelain or glass, the sight of thousands of these is quite stunning. Dress to impress and you can sometimes score an invite to a hedonistic masked ball in a private *palazzo*. As well as walking around in costume and masked anonymity, there are concerts, dances and processions through the city. First held in the 11th century, it consisted of over two months of revelry until it fell into decline during the 18th century. It was revived in 1979 with great success.

Where: Venice, Italy
When: Two weeks leading up to Lent
....

CARNEVALE DI VIAREGGIO
Viareggio

It is hard to make your carnival the best when you have to compete with Venice, but the elegant Tuscan town of Viareggio uses its wide seaside streets to host some of the world's most spectacular parades. The largest of the floats are a staggering 20m high, 14m wide and weigh around 35t. Some carry up to 200 people. They feature papier-mâché merry-go-rounds, clowns, opera divas, skeletons, kings and more, and many have giant satirical effigies of political and other topical figures. This is an echo of the very first carnival, in 1873, when masked protesters against taxation joined the procession organized by the city authorities. The parades take place every Sunday for the four weeks leading up to Carnival Sunday, and there are fireworks, masked balls and concerts all over the city.

Where: Viareggio, Italy
When: Four Sundays leading up to Lent
....

CORSA DEI CERI
Gubbio

This frenetic race dates back to the 12th century and sees three teams racing up a hill, each bearing a saint mounted on a stand 4m high. The stand, often referred to as a candle, looks rather like an hourglass and weighs almost 280kg. The saints they carry are St Ubaldo, the patron saint of this Umbrian town, St Giorgio and St Antonio. The bearers wear yellow, blue and black shirts respectively, along with white trousers and a red scarf. The statues are paraded around the town before the race starts at 6.00 p.m. They race through the streets and up the steep Mount Ingino to the Basilica di St Ubaldo. Bizarrely, the winner is not the first one into the church; that honour always goes to St Ubaldo.

Where: Gubbio, Italy
When: St Ubaldo's Day, 15 May
....

A drummer in medieval costume processes towards the Arno River for the Gioco del Ponte, where opposing districts will fight for possession of the bridge, not with weapons, but in a Pisan tug of war.

FESTA DEL REDENTORE
Venice

Celebrating the city's deliverance from a plague in 1576, the Festa del Redentore (Feast of the Redeemer) is a glorious mix of the sacred and the profane. Following the plague, in thanks the Doge (the ruler of Venice) commissioned Palladio to build the church of La Redentore on the island of Giudecca. Nowaday's the festivities begin on Saturday evening, when countless small boats congregate in the Giudecca Canal and the Bay of San Marco. Decorated with balloons and coloured lanterns, they moor next to each other and the occupants feast at a lavish dinner until the colossal firework display that starts shortly before midnight. On Sunday there is a procession and mass followed by a series of gondola races. Devotees reach the church by crossing a 330m floating pontoon bridge laid across the lagoon.

Where: Venice, Italy
When: Third weekend in July
....

GIOCO DEL PONTE (GAME OF THE BRIDGE)
Pisa

The stately city of Pisa in Tuscany stages one of the most bizarre tug-of-war competitions you will ever see. More accurately described as a push-of-war, the event sees two teams representing the different districts on either side of the Arno River competing to push a huge 6t cart down a 50m track. This test of strength between the Tramontana and Mezzogiorno dates back to 1490. Before the battle, members of the districts process to the bridge in medieval costume. The contest is run a number of times by teams of 20 people who lean backwards against the cart and push against it until one of the teams is pushed backwards so far that their banner is knocked over.

Where: Pisa, Italy
When: Last Sunday in June
....

GIOSTRA DEL SARACINO
Arezzo

The Giostra del Saracino sees brave knights from the four different districts of Arezzo do battle with a metal adversary in the shape of a Saracen soldier in a fairly one-sided joust. The tradition has its roots in the Crusades of the 1400s when Saracen invaders reached this Tuscan city. The Aretins of the Middle Ages grew fond of jousting and the first known mention of the festival was in 1677. Today, the twice-yearly joust sees the competitors escorted into Piazza Grande by soldiers, knights, musicians and flag wavers in medieval dress for a solemn ceremony before the jousting begins. The competitors charge the Saracen and, as they hit it with their lances, it swings around, aiming a blow at them in return. They lose some points if they are hit, and all their points if they are knocked off their horse. The winners are awarded the Golden Lance.

Where: Arezzo, Italy
When: Saturday before last in June, 1st Sunday in September

INFIORATA
Genzano di Roma

The tradition of Infiorata, carpeting a street with a display of flowers in various ornate patterns, is popular in many places in Italy. Arguably the most extravagant displays are at the town of Genzano di Roma in Lazio, which has been holding the festival since 1778. The Infiorata is constructed by a number of artists who all work to a theme. The display runs the whole length of Via Italo Belardi, and consists of often allegorical tableaux made out of coloured flower petals. Once the whole thing is finished, there is a parade down the length of the road, with masked characters wearing medieval and other traditional costumes. Other towns that hold Infiorata include Noto in Sicily, Bolsena near Rome and Brugnato in Liguria.

Where: Genzano di Roma, Italy
When: Sunday and Monday after Corpus Christi (May or June)

L'ARDIA DI SAN COSTANTINO
Sedilo

There are a number of traditional horse races in Italy, but the wildest is surely the Ardia in Sedilo on the island of Sardinia. It commemorates the victory charge of the Emperor Constantine I over Maxentius in 312 at the Milvian Bridge in Rome. Before the battle Constantine foresaw his victory in a vision from God and was subsequently converted to Christianity. Every year this charge is re-enacted in a thrilling race around the Santuario di San Constantino. Horses and riders gather on a hill outside town, while local dignitaries give speeches and prayers. The horses then charge down the hill, the rider representing Constantine first, his two flag bearers next with the thundering herd behind. When they reach the sanctuary,

Highly skilled flag wavers add to the spectacle of the parade that accompanies the Palio in Asti, Italy.

they circle it slowly, seven times, getting blessed by the priest each time they pass. But Constantine takes off after the sixth pass, leading all challengers to the dry fountain that marks the end of the race. The townsfolk breathe a collective sigh of relief; a win means the basic tenets of Christianity have been renewed for another year.

Where: Sedilo, Italy
When: 5–7 July

IL PALIO
Asti

Asti in Piedmont has more than just sparkling wine to boast about: it holds a Palio, one whose origins date back even further than its better-known cousin in Siena. First run in 1275 in the vineyards beneath the walls of the neighbouring city of Alba, the race is preceded by a great deal of ritual today. In the days leading up to it the 21 competing neighbourhoods try to influence their horses' chances by throwing banquets, carrying out magic rituals and by nobbling the opposition. On the big day the horses are led to the race preceded by a parade of over 1,200 people dressed in medieval costume, led by flag twirlers waving the banners of the neighbourhoods. As with the race in Siena the winner receives a *palio*, a crimson banner decorated with the Asti coat of arms.

Where: Asti, Italy
When: Third Sunday in September

IL PALIO
Siena

The Palio in Siena and intrigue go hand in hand. Riders can be bribed and horses drugged or even kidnapped by competing *contrade* (districts), so both are held under virtual house arrest in the build-up. The 17 city *contrade* draw lots to decide which ten will take part in each race. Lots also allocate the horse and rider. On race day the *contrade* process to the spectacular cobbled *campo* (main square) in medieval costume, led by flag bearers who twirl their flags high into the air. In front of a packed crowd the race lasts for three adrenaline-fuelled circuits.

Where: Siena, Italy
When: 2 July and 16 August

PROCESSIONE DEI MISTERI DI TRAPANI
Trapani

The religious spectacle of the Misteri processions is known to date back as far as 1612, and features a series of floats carrying elaborate sculptures showing scenes from the Passion – the death and resurrection of Jesus Christ. In Trapani on the island of Sicily, 20 different guilds each construct a float showing a different scene from the Passion. The various guilds include shoemakers, bakers and even hairdressers. The floats are made from painted wood and canvas and are carried shoulder-high around the town in a procession for 24 hours, from 2.00 p.m. on Good Friday. The tradition is said to come from the Spanish celebration of Las Casazas, where living people represented the scenes of the Passion. This 'passion play' is regarded as the highlight of Holy Week in Trapani.

Where: Trapani, Italy
When: Good Friday afternoon to midday Easter Saturday

PROCESSIONE DEI SERPARI
Cocullo

Italy doesn't top the list of most dangerous places for snakebites, but the people of Cocullo in L'Aquila take the threat seriously, holding an annual procession to their patron saint, San Domenico Abate. After fireworks and a solemn mass, a statue of the saint is paraded around the village, liberally draped with writhing local snakes. This is supposed to save the villagers from snakebites for the next year. The somewhat incongruous thing is that the captured snakes – grass snakes, rat snakes, cervones and the struts – are all non-venomous, but have their fangs removed to stop them biting. As if this weren't bizarre enough, San Domenico has a sideline in dental work, and people attempt to ring a bell in his honour with a string tied to their teeth to protect them from toothache.

Where: Cocullo, Italy
When: First Thursday of May

REGATA STORICA
Venice

Venice is famous for its gondolas, the long black boats that are rowed around the canals of the city. The gondoliers are fiercely proud of their traditions, and every year take part in a mass regatta on the historic Grand Canal. The event dates back to the mid-13th century, and features a flotilla of gondolas carrying figures in period costume from the days when the Doges ruled the city, including characters representing the Doge and his wife. There are also four gondola races for the different styles of gondola, including a small sporty version designed for speed rather than comfort. Of course, this being Italy, the whole event is accompanied by food, wine, music and much fanfare.

Where: Venice, Italy
When: First Sunday in September

REGATA DI SAN RANIERI
Pisa

Mention Italian regattas and most people will think of Venice, not Pisa, but the city of the leaning tower gets into the boating tradition with this crazy race up the River Arno which dates back to 1290. Four teams of ten men, representing the four districts of the city, propel narrow rowing boats upstream against the current for 1,500m. Each team comprises eight oarsmen, a navigator and a climber or *montatore*. The climber is there to scale one of four 10m cables fixed to the mast of a boat at the finishing line and snatch the winning pennant (the *paliotto*). The winning team claims the blue pennant, the runners-up get white and red pennants respectively, but the team in last place gets nothing except jeers from the huge crowd.

Where: Pisa, Italy
When: 17 June

SA SARTIGLIA
Oristano

For three days during Carnival, the town of Oristano in Sardinia is transported back to medieval times in an equestrian festival that mixes 11th-century traditions with those of the period when the island was under Spanish rule. Participants dress in traditional Sardinian and Spanish knightly fashion, show off their horsemanship and compete in the Sa Sartiglia jousting tournament from which the festival takes its name. The centrepiece of the festival is the attempt to spear a hanging star with a lance at full gallop. The more holes in the star, the luckier the year ahead will be. The festival is ruled over by a masked androgynous character called Su Cumponidori.

Where: Oristano, Italy
When: Carnival Sunday and Shrove Tuesday

SCOPPIO DEL CARRO
Florence

The people of Florence see in Easter Day with a bang in a ritual thought to date back to the Crusades. The Scoppio del Carro (Explosion of the Cart) commemorates a member of the Pazzi family raising a Christian banner on the walls of Jerusalem during the First Crusade. In return he was granted three flints from the tomb in the Holy Sepulchre, which were sent back to Florence to ignite a new fire of Christianity in 1101. The arrival of the stones has been re-enacted annually, and the 'fire' element has grown. At 10.00 a.m. on Easter Day, the flints are used to light a fire that is carried around in a cart, accompanied by drummers, soldiers and flag jugglers in medieval costume. They process to the Duomo where the fire lights a dove-shaped rocket that flies on a wire from the cathedral to the cart and ignites a huge fireworks display.

Where: Florence, Italy
When: Easter Sunday morning

SIEGE OF CANELLI
Canelli

In 1613, the people of Canelli in Piedmont united with a small garrison under the Duke of Savoy to drive off the forces of the Duke of Nevers from Mantua, who had had laid siege to the town. Today, townspeople dress in the uniforms of the period and re-enact the main events of the siege along with much drinking and feasting. The first battle begins in the late afternoon on the Saturday, and the invaders lay siege to the town overnight. Sunday is victory day. The final battle begins at 11.30 a.m. when the enemy sweeps into town, only to be chased out by the townspeople. Victory is declared at noon, followed by a celebratory lunch, cart races, games and street entertainment.

Where: Canelli, Italy
When: Third weekend in June

ST VALENTINE'S DAY
Terni

Ask the good people of Terni in Umbria, and they will tell you that the mortal remains of the patron saint of love lie in the Basilica di San Valentino in the centre of town, where, it is said, he would often give gifts of flowers from his own garden to young visitors. The story goes that two of the youngsters fell in love and married, forever linking St Valentine with love and giving this city the claim to his feast day on 14 February. Terni celebrates love for the whole of February, but events peak on the big day with a feast around the Basilica, and the announcement of the Year of Loving Award in honour of a particularly worthy act of love.

Where: All over Italy, particularly Terni
When: 14 February

A pole-leaper takes to the air, using the 13m long pole fixed in the canal to get to the other side, at the Fierljeppen Championship in Friesland, Netherlands.

> NETHERLANDS

BLOEMENCORSO AALSMEER
Aalsmeer to Amsterdam

The Bloemencorso are flower pageants, which feature *praalwagens* (floats) and cars ornately decorated with flowers. A number of towns in the region hold flower parades, but the oldest and most spectacular is the Aalsmeer parade. Dating back to 1948, the parade runs almost 10km from the Aalsmeer flower auction house to Dam Square in Amsterdam. The parade is a 2.5km extravaganza of floats, trucks with bands playing and dancers in flower-related costumes. Participants act out plays and the whole event is a riot of colour and scent. Typically over half a million flowers are used to jazz up 20 massive floats. Floats tend to have themes, such as giant flower elephants, cartoon characters or comedy trains, while the cars are decorated with blooms on their roofs, bonnets and sides.

Where: Aalsmeer to Amsterdam, Netherlands
When: First Saturday of September

CANNABIS CUP
Amsterdam

There is some degree of irony in the fact that the Cannabis Cup is held in the days leading up to Thanksgiving, with its links to the Protestant Reformation, and this is probably not lost on the stoners. Organized by *High Times* magazine, the cup has been held in Amsterdam for over 25 years. A major celebration of all things to do with smoking dope, the festival features a major competition to see who can produce the best hashish and marijuana. This is judged by a panel of experts who sample the wares (no doubt with much pizza) before handing out the prizes. There are a whole host of other awards for best seeds, best pipe, best coffeeshop and so on. The cup also includes music, comedy and presentations from celebrities in the industry.

Where: Amsterdam, Netherlands
When: Five days in Thanksgiving week (4th Thursday in November)
....

FIERLJEPPEN (POLE-LEAPING CHAMPIONSHIPS)
Friesland

This is an odd sport to say the least. Athletes take a run-up towards a long pole anchored in a canal, leap onto it and shimmy up as far as they can as the pole falls forwards, then leap into a sandpit on the other side of the canal. The poles can be more than 13m long, and the record distance for a leap is over 20m. Originating in Friesland, *fierljeppen* is now a popular sport all over the country and there is a national championship held every August. This is the perfect opportunity to see some of the best pole-leapers in the country. The sport is believed to date back to the 1200s, when farmers used poles to leap across canals as they moved around their land. An alternative theory is that poachers invented the practice so that they could steal eggs and get away quickly without having to rely on fixed crossing points.

Where: Friesland, Netherlands
When: August
....

KONINGSDAG
Amsterdam

It's big, noisy and orange… very orange. Koningsdag, or King's Day, in the Netherlands is a riot of colour and partying. As it is a public holiday the whole nation gets to celebrate the birthday of its monarch. The colouring – after the name of the Dutch royal family, the House of Orange – is ubiquitous. Parties often begin the night before and continue right through the actual day. There are a number of official events, but one of the nicest things about the festival is the way it galvanizes almost everyone to celebrate in their own way – only dressed in orange, from orange-themed boat parades to street parties, through to full-on orange club nights in some of the trendiest venues in town.

Where: All over the Netherlands, especially Amsterdam
When: 27 April (unless a Sunday, in which case celebrations take place on Saturday)
....

MAASTRICHT CARNIVAL
Maastricht

For three days every year, Carnival, or Vasteloavend as it is known in these parts, takes over the city centre in a riot of partying and processions. Everyone seems to be decked out in the official carnival colours of red, yellow and green. On Saturday the Prince of Fools is chosen and given the

keys of the city by the mayor. Celebrations begin on Sunday with the hoisting of the Prince's flag and a model of the *Mooswief,* literally the 'vegetable woman', who will oversee proceedings. The Grand Carnival Parade follows, featuring hundreds of ornately decorated floats, giant puppets and spectacular costumes. Monday is family day and sees a number of different stages hosting music, dancing and singing. On Tuesday there is a brass band competition before the *Mooswief* is taken down for another year.

Where: Maastricht, Netherlands
When: Three days leading to Shrove Tuesday
....

ZOMERCARNAVAL
Rotterdam

As a summer carnival, this event in the port city of Rotterdam has more in common with Rio and Notting Hill than with the pre-Lenten frenzy of many European winter carnivals. The city has big communities from the Cape Verde Islands and Suriname, and they bring the atmosphere of their own distinctive carnivals to the streets of Rotterdam. Carnival week begins with the choosing of the Carnival Queen who is shown off at a party on a especially created beach in the city centre on Thursday. On Friday a Battle of the Drums is held, with brass bands from all over the country competing for a place in the parade. On Saturday there is a vibrant and lively street parade with music, floats and people in Caribbean costumes. After the parade a number of bands perform at stages around the city.

Where: Rotterdam, Netherlands
When: Thursday to Saturday in June or July
....

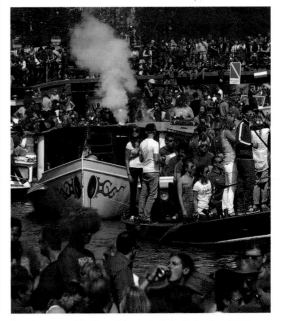

The colour orange of the House of Orange dominates Koningsdag, when the subjects of the Dutch royal family celebrate the birthday of their monarch.

> PORTUGAL

FESTA DE SANTO ANTÔNIO
Lisbon

Lisbon celebrates the feast day of its patron saint with a citywide sardine-fest. The fish are grilled and eaten on the streets with great enthusiasm. The festival is said to date back to a sermon delivered to the ocean by St Anthony in the 13th century, when all the fish lined up with their mouths open to listen. There are also a number of competing costumed parades through streets decorated with fairy lights, paper lanterns and coloured streamers. St Anthony is also known as a matchmaker. Women are supposed to write the name of their intended on a piece of rolled-up paper and then see if it unrolls in water overnight to indicate he is their true love. Men have an easier task: they simply have to present their intended with a basil plant and a love poem.

Where: Lisbon, Portugal
When: 12–14 June

FESTA DE SÃO JOÃO
Porto

Not to be outdone by the capital city, Porto has its own celebration – the Festa de São João – and the locals celebrate in style, with an all-night party and a regatta down the Rio Douro. The party on the eve of the feast day of St John gets pretty wild, with fireworks, bonfires, concerts, much drinking and dancing as well as the odd tradition of hitting each other over the head with garlic flowers or large squeaky plastic hammers. Everyone aims to head to the beach to watch the sunrise. The following afternoon the annual regatta of *barcos rabelos*, traditional sailing boats that used to transport barrels of port wine down from the mountains, sees vessels representing the various port wine shippers compete in a less-than-serious race.

Where: Porto, Portugal
When: 23–24 June

FESTA DOS TABULEIROS
Tomar

The origins of this 600-year-old festival – held as thanksgiving for the harvest and to aid the city's charity for the poor – are a subject of endless speculation, but the celebrations are suitably spectacular. The highlight of four days of music, dancing, fireworks, bullfights and feasting is a procession through the streets of this historic city of 600 girls in traditional dress, each sporting a huge *tabuleiro* (headdress) decorated with embroidered linen, small loaves of bread and paper flowers. It is stipulated that the headdress 'must be as tall as the girl who carries it' and can weigh up to 15kg. The procession ends in the main square where the loaves are blessed along with carts full of wheat, wine and oxen ready for

A procession of girls wearing traditional *tabuleiros* decorated with bread and flowers, which must be as tall as the wearer, make an impressive sight at the parade of the Festa dos Tabuleiros at Tomar, Portugal.

slaughter. The following day another procession, accompanied by bands, firecrackers, bagpipes and drums, sees the food distributed to the poor and the elderly.

Where: Tomar, Portugal
When: Four or five days in July, every four years; next in 2019

> REPUBLIC OF IRELAND

GALWAY OYSTER FESTIVAL
Galway City

Dreamed up in 1954 as a marketing tool for the city's Great Southern Hotel, the Galway Oyster Festival is now an international event, attracting more than 10,000 visitors in 2012. The oyster is king here, with all manner of oyster-based events and opportunities to eat as many as you can in a variety of guises. It is held each year in the last weekend of September at the start of the oyster harvest. The highlight of three days of fine dining on oysters and other seafood, top-class music and entertainment, street parades and legendary Irish hospitality is the World Oyster Shucking Championships, all washed down with pints of the finest creamy Irish stout, of course.

Where: Galway City, Republic of Ireland
When: Last weekend in September

GARLAND SUNDAY
Croagh Patrick

In a mass demonstration of religious fervour up to 15,000 Catholic pilgrims climb the 764m Croagh Patrick holy mountain near Westport in County Mayo. Despite often cold and wet weather, some climb barefoot, others without their shirts. The path is rough with scree underfoot in parts, and the climb is challenging, especially in poor weather. Some of the pilgrims walk over 35km from Ballintubber Abbey to Croagh Patrick before they start the climb. St Patrick is said to have fasted on Croagh Patrick for 40 days in the 5th century, and a number of masses are celebrated throughout the day at the small chapel on the summit. After the pilgrimage most people retreat to Campbell's pub at the foot of the mountain where, as publican Owen Campbell once remarked to me, 'Things can get somewhat rowdy.'

Where: Croagh Patrick, Republic of Ireland
When: Reek Sunday (last Sunday in July)

LISDOONVARNA MATCHMAKING FESTIVAL
Lisdoonvarna

The tradition of matchmaking in Ireland goes back a long way. It was established to introduce young people from remote rural communities to potential marriage partners. Matchmakers kept records of unmarried people in their area and made introductions between people they deemed suitable. One of the few matchmakers left is Willie Daly, who maintains the tradition in the town of Lisdoonvarna in County Clare, where people used to meet and be introduced on market days, and this evolved into today's Matchmaking Festival. Billed as the largest singles event in Europe, there are dances all week during September, but at weekends tens of thousands of people come to town. Some of these are local farmers looking for partners, but many are just singles from all over Europe seeking the famed Irish *craic*.

Where: Lisdoonvarna, Republic of Ireland
When: September

PUCK FAIR
Killorglin

Arguably one of the strangest festivals anywhere in the world and certainly the oldest festival in Ireland, the Puck Fair at Killorglin in County Clare sees a wild mountain goat made king of the town for three days and nights. The origins of the fair are veiled by good old Irish 'blarney', although its 'official' 400th anniversary was celebrated in 2013. Some believe that the male goat Puck is an ancient pagan symbol of fertility. A traditional Irish horse fair, it attracts buyers and sellers from far around. A parade that features the coronation of King Puck takes place on the first day. Over the next two days there are concerts, street entertainers and the ubiquitous Irish *céili*. Events finish at midnight on the final night with a massive firework display.

Where: Killorglin, Republic of Ireland
When: 10–12 August

SAMHAIN
Dublin

Encompassing Gaelic, Celtic and pagan traditions, Samhain is more than the Irish manifestation of Halloween. Along with Imbolc, Beltane and Lughnasa, it is one of the seasonal quarter days of the Celtic calendar. Seen as the beginning of winter, it is a time for meeting and settling scores, as well as storing away food and harvesting fruit before the winter, lest it be polluted by a *pooka* – a devilish horse. Traditionally, all lights and fires would be extinguished, making it the darkest night of the year. That being said, you will see a lot of ghouls, ghosties, witches and miscellaneous monsters at the Halloween Parade that scares its way through the city. A large fireworks display drives off all the bad spirits at the end of the night.

Where: Dublin, Republic of Ireland
When: 31 October

ST PATRICK'S DAY
Dublin

St Patrick is the patron saint of Ireland and is believed to have performed miracles, not least of which was clearing the Emerald Isle of snakes. The plethora of identikit Irish theme pubs around the world all hold parties on 17 March in his honour, but of all the places that hold such celebrations, the one to head for is Dublin. The city celebrates Paddy's day in a big way, stretching the events over four days, with concerts, street performances and a funfair; they even turn the floodlights of the whole city green (the colour of Ireland). The main event is a grand parade that sees thousands of people marching through the city.

Where: All over the world, particularly Dublin, Republic of Ireland
When: 17 March, but celebrations last four days

Thousands of party-goers, dressed in obligatory green, in the grand parade on St Patrick's Day in Dublin, Ireland.

Roads to Salvation

PILGRIMAGES ARE MADE FOR MANY DIFFERENT REASONS – FOR HEALING,
PENANCE, GRATITUDE, FULFILMENT, OR TO WITNESS A MIRACLE. THE JOURNEY
CAN BE A RITE OF PASSAGE AND A LIFE-CHANGING SPIRITUAL EXPERIENCE,
AND WHEN PILGRIMS REACH THEIR DESTINATION THERE IS OFTEN A FESTIVE
HOLIDAY ATMOSPHERE WITH MUSIC, DANCING AND THE SHARING
OF STORIES AND FOOD.

ABOVE A radiant pilgrim joins the Lord of Miracles procession in Lima,
Peru, to worship at the Sanctuary of Las Nazarenas.

OPPOSITE Two of the three giant chariots carrying the statues of Jagannath,
Balabhadra and Subhadra are drawn by Hindu devotees at the Rath Yatra
(chariot journey) at Puri on the Bay of Bengal.

OPPOSITE TOP LEFT Inside a glass case in the Sayyid Badawi mosque is a large stone with two footprints believed to be those of the Prophet Mohammed. Pilgrims at the Moulid of Sayyid Ahmed al-Bedawi in Egypt touch the glass in veneration.

OPPOSITE TOP RIGHT Muslim pilgrims on the island of Lamu, Kenya, chant religious verses at the Maulid festival.

OPPOSITE BELOW Pilgrims from all over Spain take part in the procession of the Nuestra Señora del Rocío.

ABOVE Barefoot and supported by two sticks, a Christian believer climbs the arduous route to the summit of Croagh Patrick in Ireland on Garland Sunday.

For many believers life itself is a form of pilgrimage – a journey from an imperfect condition to a state of holiness – and regular communal worship in a church, mosque, synagogue or temple is the conventional path to their goal. For deeply religious people, however, the act of going on a physical journey to a particular sacred place takes them out of their everyday life and creates a heightened religious experience. Their destination might house an object that can help them, such as a relic. It could be the birthplace of their religion's founder, or the scene of a miracle or the death of a martyr. The more challenging and arduous is the journey, the greater the chance of spiritual enlightenment and reward.

Some of the world's greatest pilgrimages, such as El Camino de Santiago in Spain and the Muslim Hajj, are either not festivals or not open to non-believers and so are not included here. But there are other Muslim pilgrimages that attract vast numbers of people to shrines and sites throughout the world. The Moulid of Sayyid Ahmed al-Bedawi (see p. 15) in Egypt, for example, attracts up to two million to the shrine of this Sufi saint. Devotees enter trances and whirl in circles in order to get closer to God. Another Sufi pilgrimage, the Moussem Ben Aissa (see p. 16), is held at the holy town of Meknes in Morocco. In former years pilgrims were noted for eating snakes and even glass while in a trance. These days things are a little more sedate, although in the accompanying festivities, you can still witness a traditional horseback charge, complete with firing muskets.

Not all Muslim pilgrimages are to Sufi shrines: the Maulid (see p. 14) held on the island of Lamu off the coast of Kenya is a four-day festival involving music, veneration, dancing and dhow and donkey races to celebrate the birth of the Prophet Mohammed. Pilgrims chant religious verses, called *maulidi*, and beat tambourines as they process along the historic dhow-lined waterfront.

Robert Louis Stevenson once famously said: 'To travel hopefully is a better thing than to arrive', and there are some pilgrimages where the journey seems more important than the destination. In the weeks and days before Pentecost, members of up to ninety Christian pilgrimage societies travel on foot and by horse cart from all over Spain to the church in the village of El Rocío, for the procession of the statue of Nuestra Señora del Rocío (Our Lady of El Rocío) (see p. 224). Pilgrims dress in traditional Andalusian clothes and decorate their carts with flowers, giving the effect of travelling back in time.

ABOVE There is a feast of colour and spectacle for pilgrims at the ten-day festival of Onam in the southern state of Kerala, India.

OPPOSITE TOP The monolithic statue of the Siddha Bahubali, voted by Indians as the first of India's Seven Wonders, is bathed in libations of milk, sugarcane juice and saffron paste at the Jain festival of Mahamastakabhisheka at Karnataka, India.

OPPOSITE BOTTOM The Changpa nomads make their annual pilgrimage to the Korzok Gompa (monastery) in northern India to enjoy *cham* dances performed by the monks.

The act of taking part in such a long and traditional journey is as vital a component of the pilgrimage as the rituals at the village on arrival. The Procession de San Lázaro in Cuba, the Black Christ Festival in Panama and the Garland Sunday pilgrimage up Croagh Patrick in Ireland (see pp. 45, 57 and 210–11) are all Christian pilgrimages that centre on the journey. For these events, penitents often make the journey barefoot or on their hands and knees.

For the majority of pilgrimage festivals, however, communal devotion is the main form of expression. Believers travel simply to attend, and some festivals attract vast numbers of pilgrims from far afield. India is arguably the greatest nation for pilgrimages. Its expansive network of railways means that even the poorest can travel long distances for their faith. Going on a pilgrimage is a major part of the Hindu religion, and there are temples and sacred bathing spots all over the country, and many days when worshipping at them is deemed to be particularly auspicious. These days can be fixed by historical events, but are more usually determined by the phases of the moon and by the movement of the stars. By going on a pilgrimage, Hindus believe that they can gain merit (*karma*), wash away sins and free themselves from the endless cycle of rebirth to approach enlightenment.

Little wonder, then, that pilgrims will undertake long journeys and endure considerable discomfort for their faith. I once spoke to pilgrims at the Kumbh Mela festival in Allahabad (see p. 124), which only takes place every twelve years, who had travelled from South India for three days in third class on a special pilgrim train. They made their way from the station amid the huge crowds to the festival ground, bathed at the holy *sangam* and then caught a train home after just twenty-four hours: a round trip of a week.

There are many astonishingly large Hindu bathing festivals, but Indian pilgrimage festivals are not just about bathing. The faithful are drawn to temples all over the country. The southern state of Kerala sees the Onam Festival (see p. 126), which includes impressive parades of elephants, each wearing a golden headdress and mounted by

acolytes brandishing Aalavattom fans of peacock feathers; the Igitun Chalne (see p. 123) brings pilgrims to fire-walk at the Sirigao Temple in Goa; and at the Jagannath Rath Yatra in Orissa (see p. 123) massed ranks of devotees haul gargantuan chariots through the streets.

India is home to several great religions, many of which revere the pilgrimage. The Mahamastakabhisheka Festival (see p. 126) takes place every twelve years and draws Jain pilgrims who anoint an 18-metre-high statue of the Siddha Bahubali with milk and sugarcane juice, and the Nanak Jayanti (see p. 126) brings Sikhs from all over the world to pray at the Golden Temple in Amritsar.

ABOVE Pilgrims climb the steep steps to a holy sanctuary in the ancient ruins of Wat Phu, Champassak in Southern Laos, where offerings are made to the Buddha.

ABOVE RIGHT Hundreds of thousands of Catholic pilgrims mark their devotion to the crucified Christ at the Lord of Miracles procession in Lima, Peru.

In northern India many people follow Tibetan Buddhism. Ladakh lies sandwiched between the Karakoram and Greater Himalayan ranges, and is the seat of numerous ancient monasteries. Each will hold at least one festival, attracting pilgrims from miles around to see the monks performing masked religious *cham* dances, which are considered a form of meditation and an offering to the gods. One of the most atmospheric of these festivals is the Korzok Gustor (see p. 124), which takes place on the shores of Lake Tsomoriri. Held in the somewhat tumbledown Korzok Gompa (monastery), the two-day festival is popular with the Changpa nomads who use the plateaus above the village for their summer grazing. Dances include the remarkable Black Hat Dance, and the monastery animals, including a yak, are symbolically released.

Buddhism has a tradition of pilgrimage, often attracting followers to ancient monuments. The festival of Waisak (see p. 148) draws countless monks and pilgrims to Borobudur in Indonesia. Celebrating the life and enlightenment of Lord Buddha, devotees circle a massive stone structure constructed in the ninth century to represent the Buddhist cosmology. An annual pilgrimage is held at the ancient ruins of Wat Phu Champassak in Southern Laos (see p. 149). The site was originally a Hindu temple, built as part of the Cambodian Khmer Empire. Thousands of pilgrims climb the steep and uneven steps to the sanctuary on the summit of a hill, where they make offerings to images of Buddha. A 'holy' spring emerges in a nearby cave and pilgrims catch drips of water in plastic bottles.

The Roman Catholic Church spread the notion of pilgrimage to South America, where it has been fervently embraced by the faithful. The Círio de Nazaré (see p. 88) in

ABOVE A pilgrim carries his personal shrine to Mamacha Carmen, patron saint of the *mestizo* people at the Festival of the Virgen del Carmen in the Peruvian town of Paucartambo.

ABOVE RIGHT Pilgrims follow the statues of the saints Sara, Marie-Jacobé and Marie-Salomé to the sea at the Pèlerinage des Gitans at Saintes Maries de la Mer in the Camargue, France.

Brazil is said to be the largest Catholic pilgrimage in the world, attracting some two million pilgrims, who crowd together to help pull, with enormous ropes, the cart on which the venerated statue of Our Lady of Nazareth is carried. The crush over the three-kilometre procession route is fraught with intense emotion and people are often injured in their desire join in. The Lord of Miracles (see p. 92) is another spectacular pilgrimage procession. Held in Lima, Peru, it involves the epic twenty-four-hour parade of a statue of the Black Christ carried on a silver litter by penitents dressed in purple robes.

A smaller but more colourful Peruvian procession takes place at Paucartambo, where the figure of the Virgen del Carmen is carried around the village accompanied by dancers wearing painted masks (see p. 93). A blend of original Andean pre-Christian belief and Catholicism, the Virgen is reputed to grant the wishes of pilgrims who come to pray to her.

One of the most moving Catholic pilgrimages I have seen is the annual Pèlerinage des Gitans at Saintes Maries de la Mer on the Camargue coast in France. Gypsy communities from all over Europe flock to the fortified church in the middle of town to worship the statues of Saint Marie-Jacobé and Saint Marie-Salomé, who were said to have landed there when they fled the Holy Land after the Crucifixion. They brought with them the dark-skinned Egyptian Saint Sara, who became the patron saint of the gypsies. Over two days the statues, first of 'Black Sara', then of the two Maries, are lowered from the loft of the church and processed around the town and into the sea by gypsy pilgrims, escorted by *gardians*, the cowboys of the Camargue, on their famous white horses. The fervent pilgrims make an incongruous sight as they weave past holidaymakers on the beach, accompanied by music and singing. In the sea a blessing is held, before the statues are returned to the church.

> SAN MARINO

MEDIEVAL DAYS
San Marino City

Known as 'The Old Land of Freedom', San Marino is a tiny landlocked city-state in Italy, near the seaside town of Rimini. During its annual Medieval Days festival, San Marino turns the clock back as historical societies convert the city centre into a village from the Middle Ages, populated, amongst others, by the Courtesans of Serravalle, the San Marino Federation of Crossbowmen, the Corporation of Nobles, and the Group of Charlatans. Everyone dresses up in period costume. Expect medieval theatre performances, archery and jousting competitions and parades accompanied by the sounds of trumpets and drums. Other highlights include fire-eating displays, jesters, minstrels, the *palio* of the crossbowmen and a flag-waving exhibition.

Where: San Marino City Centre
When: Four or five days towards end of July

> SPAIN

BASQUE CARNIVAL
Ituren and Zubieta

No one is quite sure of the whys and wherefores of the ancient ritual that is practised in the Basque villages of Ituren and Zubieta in the last week of January. In what is generally thought to be some kind of purification rite, processions take place in both villages: Ituren on the Monday and Zubieta the following day. They feature a company of odd characters called *Zanpantzar* who are dressed in lace petticoats, with sheepskins wrapped around their shoulders and waists, sandals, bandanas and tall conical hats. On their belts they wear large cowbells (*joaleak*) that swing against their backs as they walk, making such a racket that it awakens nature from its winter slumber.

Where: Ituren and Zubieta, Spain
When: Monday and Tuesday of the last week of January

BATALLA DEL VINO
Haro

This annual ritual is surely one of the oddest ways to commemorate a boundary dispute. Centuries ago Haro in Rioja and Miranda de Ebro in Burgos engaged in a dispute over the ownership of Mount Bilibio. On the feast day of its patron saint, San Pedro, the mayor of Haro, on horseback, leads a procession of people carrying a great quantity of red wine, provided by the local council, through the town to the Hermitage of San Felices de Bilibio. There mass is celebrated, after which a grand battle commences. People sport jugs, wineskins and even water pistols of wine. The battle lasts for around three hours until everyone has turned

a rather fetching violet colour. Then they return to the town to have tapas and drink more wine (if there's any left) around bonfires.

Where: Haro, Spain
When: 29 June

(BOUS A LA MER) SANTÍSIMA SANGRE
Denia

During Bous a la Mer (roughly translated as 'bulls to the sea', although it means 'oxen to market' in Catalan) the locals try to 'encourage' the furious beasts to take a dip. The Santísima Sangre, or Holy Blood, festival originated in 1633 when a monk called Pedro Esteve delivered the town from the plague by making the people share their bread. What this has to do with dunking bulls is anybody's guess, but this 'game' has been staged twice a day during the nine-day festival since 1926. A bullring is created on the harbour with one side open to the sea. The bulls are released one by one and foolhardy locals try to get the bulls to chase them over the edge and into the sea. The bulls are canny and try not to take the plunge, until one gets too close and falls into the sea, at which point it is promptly rescued and another bull is released.

Where: Denia, Spain
When: Nine days from 2nd Saturday in July

CARNAVAL DE VILANOVA I LA GELTRÚ
Vilanova i la Geltrú

One of the few towns to have defied the iron rule of the Franco era, the carnival in the Catalonian seaside town of Vilanova i la Geltrú maintains some of its unique traditions at Carnival. Thursday before Lent sees *La Merengada*, a huge meringue fight that leaves everyone covered in a sticky mess. Friday hosts the masked street procession of the Carnival King, and Saturday sees the arrival of the *Moixó Foguer,* a human bird covered in honey and feathers, and the *mascarots* who wear masks and to try to guess each other's identity while preserving their own. Sunday sees traditional parades converging on the Plaza de Coles, where the *Batalla de Caramellos* (Battle of the Sweets) breaks out. There are more parades on Monday and Tuesday before the ritual burial of the sardine on Ash Wednesday that marks the official start of Lent.

Where: Vilanova i la Geltrú, Spain
When: Week before Lent

EL COLACHO (BABY JUMPING)
Castrillo de Murcia

Spain seems to specialize in odd festivals. This one, in which a man dressed as the Devil (El Colacho) jumps over

Despite the goading and cajoling from locals to chase it into the sea, this bull stands firm at the water's edge; others are not so cautious and find themselves swimming with their antagonizers at the Santisima Sangre Festival at Denia, Spain.

babies to cleanse them of evil spirits, might well be the oddest. Dating back to 1621, the baby-jumping ceremony is the culmination of a four-day celebration following the feast of Corpus Christi. The festival begins with a procession in which El Colacho is escorted through the village by a group of solemn acolytes dressed in black. He chases after the villagers, smacking as many bottoms as he can reach and generally making a nuisance of himself. When they reach the central square, solemn parents place their wailing, one-year-old babies on a mattress. As a grim man dressed in black marches around beating a drum, El Colacho runs up and jumps over them.

Where: Castrillo de Murcia, Spain
When: Corpus Christi (May/June)

ELS ENFARINATS
Ibi

Many people use the lull between Christmas and New Year to visit relatives, hit the sales or generally sleep off the festive excesses. In the town of Ibi near Alicante local married men throw a massive flour and egg fight. One group, the *Els Enfarinats,* dresses up in mock military uniforms and stages a 'coup', taking over the town and instituting a series of bizarre laws. They catch any miscreants with a net and fine them for charity. Another group tries to overthrow the new rulers and battle ensues. The festival is said to date back 200 years. Though its precise origins are unknown, it falls on 28 December, which is the Feast of the Holy Innocents, a day traditionally celebrated in Spain and Latin America with childish pranks (*inocentadas*).

Where: Ibi, Spain
When: 28 December

FERIA DE ABRIL
Seville

In contrast to many of the hectic Spanish fiestas, the week-long Feria de Abril in Seville is a stylish and refined affair. Women dress in *trajes de flamenca* (flamenco dresses) and men in *traje corto* (short jackets, tight trousers, boots and hats). The feria begins with a grand parade of horse-drawn carriages and riders. There is a programme of *corridas* in the exquisite bullring, but this is decidedly not a bullfighting festival. The city is noted for its flamenco, and the fiesta attracts flamenco dancers and musicians from all over Andalucía – including some of the biggest names in the business. A vast area of tented bars and dance halls called *casetas* is constructed, and plays host to parties and flamenco performances.

Where: Seville, Spain
When: April

FERIA DEL CABALLO
Jerez de la Frontera

Another sophisticated Spanish festival is the Feria del Caballo, the annual horse fair in Jerez, one of the biggest events in Europe's equine calendar. It features all kinds of horse-related activities, including international show-jumping competitions, dressage, horse rallies, livestock exhibitions and auctions. At the centre of things each day, the Parque González Hontoria fills with hundreds of riders dressed in traditional Andalucían riding outfits displaying their incredible horsemanship. Another of the attractions of this week-long spectacular is the *Cómo Bailan los Caballos Andaluces* – the dancing horses of Andalucía, whose performances inevitably bring the house down.

Where: Jerez de la Frontera, Spain
When: Seven days in May

FESTIVAL OF NEAR DEATH
Las Nieves

If you have had a narrow scrape over the past 12 months and cheated death in some way, then you can both celebrate and give thanks to Santa Marta de Ribarteme, the patron saint of resurrection, by heading to the town of Las Nieves in Galicia. You will need to take your family with you though, as it will be their job to carry you around the town in a coffin. If you travel solo, then you will have to carry your own. This bizarre ritual starts around 10.00 a.m. as the lucky few are carried to mass in the church, and then in a procession with a statue of St Marta, which includes a quick stop at the local cemetery. Back in town the 'almost dead' ceremonially rise from their coffins amidst a chanting crowd, before regaling those present with tales of their survival.

Where: Las Nieves, Spain
When: 29 July

FESTIVAL OF THE HOLY CROSS
Caravaca de la Cruz

The Sanctuario de la Vera Cruz in the Murcian town of Caravaca houses a piece of wood said to have been part of the cross on which Christ was crucified. The people of the town venerate and celebrate this relic during the Festival of the Holy Cross by racing riderless *caballos del vino* (wine horses) from the bottom of town to the Sanctuario, which sits at the top of a steep hill. The horses are decorated with ornately embroidered robes and carry wine skins, a tradition reputed to date back to the mid-13th century when the Knights Templar galloped through Moorish territory to take wine to those guarding the Vera Cruz (True Cross).

Where: Caravaca de la Cruz, Spain
When: 2 May

FIESTA DE LA VIRGEN DE LA SALUD
Algemesi

It might seem odd to celebrate the day of Our Lady of Good Health by taking part in a ritual that can end in physical pain, but the people of Algemesi near Valencia do just that. As part of their saint's day, they hold processions and traditional dances around the town that end with the creation of a series of spectacular human pyramids. Some of these pyramids, or towers as they are known, are formed by as many as 200 *muixeranga* (acrobats) and can be up to six levels high. The celebrations also feature masses, processions, dancing, music and local food and wine.

Where: Algemesi, Spain
When: 7–8 September

FIESTA DE MOROS Y CRISTIANOS
Alcoy

Many festivals in the area south of Valencia commemorate the period of Moorish rule between AD 700 and the fifteenth century. The most striking of these is the Fiesta de Moros y Cristianos at Alcoy near Alicante, which recreates a great battle between the Moors and the Spanish in 1276. The three-day fiesta begins with a procession of the opposing armies, when over 5,000 people in traditional dress set the scene. The second day is devoted to San Jorge (St George) who was said to have helped the Spanish to victory. On the final day there is a re-enactment of the great battle. In the morning the Moorish army takes the castle constructed for the occasion in the Plaza de España. In the afternoon the Christian forces retake it before defeating the Moors in a final battle, after which San Jorge fires arrows from the castle to celebrate another year of Christian rule.

Where: All over southern Spain, particularly Alcoy
When: 22–24 April

FIESTA DE SANT JOAN
Ciutadella, Menorca

Rearing horses, medieval tournaments, a pampered ram and battles with hazelnuts – all washed down with gin and lemon – the people of Menorca mark the Fiesta de Sant Joan in eclectic style. Little has changed since medieval times. The fiesta that honours John the Baptist follows an elaborately involved programme. At its centre are the beautiful black Menorcan horses that give this fine equestrian festival its unique quality. Three days of festivities include a cavalcade of horses, the *Jaleo* (Commotion) where the horses rear up and walk on their hind legs while brave locals run underneath them to touch their hearts for luck, horse races and the *Jocs des Pla* medieval equestrian tournament. Much of the local *pomada* (gin and lemon) is drunk, before an immense firework display brings to an end the celebrations.

Where: Ciutadella, Menorca, Spain
When: 23–25 June

LA GRAN BATALLA DE RAIM
Binissalem, Mallorca

What could be more natural as a way of celebrating the grape harvest than hurling handfuls of surplus grapes at each other? This is the logic behind La Gran Batalla de Raim (the Great Battle of Grapes), the undisputed highlight of La Festa des Vermar that marks the end of the year's harvest in Binissalem on the Balearic island of Mallorca. On the final Saturday of the festival, two great piles of grapes are dumped in the church square and then thrown at anyone wearing a neckerchief until all the participants and the streets are awash with grape juice. If you are not much of a fighter then the grape-treading competition, in which you see how much juice you can tread out of the grapes in the traditional way in three minutes, might be more your thing. The juice will be used in that year's wine production.

Where: Binissalem, Mallorca, Spain
When: Two weeks towards end of September

LA PATUM DE BERGA
Berga

Against a backdrop of the fires of hell, the hordes of Hades take over the town of Berga near Barcelona. This festival marries religious and pagan roots with Catalan heritage in a series of spectacular parades (*patum*) and dances that date back to the Middle Ages and which act out the triumph of good over evil. Thursday sees the Ceremonial Patum that features the *Salto de Plens* (Jump of the Devil), Friday hosts a children's parade and Sunday features the Tirabol, in which hundreds of traditional folkloric characters dance through the streets to the beat of tambourines and a huge

Downtime after the hectic mêlée of hurling, and receiving, blows from ripe tomatoes at La Tomatino, the world's reddest festival at Buñol, Spain.

drum called the *tabal*. These allegorical figures have evolved over the years and include *cavallets* (papier-mâché horses), *maces* (demons wielding maces and whips), *guites* (mule dragons), eagles, giant-headed dwarves, *plens* (fire demons) and giants dressed as Turks and Saracens.

Where: Berga, Spain
When: Thursday to Sunday, Corpus Christi (May/June)
················

LA TAMBORRADA
San Sebastián
··

If you enjoy drumming then this festival in the Basque Country of northern Spain will be right up your street. Brief, intense and very, very loud, it features teams of drummers combing the town for an ear-splitting 24 hours, banging drums and wooden barrels in honour of the town's patron saint, Donostia de San Sebastián. The action starts on the evening of 19 January as uniformed companies of drummers start to march through the old town from the Plaza de la Constitutíon. They carry on for the next 24 hours, apart from a break around dawn for brandy and *churros*, passionately trying to outdo each other in sheer volume. Popular legend has it that the first drummer was a baker in 1720, who serenaded some young ladies while filling barrels at a water fountain. The girls banged out a beat to accompany him on the barrels and a noisy tradition was born.

Where: San Sebastián, Spain
When: 19–20 January
················

LA TOMATINA
Buñol
··

The largest food fight in the world, La Tomatina is the perfect antidote for anyone who has ever been told not to play with their food. Lasting for less than an hour before the big clean-up, this frenetic burst of activity begins as a dozen large trucks inch their way into the main square loaded with tomatoes and, often, some of the more adventurous (or drunken) locals. The square is packed with thousands of revellers, many of them the worse for wear even though it is 11.00 a.m., and all of them ready for a fight. One by one the trucks dump their tomatoes on to the ground, where they are grabbed, thrown and thrown again, until the ground and everyone in the square is covered with a thick red juice. Municipal fire hoses are used to keep the crowds cool. Against the rules of the fiesta, drenched T-shirts are inevitably ripped off and thrown as missiles when the tomatoes start to run out.

Where: Buñol, Spain
When: Usually the last Saturday in August
················

LAS FALLAS
Valencia
··

If you are of a nervous disposition, or hate loud noises, this Spanish fireworks festival is certainly not for you. It is probably one of the loudest festivals in the world, featuring great firework displays, random firecrackers and the burning of giant effigies on pyres. The build-up starts at the beginning of March, when the townspeople start to construct the effigies, known as *ninots*. For four nights there are massive firework displays after midnight along the Paseo de la Alameda, between Exposición Bridge and Las Flores Bridge. On the middle two evenings of the four-day festival the *ninots* are paraded around town, and just after midnight on the last night they are burned. The fires are incredible, and are often set dangerously close to buildings in relatively narrow streets.

Where: Valencia, Spain
When: 15–19 March
················

LAS LUMINARIES DE SAN ANTON
San Bartolomé de Pinares

Horses have always been important in Spain, and they take pride of place in the celebrations on the feast day of San Anton (St Anthony), the patron saint of animals, in the village of San Bartolomé de Pinares near Avila. In a tradition said to date back to medieval times, daring riders jump their steeds through a string of roaring bonfires lining the narrow streets. What might seem like a cruel tradition is said to cleanse the animals and protect them from illness over the coming year. The horses are doused in water first to prevent immolation, and they make a spectacular sight leaping through the flames, often sending up clouds of sparks. Despite accusations of cruelty, the villagers remain fiercely attached to the tradition, which is said to have begun during a time of sickness some 500 years ago.

Where: San Bartolomé de Pinares, Spain
When: 16 or 17 January

LES FESTES DE LA MERCÈ
Barcelona

Although it is dedicated to one of the patron saints of Barcelona, the Virgin of Mercy, your tired limbs can expect little mercy during this major festival of the city and of all things Catalan. Over 600 events vie for your attention, including concerts, fireworks, sporting events and cultural performances, washed down with litres of fizzy *cava* (the local sparkling wine). If you feel fit enough you can even compete in a swimming race across the harbour. Although a modern city, Barcelona still relishes its traditions. These include the parade of *gigantes* (giant human figures) and the procession of the *correfocs*, fire-breathing dragons accompanied by fireworks and firecrackers. The festival is also noted for the great human towers called *castells*, which are 'constructed' in the Placa de Sant Jaume and can be up to nine storeys high.

Where: All around Barcelona
When: Four days around 24 September

ROMERIA DE LA VIRGEN DE ALHARILLA
Porcuna

This pilgrimage (*romeria*) in honour of the Virgen de Alharilla, the patron saint of Porcuna, is believed to date back 800 years, and attracts tens of thousands of pilgrims to a small shrine commemorating the Virgin Mary in the olive grove just below this small Andalusian hill town. The fiesta begins on the Saturday evening with a mass at the shrine. Some stay in olive groves all night, while others return to town to eat, drink, sing and dance the *Sevillanas*. On the Sunday, the main street is covered in sand for a mass procession of horses and carriages. All the people are dressed in Andalusian style, which some describe as flamenco chic. In the afternoon,

One of many *castells*, human towers, which add to the drama at Les Festes de la Mercè, a festival that celebrates Barcelona and Catalan culture.

the statue of the Virgin is processed through the town before being returned to the shrine for another year.

Where: Porcuna, Spain
When: Second weekend in May

ROMERIA DEL ROCÍO
El Rocío

Drive around the village of El Rocío in the days leading up to Pentecost, and you might imagine that you have gone back in time, as you'll come across hundreds of thousands of pilgrims in traditional Andalusian dress on foot, on horseback and with brightly coloured carts. In this unique pilgrimage the members of some 90 societies called *hermandades* converge on the colonial-style church of Ermita del Rocío for Pentecost weekend. Many travel for days from neighbouring towns and villages all over Andalusia. In the early hours of Monday they carry the statue of Nuestra Señora del Rocío (Our Lady of El Rocío) around the village. This is not a sedate affair: members of the Almonte *hermandad*, who lay claim to the statue (also referred to as La Blanca Paloma, or the White Dove), snatch it from the church, fighting off others for the privilege. After a long and chaotic procession La Blanca Paloma is returned to the church for another year.

Where: El Rocío, Spain
When: Concludes at Pentecost (50 days after Easter)

SAN FERMIN
Pamplona

There are festivals that feature bull runs all over Spain and southern France, but the most famous is the San Fermin of Pamplona. Hemingway popularized the *encierro*, where people run through streets chased by fighting bulls, in his novel *The Sun Also Rises*, and there is a statue to the writer here put up by a grateful municipality. San Fermin is essentially a bullfight festival, but there are a host of other attractions in this week-long fiesta. Highlights are the processions of *gigantes y cabezudos* (giants and big-heads), traditional characters with large papier-mâché heads who walk around the town causing mischief and scaring small children, and the nightly firework displays. There is also much general partying and merriment in the streets and in the bars, washed down with sangria, cheap red wine and *kalimotxo* – a mix of red wine and cola.

Where: Pamplona, Spain
When: 6–14 July

SANLUCAR BEACH HORSE RACES
Sanlucar de Barameda

More than just a sporting event, the horse races at Sanlucar de Barameda on the Andalucían coast combine the Sport of Kings with a day out at the beach. But this is no donkey-derby. The event attracts professional jockeys and top horses and is a part of the Spanish horse-racing season. The first official series of races was held in 1835, although the tradition of racing on the beach seems to have been well established by then. The whole setting for the races is somewhat incongruous. As the horses thunder down the beach they are watched casually by a crowd of holidaymakers dressed in the usual range of skimpy Euro-beach attire. A feature of the festival are the bookmakers' stalls set up by local children, who take bets on the races from passing adults.

Where: Sanlucar de Barameda, Spain
When: Second and 4th weeks of August: Thursday to Sunday

SEMANA SANTA
Seville

The week leading up to Easter sees 58 spectacular religious processions pass through the streets of Seville. Organized by members of the city's ancient religious brotherhoods, called *hermandades* and *cofradías*, the processions of floats feature wooden statues (*pasos*) of scenes from the Passion (the death and resurrection of Christ) and the Virgin Mary, and are carried shoulder-high by penitents wearing robes with pointed hoods. Some of these are black, some white and some brightly coloured. Up to 50,000 people don traditional robes to take part. Processions are held in the evening, and go from the city's many churches to the cathedral and back. They take different routes, but all must pass a particular area from Calle Campana to the cathedral. Thousands of people line the route, especially on Good Friday to mark the Crucifixion, and the feeling of religious devotion is palpable.

Where: Seville, Spain
When: Six days leading to Easter Weekend

TENERIFE CARNIVAL
Santa Cruz, Tenerife

Vibrant and sexy, the Tenerife Carnival brings the costumes of Rio and rhythms of Africa to the Canary Islands in an exuberant prelude to the austerity of Lent. There is nothing religious about this month-long fiesta. The main parade happens on Shrove Tuesday. Led by the Carnival Queen, this sees floats, marching bands and members of carnival clubs taking to the streets of the city of Santa Cruz. These include the masked *mascarillas*, and the satirical bands of the *murgas*. As with many Spanish carnivals, the final act on Ash Wednesday is the *entierro de la sardina* (burying of the sardine). Tenerife makes this dramatically emblematic: an effigy of a giant sardine perched on top of a throne is processed to its burial, followed by a group of mourners. On the first Sunday of Lent, a fireworks display called *La Piñata Chica* marks the end of the festivities with an emphatic full stop.

Where: Santa Cruz, Tenerife, Spain
When: Week leading to Ash Wednesday

VIANA DO BOLO
Ourense

Some people may dream of a white Christmas, but if you are hoping for a white Lent then you might have to head for Ourense in Galicia. Don't bother packing your skis, though. Although the streets will be awash with white – it will be flour and not snow. Everyone gets completely covered in the stuff, usually having it playfully rubbed into their faces by members of the opposite sex. The Viana do Bolo is not just about chucking food, though, it's about eating and drinking as much as possible before the austerity of Lent. There are plenty of opportunities to sample local delicacies such as *chorizo*, *lacon* and *androlla*, which are often handed out free and washed down with red wine. On the Sunday before Lent, there is a drumming procession called the *Folion*, where colourful masked carnival characters called *peliqueiros* run riot in the streets.

Where: Ourense, Spain
When: Three weeks before Lent, peaking in the last 5 days

Food Fights

MANY FESTIVALS AROUND THE WORLD INVOLVE RITUALIZED FORMS OF FIGHTING –
WHETHER CELEBRATING PAST VICTORIES, APPEASING ANGRY GODS OR SIMPLY STIRRING
UP ANCIENT GRUDGES – AND IT'S NOT ALWAYS FISTS, FIREBALLS OR FIREWORKS. TO THE
DELIGHT OF ALL OF US WHO REMEMBER BEING TOLD NOT TO PLAY WITH OUR FOOD, SOME
FESTIVALS ARE LITTLE MORE THAN AN EXCUSE TO RELEASE OUR INNER CHILD
AND THROW THE STUFF AROUND.

ABOVE A combatant, orange in hand, seeks a target for her next
volley of missiles at the Battaglia delle Arance in Ivrea, Italy.

OPPOSITE A mock coup, executed with eggs and flour, unseats the status quo
for a day at Els Enfarinats in the town of Ibi in Spain.

OPPOSITE The madness and mess of the communal tomato fight at La Tomatino Festival at Buñol, Spain.

BELOW A tray of eggs smashed into the face of your assailant adds to the mayhem of Els Enfarinats in Ibi, Spain.

One of the most embarrassing moments of my life occurred while watching TV with some of the locals in the foyer of a low-rent hotel in Addis Ababa, when a report came on about an American hamburger-eating contest. About thirty shocked Ethiopians turned to me for an explanation of this extraordinary event. The best I could come up with was that in the West we have too much food, so are free to indulge in gluttony. In most of the rest of the world, particularly in Africa, people eat the food they produce to stay alive.

That being said, I have wallowed in tomato slops with thousands of others at the chaotic mayhem of La Tomatina in Spain, and thoroughly enjoyed myself – although I was picking bits of tomato out of my hair, ears, nose and clothes for days afterwards. La Tomatina (see p. 223) is the best known of all of the food fight festivals. Taking place every August in the tiny Valencian town of Buñol, this frenetic event sees around a dozen

trucks driving into the cramped main square and dumping their load of tomatoes. The assembled horde pounces on the deposit of free ammunition and indulges in an hour of communal madness.

There must be something about the Spanish, as they have an inordinate number of food fight festivals. At the Els Enfarinats festival in the town of Ibi (see p. 221), the weapons of choice are flour and eggs. The festival dates back over 200 years and only married men are supposed to take part. Although its origins are shrouded in mystery, a mock coup d'état, which involves the liberal use of ingredients more usually associated with making pancakes, takes place, and the town comes under a regime of 'new justice'. Flour and eggs are also a feature of the Carnaval at Cuenca in Ecuador

(see p. 91), where so-called *diablillos* try to cover everyone in the stuff, adding water to make a very fine mess. The tradition started off as part of the indigenous Indian population's celebrations to mark the second moon of the year, but was subsequently incorporated into Catholic pre-Lenten festivities.

On the island of Mallorca, the people of Binissalem join in the great Spanish food-fighting tradition by lobbing each other with grapes in the great Batalla del Vino (see p. 220). This forms part of the Festa des Vermar – an annual celebration of the wine harvest. Going one stage further, the people of Haro and Miranda de Ebro in La Rioja arm themselves with thousands of litres of wine. The tradition harks back to a dispute between these two neighbouring villages over who owned the mountain that separates them. In this annual re-enactment, everyone dresses in white clothes, packs whatever weapons they can muster – cups, buckets, jugs, water pistols and watering cans – all filled with the local Rioja – and heads to the top of the hill for a battle royale. Predictably not all of the wine is thrown (much of it is drunk), but enough is hurled around to make this a very colourful occasion.

After all of this craziness, the carnival at Vilanova i la Geltrú (see p. 220) seems almost refined. As part of the traditional Carnival blowout before the start of Lent, the town celebrates *La Merengada*, where meringues are tossed about with predictably sticky results. The heat is turned up later in the day with the *Batalla de Caramellos*, in which sweets are used as missiles. These are sticky, too, and they hurt. At the end the streets are coated with sweets that are swept up into great piles.

The Italians get in on the act with the Battaglia delle Arance at Ivrea in Piedmont (see p. 204). Commemorating a twelfth-century rebellion against the ruler of the town, this is more ritualized than most food fights. Thousands of locals dressed in medieval costume form nine teams who then bombard each other with oranges on the three days leading up to Fat Tuesday, when the festival concludes with a sombre funeral procession. Oranges are also thrown during the Carnaval de Binche in Belgium (see pp. 188–9) by up to a thousand *Gilles* who make up the costumed parade. They wear distinctive wax masks and roam the streets dancing and hurling the citrus. It is good luck to catch the oranges and very bad manners to throw them back, making the fight a rather one-sided affair.

Apokriatika is the Greek version of Carnival, and is celebrated with Dionysian excess by many towns, each of which seems to put its own interpretation on the party. The

ABOVE Citizens of the Greek village of Galaxidi hurl coloured flour at each other on Clean Monday to mark the start of Lent.

OPPOSITE Silly fancy dress is obligatory at the World Custard Pie Championships held in Coxheath, England, where special 'custard' with particularly good sticking power is flung at the opposition.

OPPOSITE BELOW A little mucky but clearly victorious, this contestant displays the winning qualities of a pie-fighting champion.

town of Galaxidi (see p. 203) delights in a mass flour fight, where townspeople battle it out until everyone is dusted. The flour is provided by the municipal authorities who often add colouring to make things even more spectacular. The so-called Flour Wars take place on the Monday of Carnival week, incongruously known as 'Clean Monday'.

The Wasserschlacht (see p. 202) in Berlin began as a food fight in 2001 with flour being hurled in a mock battle between the rival districts of Friedrichshain and Kreuzberg that lie on opposite sides of the Oberbaumbrücke bridge, but things have since moved on. Originally a protest at the civic authority's attempt to merge the two districts, part of the motive for the fight has become to be as outrageous as possible, and salted herrings, rotten fruit, bad eggs, dirty nappies and other smelly nasties have joined the arsenal of weapons used to dislodge the opposing side from the bridge. Luckily, and as the name suggests, the festival is also a water fight, and so help is usually at hand to rinse yourself down.

The crazy English take their love of slapstick to international levels using a secret recipe for the World Custard Pie Championships (see p. 241), held in Coxheath, Kent, since 1967. Unfortunately, the pies are not edible, because delicious creamy custard is just not sticky enough, and special 'sticking' ingredients need to be added. A number of teams take part in this pie-flinging fiesta said to have been inspired by Charlie Chaplin, and to make matters even more bizarre, everyone dons fancy dress, depending on the

theme of their team. Protagonists line up, two and a half metres apart, with their pie ammunition on tables behind them. At the signal they begin to throw, winning points for hitting an opponent and losing points when they miss. The winners go through several heats until a championship team emerges. Current holders are Pie of the Tiger.

One of the few food fights to take place outside the privileged West has a laudable aim. Perang Topat (see p. 147) is an Indonesian harvest festival that ends up in a three-day 'rice cake' fight. Rather than having a purely pugilistic motive, however, the event celebrates the harmony between Hindus and Muslims on the island of Lombok. In the run-up to the good-natured battle, which is believed to bring blessings, people from the two communities pray at the same temple and together, ceremonially, prepare the *topat* (boiled rice parcels wrapped in coconut leaves). If only the entire world's religious problems could be sorted out by lobbing food at each other.

> SWITZERLAND

BASEL CARNIVAL
Basel

The Swiss like to get up early – just as well, as the madness of the Basel Carnival begins at 4.00 a.m. on the Monday after Ash Wednesday, when masked pipers and drummers take to the streets in the *Morgestraich* (Morning Tatoo). With all the streetlights extinguished, masked *cliquen* (carnival groups) carrying lanterns join the musicians in a spectacular procession. On Monday and Wednesday afternoons the *cliquen* take to the streets again. In smaller groups they move around different bars acting out *Schnitzelbängg*, or topical satirical songs and verses. Tuesday is the night of the *Guggenmusik*, when masked musicians all seem to play different tunes to create a racket. Each night masked locals perform the *Gässle*, wandering through the narrow streets and alleyways of the old town, dancing and marching to the pipers and drummers, till the early hours of the morning.

Where: Basel, Switzerland
When: Monday to Thursday after Ash Wednesday

CHIENBÄSE
Liestal

For over 100 years the town of Liestal has been sending the Carnival spirit up in smoke with a parade of fire that reflects off the town's rivers and canals. The parade comprises some 20 wagons topped with great bonfires. These are constructed and dragged almost 2km by *füürwägeler* (fire-carters) to the sounds of fifes and drums. Over 300 people process alongside the carts carrying huge flaming torches made of bundles of pinewood chips called *chienbäse* (pinewood besoms) in the shape of traditional brooms. In total almost 100 cubic metres of pinewood are torched each year and, in a uniquely Swiss way, this is all provided by the civic authorities.

Where: Liestal, Switzerland
When: First Sunday after Ash Wednesday

COMBAT DES REINES
Martigny

The Spanish have their bullfighting, but the Swiss have their cow fights. The protagonists are the local Hérens cows, popular in the Valais region. They are short-legged with strong chests and a fearful temper – especially if their fodder has been spiked with the odd bucket of local wine. Put two of these Daisies together and they will naturally fight. Of course, there's no blood; the winner is the one who pushes and dominates the other into yielding. Local farmers have been staging cow fights here since the 1920s. These are held a couple of times a month on Sundays between March and September and originated in a contest to find a cow to lead the others up to the higher alpine pastures for their summer grazing. Local winners go through to a tournament at the town of Aproz in mid-May, followed by the grand championship in the ancient Roman amphitheatre at Martigny. The winning owner gets a bunch of Swiss Francs and his beast receives the title Queen of the Herd.

Where: Martigny, Switzerland
When: First week of October

INTERNATIONAL ALPHORN FESTIVAL
Tracouet

Its geographical position means that Switzerland is a melting pot of French, German, Austrian and Italian cultures, the results of which can be seen in its surprisingly eclectic range of festivals. The International Alphorn Festival is one such event and celebrates the long and booming traditional Alpine horn with a series of competitions, parades and folk performances of alphorn music. The 3m-long carved wooden horns are thought to date back over 600 years and were invented for communicating in the mountains. Tracouet, near Verbier, is 2,200m high, and the sound of the alphorns echoes around the breathtaking scenery during the course of a weekend that also celebrates other mountain traditions and folklore. One of the highlights is the mass *morceaux d'ensemble*, which features an orchestra of up to 150 horn players.

Where: Tracouet, Switzerland
When: July

KLAUSJAGEN
Küssnacht

If you don't like Christmas then head to Küssnacht on the northern shore of Lake Lucerne where, you can chase down Santa Claus with a cowbell and give him a sound thrashing. Dating back to the medieval pagan ritual of scaring off evil spirits with noise, the practice was banned in the 18th century, only to be revived under the guise of a Christian festival featuring St Nicholas. The night before St Nicholas' Day the whole village turns out for a parade led by men cracking whips and wearing the characteristic *iffele* hats. These are translucent paper and card, ornamental headdresses in the shape of a bishop's mitre, which are lit by candles giving the village a warm glow. Next comes a man dressed as St Nicholas, who is chased and beaten by up to 500 people carrying cowbells and horns. It's perfect revenge for the time you didn't get the bike you wanted for Christmas.

Where: Küssnacht, Switzerland
When: 5 December

LUCERNE CARNIVAL
Lucerne

The Fritschi family have been at the helm of the Lucerne Carnival since the 15th century, when old Mr Fritschi was nothing more than a straw puppet and a symbol of one of the city guilds. Time has moved on and Fritschi and his wife are now elderly figures with a child (Fritschikind) who parade around town in their wagon. The family kick off the festival with a gunshot from the City Hall on *Schmutziger Donnerstag* (Dirty Thursday), and lead noisy parades on the Thursday and Tuesday nights before Ash Wednesday. Lanterns light the parade route as bands and masked revellers take to the streets. Lucerne Carnival is noted for its *Guggenmusik*, where impromptu bands of masked musicians march around the streets playing brass and percussion instruments comically badly to amuse spectators, and for its masked and costumed dances.

Where: Lucerne, Switzerland
When: Thursday to Shrove Tuesday

RÄBECHILBI (TURNIP) FESTIVAL
Richterswil

A sort of *son et lumière* for a humble vegetable, this is the largest turnip festival in Europe. The streets of the small town of Richterswil on the banks of Lake Zurich are lit up by 50,000 candles, turnip lanterns and other illuminations for a parade of floats carved from 26t of turnips by local schools, clubs and societies – some resemble Roman temples, others giant animals, flowers, Viking boats or even chariots. There are carved turnip lanterns on display in the windows of homes and buildings along the route, like a fairytale come to life. The custom is said to date from the mid-19th century when the wives of farmers living in the hills above the town used turnip lamps to find their way home from evening church services in the wintertime, and it symbolically marks the transition from autumn to winter.

Where: Richterswil, Switzerland
When: Second Saturday in November

SECHSELÄUTEN
Zurich

Ringing in the change from winter to spring, the Sechseläuten (Ringing the six o'clock) gets its name from the 14th-century tradition of marking the end of the working day by ringing the Grossmünster bell. The main event of the festival is an afternoon parade with 3,000 members representing the 25 city guilds in 18th- and 19th-century costume marching with up to 30 brass bands. They take with them a giant snowman called the *Böögg*, which is made of wadding and represents winter. The parade is timed with Swiss efficiency to arrive at Sechseläutenplatz on the shores of Lake Geneva at 6.00 p.m., where the *Böögg* is torched

Flaming pinewood besoms, from which the festival takes its name, are carried through the city centre to celebrate the start of Chienbäse, the pre-Lenten carnival in Liestal, Switzerland.

as members of the guilds on horseback gallop around it to music. The *Böögg* is packed with fireworks, and the quicker it explodes the sooner spring will come.

Where: Zurich, Switzerland
When: Third Monday in April, unless this clashes with Easter Monday

UNSPUNNEN FESTIVAL
Interlaken

The Unspunnen Festival happens only every 12 years. This celebration of Swiss folklore is most famous for the *steinstossen* (stone throwing) competition in which a huge boulder of up to 76kg is hurled as far as possible, but there is also a tournament of *schwingen* (Alpine wrestling) where burly mountain types attempt to grapple their opponents on to their backs. Less macho and more cultural pursuits include a gathering of alphorn players and demonstrations of folk dancing, singing and yodelling. On the last day of the festival a grand parade showcases the culture and traditional costumes of participants from all over Switzerland, culminating at the Höhematte green in the centre of town.

Where: Interlaken, Switzerland
When: Every 12 years in September, next in 2017 (as the 2005 festival was postponed a year due to local flooding)

> UK > ENGLAND

BOLNEY WASSAIL
Bolney

Wassailing is an Anglo-Saxon pagan custom still practiced in many of the cider-producing counties of England. It involves driving evil spirits out of the orchards in the hope of a good apple harvest. The ceremonies are often carried out by morris Dancers – men, generally dressed in white and wearing tiny bells on their legs, who perform an ancient folk dance. After dark, farmers, villagers and morris men head to the orchard and select the largest tree. Cider is poured on the roots, a bonfire is lit and the tree trunk is beaten with sticks. The Bolney Wassail, at Bolney in Sussex, is held on the first Saturday in January, though traditionally most Wassails are held on the Old Twelfth Night, which is 17 January. This disparity began in 1752 when Britain moved from the Julian to the Gregorian calendar, effectively losing 11 days.

Where: Old Mill Farm, Bolney, England
When: First Saturday in January

BONFIRE NIGHT
Lewes

Commemorating the foiling of the Gunpowder Plot in 1605, when Guy Fawkes attempted to blow up the House of Lords and King James I, Bonfire Night is celebrated throughout England. Traditionally bonfires with effigies of Guy Fawkes on top are ritually burned. There are firework displays all over the country, though families often let off fireworks at home. The most extravagant celebrations take place at Lewes in East Sussex, where Bonfire Societies from the area process around the town to the site of their own bonfires. They carry flaming crosses (in memory of 17 Protestant martyrs who were burned at the stake in the town between 1555 and 1557) and wear themed fancy dress, such as Vikings, Zulu warriors or English Civil War soldiers.

Where: All over England, particularly Lewes, England
When: 5 November (unless a Sunday then held the day before)

BRIDGWATER CARNIVAL
Bridgwater

As a child watching a local West Country carnival, I had no idea of its heritage. I simply stared at the endless line of floats. Each one was covered in hundreds of brightly illuminated light bulbs; some had intricate moving parts and most had costumed dancers performing jaunty routines. The Bridgwater Carnival grew out of celebrations ordered by James I over the foiling of the Gunpowder Plot in 1605. Staunchly Protestant, the citizens of this Somerset town took the king's orders to heart. In the early days Bridgwater celebrated with a massive bonfire of an old wooden boat and

tar barrels, as well as homemade fireworks called squibs. These celebrations became increasingly rowdy, until 1880, when the fires were substituted with a carnival procession. Over the years, the procession grew in size and inspired similar carnivals throughout the West Country, although Bridgwater remains the largest and most spectacular.

Where: Bridgwater, England
When: First Saturday in November

BRISTOL INTERNATIONAL BALLOON FIESTA
Bristol

Featuring the largest mass lift-off of hot-air balloons in Europe, the annual Bristol International Balloon Fiesta at Ashton Court fills the sky over the city with balloons of all colours, shapes and sizes. It is a truly spectacular sight. Many are traditionally shaped; others are giant animals or objects such as eggs, bananas, houses and even a sponsored shopping trolley. Launches are at 6.00 a.m. and 6.00 p.m. each day, depending on weather conditions. The wind controls the direction of the balloons, but they often drift across the city. On Thursday and Saturday nights there are 'nightglows', when tethered balloons are inflated but not launched. The burners make them glow atmospherically, often in time to music, as they illuminate the festival ground.

Where: Bristol, England
When: Early August, Thursday to Sunday

COOPER'S HILL CHEESE-ROLLING AND WAKE
Brockworth

Would you race down an impossibly steep hill, just for a bit of Double Gloucester cheese? Plenty of people would in the madness that is cheese rolling in an activity that dates back to the early 1800s, a 3.5kg cheese wheel is rolled down the 1:1 gradient of Cooper's Hill in Gloucestershire by an official Master of Ceremonies. The first person over the finish line at the bottom wins the cheese. There are events for men and women, with breakneck downhill races and predictably slower ones uphill. The kamikaze downhill racers start off on their feet, but end up falling and tumbling down the hill. Some are injured and carried off in ambulances. In recent years the official event has been cancelled due to the huge crowds and the ubiquitous health and safety concerns, but an unofficial event persists.

Where: Cooper's Hill, near Brockworth, England
When: Spring Bank Holiday (last Monday in May)

COTSWOLD OLYMPICK GAMES
Chipping Campden

Forget everything you thought you knew about the modern Olympics. The Ancient Greek Olympic Games were not

The Haxey Hood Fool, raised above the crowd on the Mowbray stone in front of the village church in Haxey, gives his welcome speech before the leather hood is thrown into the air for the game to begin.

revived by Baron Pierre de Coubertin in Paris in 1894, but by one Robert Dover in a Cotswold village in 1612. Today's events, which are taken from those early days, include morris dancing, piano smashing and 'dwile flonking', which involves two teams throwing a beer-soaked rag at each other. The Games also host the World Shin-kicking Championships, where two men dressed in white coats attempt to kick each other's shins to force the other into submission. The games haven't been held without interruption every year. Events like the English Civil War (1642–51), and an outbreak of foot and mouth disease (2001), have caused varying gaps. Unlike the Olympic Games, there is not an expensive finale: the Cotswold Olympicks end with a large bonfire and a procession to the town square.

Where: Chipping Campden, England
When: Friday after Spring Bank Holiday (May or June)

EGREMONT CRAB FAIR
Egremont

This ancient West Cumbrian harvest fair dates back to 1267 and is most famous for the World Gurning Championships, where people compete to see who can pull the strangest, most grotesque face while wearing a horse collar around their neck. There are a number of other odd sporting events including a Cumberland wrestling tournament, which has been practised in the Lakeland area for hundreds of years, greasy pole climbing, a wheelbarrow race and a pipe-smoking competition. The Crab Fair also features the Parade of the Apple Cart; this commemorates the Lord of Egremont, who handed out crab apples to the populace and gave the fair its name. Hang out on Main Street and you might be lucky enough to catch one.

Where: Egremont, England
When: Around the third Saturday in September

GOOSE FAIR
Nottingham

Just edged out by the Egremont Crab Fair for the title of the oldest fair in England, the Nottingham Goose Fair is a relative newcomer, only dating back to 1284. Although now effectively a large funfair with a huge assortment of rides and sideshows set up by travelling showmen, it was once a large trading fair where people from miles around came to buy and sell livestock and rural produce, and also to enjoy themselves and socialize. As the name suggests, the Goose Fair attracted goose farmers who drove their charges over 80km from Lincolnshire to be sold. It was apparently also famous for its high-quality cheese.

Where: Nottingham, England
When: First week in October

GYPSY HORSE FAIR
Stow-on-the-Wold

Gypsies from all over England have been attending the twice-yearly horse fair at Stow-on-the-Wold in Gloucestershire since 1476. Originally it was much more of a trading fair, with farm produce, handicrafts, livestock and, of course, horses being bought and sold. These days, although horses are still traded and raced, the main purpose is as a social gathering for people who live in various parts of the country and don't normally get to meet up. As such, the fairs fulfil an important role in the gypsy and traveller communities, allowing relationships to be established and maintained. Gypsies dress to impress, and some even arrive in traditional wooden horse-drawn carriages.

Where: Stow-on-the-Wold, England
When: Nearest Thursdays to 12 May and 24 October

HAXEY HOOD
Haxey

This madcap tradition, which dates back to the 14th century, is essentially a violent game of rugby between four local North Lincolnshire pubs, using a 0.6m tube of stout leather known as a 'hood'. Steeped in ritual, preparations are led by the Lord of the Hood and his Boggins, or fool. The hood is taken to each of the four pubs in the parish, where traditional songs are sung. It is then taken to the village church where there is a ritual 'smoking of the fool'. The game begins in a field on a nearby hill. The hood can't be thrown and no one can run with it. Instead a massive scrum forms, in which the opposing teams made up of patrons of the four pubs try to push or pull the hood towards their favoured hostelry. Games can go on for hours, and invariably end in a massive drinking session.

Where: Haxey, England
When: 6 January (unless a Sunday, then held the day before)

HENLEY REGATTA
Henley-on-Thames

Although it has a reputation of being a sporting (and drinking) event for the British upper classes, the Henley Regatta in Oxfordshire is open to the public. The regatta is a knockout rowing tournament where you can see some 200 races over a five-day period, featuring Olympians and other world-class rowers. Henley is also a great opportunity to see people who still follow the 'social season' – as interesting a minority (albeit a privileged one) as you will see at any festival anywhere in the world. Entry to some enclosures is by invitation only, and there are others for which you need tickets, but many people just picnic by the river, watch the races and sometimes jump in after having one too many Pimms.

Where: Henley-on-Thames, England
When: Wednesday to Sunday of first weekend in July

HORN DANCE
Abbots Bromley

First performed at the Barthelmy Fair in August 1226, this 16km procession of 12 dancers through the village of Abbots Bromley in Staffordshire and its surrounding farms and pubs is one of the few rural customs to have survived in this area. The dancers, all male and all from the local Fowell family, include six characters wearing 11th-century reindeer antlers, plus the Fool, the Hobby Horse and a man dressed as Maid Marion. They are accompanied by an accordion player and two youngsters, one with a triangle and the other with a bow and arrow. The procession starts at 8.00 a.m. with a blessing at the local church, before continuing through the village.

Where: Abbots Bromley, England
When: 'Wakes Monday', 1st after 4 September

HUNTING OF THE EARL OF RONE
Combe Martin

The true origins of this festival are shrouded in legend and hyperbole. The most accepted version is that it celebrates the hunting down and killing of Hugh O'Neill, Earl of Tyrone, who was run out of Ireland in 1607 by the English forces of King James I and shipwrecked off the coast of North Devon near the village of Combe Martin. The only problem with this theory is that O'Neill wasn't killed; he fled to Spain and died of old age. Still, the festival is enthusiastically celebrated and sees various characters hunting down the Earl of Rone all around the village from Friday to Sunday. These include the Hobby Horse and the Fool, along with the Grenadiers and most of the villagers. On Monday night O'Neill is 'discovered' and taken down to the beach, where he is ceremonially shot and cast into the sea.

Where: Combe Martin, England
When: Spring Bank Holiday weekend at the end of May

HURLING THE SILVER BALL
St Columb Major

The game of hurling, or *hyrlïan*, used to be played all over Cornwall. Now it has all but died out, with the tradition only surviving in a couple of places. One such place, the town of St Columb Major, forms a team to take on a team of 'outsiders'. After a cry of 'Town and Country do your best; But in this parish I must rest', a silver ball of about 7cm diameter is thrown into the crowd, who then battle to carry it to their goal while the opposing team tries to wrestle it from them. The goals are about two miles apart, and there are no rules or referees. A team wins if they get the ball to their goal, or if they carry it over the parish boundary.

Where: St Columb Major, England
When: Shrove Tuesday and again on the Saturday 11 days later

MALDON MUD RACE
Maldon

As with many recent festivals, this charity fun race, across the mudflats of the River Blackwater in Essex, seems to have originated in a pub bet. First held in 1973, it has since grown into an internationally recognized event. The course is 200m through the deep sticky mud left behind by this tidal river. Many contestants wear fancy dress as they struggle across the river and back to the starting point. A variety of techniques is employed, from simple wading to slithering along on your stomach. The fastest competitors take a few minutes; others far longer, and some have to be rescued by race marshals in wetsuits. All come out completely covered from head to toe in thick dark brown mud. The race is open to anyone, but you will need to register in advance to compete.

Where: Promenade Park, Maldon, England
When: April or May depending on tides

MARSDEN IMBOLC FESTIVAL
Marsden

Dating back some 2,000 years, Imbolc is a Celtic pagan festival that marks the midpoint between the winter solstice and the spring equinox. The festival is celebrated in various parts of Britain, but perhaps the best known is held in Marsden in the Pennine Hills of West Yorkshire. The festival has a somewhat fiery theme, which represents the purification of the awakening land and the return of the warmth of spring. The main event is a torchlight procession, with great flaming torches, fire sculptures and fire-based entertainers. There is a ritual battle in which the Green Man of spring defeats Jack Frost, and everything winds up with a spectacular fireworks display.

Where: Marsden, England
When: Saturday nearest to 1 February; even years only

NOTTING HILL CARNIVAL
London

Since its inception in 1964 to celebrate Afro-Caribbean culture, the Notting Hill Carnival has become the largest carnival in Europe, attracting over a million revellers to the streets and squares of Notting Hill in London. The main focus of the carnival is the processions of floats, incredible costumes and steel bands. Sunday sees the children's procession and the main parade is on Bank Holiday Monday. Costumes are sometimes impossibly large and ornate, barely fitting through the crowded and sometimes narrow streets on the carnival route. As well as the processions there are countless stalls selling alcohol and Caribbean food, and spread around the vast carnival area there are small, independent sound systems, each functioning like a mini nightclub.

Where: Notting Hill, London, England
When: Sunday and Monday of August Bank Holiday weekend

NUTTERS DANCE
Bacup

In a world of political correctness, the Bacup Nutters Dance is refreshingly old school. However, the word 'nutter' does not refer to the mental health of the dancers, but to a set of maplewood discs or 'nuts' that are worn on knees, hands and belt, which are hit together to make a percussive beat. The 'Nutters' blacken their faces, a tradition that is either pagan in origin or comes from Moorish pirates who settled

in Cornwall, and who later went to work in the quarries and mines of Lancashire. The official name of the club that performs the dances is the Britannia Coconut Dancers, or Coco-nutters. They wear red and white kilts, black tunics with white sashes and wooden clogs. Starting at 9.00 a.m. on Easter Saturday, they dance from one town boundary to the other, performing seven different dances.

Where: Bacup, England
When: Easter Saturday

OTTERY ST MARY TAR BARRELS
Ottery St Mary

The town of Ottery St Mary in Devon has a unique way of celebrating Bonfire Night. Not content with fireworks and a bonfire, people compete to carry burning tar barrels on their shoulders as they run through the streets. The West Country once had a tradition of rolling barrels of tar, but somewhere down the line most towns decided it was too dangerous and the practice died out. However, the people of Ottery St Mary decided that it wasn't dangerous enough and hoisted the barrels on to their shoulders. In a custom thought to date back to the 17th century, 17 barrels of ascending sizes are lit outside each of the village pubs in turn, and then carried until they become too hot, when they are passed on to someone else. The largest of the barrels is 30kg.

Where: Ottery St Mary, England
When: 5 November, unless a Sunday, then held on the Monday

The biggest carnival in Europe, Notting Hill Carnival provides an exciting spectacle of colour against a backdrop of steel band music.

PEARLY KING HARVEST FESTIVAL
London

The tradition of the Pearly Kings and Queens of London dates back to the 19th century when a street sweeper called Henry Croft decorated his work-clothes with buttons and started fund-raising for charity. These buttons used to be made of mother of pearl – hence the name. The Pearlies' Harvest Festival, celebrated by the Cockneys of East London, starts with a parade from the Guildhall to the church of St Mary-le-Bow and, after a service, moves on to a local pub for pints of ale, jellied eels and a spot of morris dancing. The Pearlies are larger-than-life characters, and this lively and traditional London event is still held in aid of the poor.

Where: St Mary-le-Bow church, London, England
When: Last Sunday in September

SHROVETIDE FOOTBALL
Ashbourne

The ancient and somewhat violent game of Shrovetide football used to be played in many parts of England, but the market town of Ashbourne in Derbyshire is one of the few to continue the tradition. The town is split into two teams depending on where the players live: Down'ards from the south and Up'ards from the north. Games can last all day as the goals are set at two old mills, three miles apart. The teams attend a pre-game ceremony, where the game's anthem is sung with the chorus: 'Tis a glorious game, deny it who can, that tries the pluck of an Englishman'. The teams form a large crush, euphemistically called a hug. A leather-covered cork-filled ball is thrown into the hug, and the players try to move it to their goal by pushing against the opposition. Once there it needs to be tapped on the mill three times to win.

Where: Ashbourne, England
When: Shrove Tuesday and Ash Wednesday

STRAW BEAR FESTIVAL
Whittlesey

In a revival of an ancient Fenland custom of making a straw bear for Plough Monday (the start of the agricultural year), the small village of Whittlesey in Cambridgeshire plays host to a festival of traditional dancing, music, storytelling and poetry. The highlight is the Saturday parade led by the strangest looking 'bear' you've ever seen: wrapped in straw, it has a pointed head and a tail made of chain, and who dances for gifts of money or beer. The bear is accompanied by an eclectic entourage including a keeper, morris dancers, clog dancers and musicians. They stop at various points around the village and perform. There can be up to 350 people escorting the bear. Banned in 1909 by the local police inspector who considered it a form of begging, the

tradition was resumed in 1980. On the Sunday lunchtime the straw costume is ceremonially burned on the beach.

Where: Whittlesey, England
When: Second or third weekend in January

SUMMER SOLSTICE
Stonehenge

Attracting hippies, ravers and self-appointed Druids to the Neolithic stones of Stonehenge on the Salisbury Plain, the Summer Solstice on June 21 sees the sun rising over the Heel or Slaughter Stone just outside the entrance to the henge. Once it was the scene of battles with the police, who tried to stop people gathering here; now the ceremony is encouraged by English Heritage, which runs the site. People gather overnight, drumming and dancing, before watching a Druidic ceremony as the rays of the rising sun over the Heel Stone align it with the central Altar Stone. If you can deal with the crowds, you can marvel at how our prehistoric ancestors were able to create this extraordinary feat of engineering.

Where: Stonehenge, England
When: Summer Solstice, 21 June

SWAN UPPING
Sunbury Lock to Abingdon

All mute swans in England used to belong to the monarch and the tradition of conducting an annual swan census dates back to the 12th century. Over five days, a team of scarlet uniformed Uppers, led by the Queen's Swan Marker, row up the River Thames in six skiffs from Surrey to Oxfordshire looking for mute swans. When they find the swans, they encircle them, before catching and inspecting them for any injuries. Cygnets are weighed and ringed before being released. Predictably, it's not easy catching swans from a boat. There is an underlying element of danger as the Uppers attempt to grab the cygnets while avoiding the powerful beaks and flapping wings of their parents. The entourage stops off for lunch at riverside pubs along the way, and as they pass Windsor Castle everyone stands to attention and salutes 'Her Majesty The Queen, Seigneur of the Swans'.

Where: From Sunbury Lock to Abingdon, England
When: Monday to Friday of third week in July

WHITBY GOTH WEEKEND
Whitby

Said to have been the setting for Bram Stoker's novel *Dracula*, the impressive ruins of the Gothic abbey perched on the cliffs of the North Yorkshire seaside town of Whitby seem to be the reason that the Goths hold their twice-yearly weekend festival here. Of course, it's not just for Goths and has become something of a celebration of non-conformity,

Thousands of visitors gather to watch the summer solstice sunrise over Stonehenge, the main religious site of pagan Britain.

diversity and freedom, also attracting punks, steampunks, emos, bikers and metallers for a weekend of music, dancing, drinking and shopping. It's quite a sight and most people seem to spend the time dressing up in black finery and walking around the picturesque streets showing off and admiring other people's outrageous attire.

Where: Whitby, England
When: Friday to Sunday in April and at Halloween
....

WORLD CONKER CHAMPIONSHIPS
Southwick
....

One day, back in the autumn of 1965, rain postponed a fishing trip. The thwarted fishermen retired to the pub wondering what to do. They decided to have a conker fight; something English boys have done since time immemorial. 'Conkers' involves threading the brown nut of the horse chestnut tree on a string and taking it in turns to hit the other person's conker, until one breaks. The last man standing, as it were, is the winner. From these humble roots has grown the World Conker Championships, which take place each year in a picturesque corner of Northamptonshire and now attract competitors from over 20 countries. The event also features food, beer and other local entertainments and any profits are donated to the Royal National Institute for the Blind.

Where: Southwick, near Oundle, England
When: Second Sunday in October
....

WORLD CUSTARD PIE CHAMPIONSHIP
Coxheath
....

Since its first on-screen appearance in the 1909 silent film *Mr Flip*, a custard pie in the face has become slapstick

gold, a protest staple and a charity fund-raising classic. Such is its appeal that there is even a World Custard Pie Championship where teams from all over the world compete to be recognized as the best 'flan-flingers' (pie-throwers) on the planet. First held in 1967, the championship normally takes place in the village of Coxheath in Kent. There are 32 competing teams, each wearing fancy dress. Two teams, standing 2.5m apart, face off against each other, with their pies behind them on trestle tables. In a frenetic burst of slinging they score points for a direct hit, but lose points for a miss. The winning teams go through to the next rounds until the champion emerges.

Where: Coxheath, England
When: Variable, usually May/June
....

WORLD MARBLES CHAMPIONSHIP
Tinsley Green
....

Another longstanding British tradition that started life in a pub, the World Marbles Championship has been held at the Greyhound Inn at Tinsley Green in West Sussex since 1932. The game, which reached its peak of popularity in the 1950s, has been played in the region for centuries. It has been traced back to 1588, although marbles date back to the ancient Indus Valley civilization. The game has complicated rules and its own vocabulary. It is also taken very seriously, so if you don't know your fudging from your cabbaging, it might be best stick to spectating. At Tinsley Green a dozen players compete in a 1.8m concrete ring containing 49 marbles. Players take it in turns to flick their Tolley (shooting marble) into the ring, receiving a point for each marble they knock out. First to score 25 is the winner.

Where: Greyhound Inn, Tinsley Green, England
When: Good Friday
....

Bizarre Britain

ANY NOTION OF BRITISH RESERVE AND 'STIFF UPPER LIP' WILL SURELY BE DISPELLED BY THE REVELATION OF THE SHEER RANGE AND NUMBER OF MADCAP FESTIVALS THAT CAN BE FOUND THROUGHOUT ENGLAND, SCOTLAND AND WALES. LITERALLY HUNDREDS OF STRANGE AND QUIRKY TRADITIONS, FESTIVALS AND EVENTS TAKE PLACE ALL OVER THE COUNTRY, MANY OF THEM DATING BACK CENTURIES.

ABOVE Like some water monster covered with bog weed, an entrant in the World Bog Snorkelling Championships surfaces at the end of her timed 'swim'.

OPPOSITE The Straw Bear and his keeper parade through the Fenland town of Whittlesey in Cambridgeshire on Plough Monday to mark the start of the agricultural year.

BELOW On Guy Fawkes Night, flames light up Lewis, a small rural English town that has been crowned the bonfire capital of the world.

Some of Britain's more eccentric festivals have their origins in historical events; the roots of others are more opaque. The Hunting of the Earl of Rone (see p. 238) at Combe Martin in Devon is one such event. This annual tradition is based on the search for the rebel Earl of Tyrone who was supposedly shipwrecked off the North Devon coast when forced to flee Ireland in 1607. Over four days, various characters, including the Grenadiers, the Fool, and the Hobby Horse, and the villagers comb the area for the Earl of Rone, who when 'found' is taken to the beach to be 'shot'. The only spoiler for this legend is that the Earl actually ended his days peacefully in Rome.

OPPOSITE TOP The villagers of Combe Martin in Devon join the Hobby Horse to hunt the Earl of Rone, who was allegedly shipwrecked on their coast.

OPPOSITE BOTTOM The six Deer-men, each wearing ancient antlers, perform the Horn Dance in the village of Abbots Bromley in Staffordshire.

One historical event celebrated all over England is the failed Gunpowder Plot to blow up the Houses of Parliament on 5 November 1605. Known as Guy Fawkes Night, after one of the plotters, or Bonfire Night, it is celebrated with fireworks and bonfires on which effigies of Fawkes are burned. Some places have developed their own versions of this popular festival. At Lewes in East Sussex, for example, there are great processions of burning torches organized by several local bonfire societies (see p. 236), culminating in firework displays and massive bonfires. Another feature of the festival involves dragging burning barrels, the insides of which have been coated with tar, on sleds through the town. The people of Ottery St Mary in Devon also uphold this tradition, but dramatically carry the burning barrels through the streets on their shoulders (see p. 239).

ABOVE A modern Druid at Stonehenge celebrates the summer solstice.

ABOVE RIGHT At the World Marble Championships in Tinsley Green, England, a contestant takes his turn to drive the marbles off the ring by shooting his larger 'tolley' marble.

Before the arrival of Roman Christianity with Saint Augustine in 597, Anglo-Saxon Britain (though not the native Christian Celts) was a pagan country, and a number of the fire festivals celebrated today have their roots in ancient pre-Christian religion. The Up Helly Aa festivals that take place in January in the Shetland Islands mark the end of the pagan midwinter celebration of Yule. The most impressive of these is in Lerwick (see p. 251), where a procession of flaming torches ends in the ritual burning of a replica Viking longboat, commemorating the Islands' Viking heritage. The name is said to derive from Old Norse. In Stonehaven, near Aberdeen, at Hogmanay (New Year) there is a spectacular procession through the town in which more than forty men and women swing great fireballs above their heads (see p. 251).

Other festivals which claim pagan origins include the Abbots Bromley Horn Dance (see p. 238). Here a small group, made up of six Deer-men wearing ancient antlers, a Fool, a man dressed up as Maid Marion and a Hobby Horse, dance at various locations in the village and the surrounding farms and pubs.

The tradition of wassailing, driving evil spirits out of apple orchards to ensure a good harvest, is said to have started sometime in the fifth century. Still practised today in a few of the apple-growing counties of southern England – for example in Bolney, West Sussex (see p. 236) – traditions vary depending on where the wassails are held, but they usually involve dressing up, singing, a spot of morris dancing and, of course, drinking.

Perhaps the most famous neo-pagan tradition is the Summer Solstice celebration at Stonehenge (see p. 240). The prehistoric ring of monumental stones, which retains its air of ancient mystery for most of the year, becomes a seething mass of humanity at dawn on the morning of 21 June as New Age Druids and a host of others gather to welcome the first day of summer.

Britain has a long history of inventing sports, such as rugby, football and cricket, and spreading their popularity to other countries, which then beat the British at their own game. This, however, has not stopped the flow of new ideas. Take the World Conker Championships at Tinsley Green or the World Marbles Championships at Oundle, for example, both very English competitions, which have seen strong challenges from Germany in recent years (see p. 241). For their part, the Welsh invented the 'sport' of bog snorkelling in the 1970s, and remain at the top of the leader board in this time trial to complete two lengths of a water-filled trench in a peat bog without swimming (see p. 251).

BELOW Contestants, kitted out in the obligatory white coat of the games, battle it out in the World Shin-kicking Competition at the Cotswold Olympick Games.

ABOVE The town's 'Down'ards and 'Up'ards' try to move the ball to their goal in the unique game of Shrovetide football, played at Ashbourne, England.

OPPOSITE AND INSET Crazy and dangerous, and traditionally only for the citizens of the local village of Brockworth, the May Day Cooper's Hill Cheese-Rolling and Wake attracts participants from all over the world.

Some would argue that shin-kicking and piano smashing (which are what they say they are) and 'dwile flonking' (the throwing of beer-soaked rags), which have been played in the Gloucestershire village of Chipping Campden since 1612, are the earliest forerunners of the modern Olympic games; others are sticking to the story of Baron de Coubertin and the Paris Olympic Congress in 1894. A visit to the annual Cotswold Olympicks (see pp. 236–7) will definitely be entertaining, but will probably not provide all the answers.

Rowdy ball games also have a long history in England. Some are said to date back a thousand years or more. Many of these games are now codified and a lot more civilized, but Ashbourne in Derbyshire still plays host to an annual two-day game of Shrovetide football (see p. 240). The game consists of a massive scrum between teams contesting an area of three miles between two disused water mills. The winners are the first to transport a cork-filled ball to their goal. There are similar traditions between pubs in Haxey, North Lincolnshire (see p. 237) and St Columb Major in Cornwall (see p. 238), which sees a contest between the Countrymen and the Townsmen to carry a silver-covered applewood ball to their goal.

Pride of place in the bizarre stakes, however, must go to the sport of cheese rolling, an event so peculiar that it has now spread around the world with a number of copycat events. The May Day Cooper's Hill Cheese-Rolling and Wake (see p. 236) is held to be the original and the best. It involves a race down an impossibly steep hill chasing after a large wheel of double-Gloucester cheese. Mad? Yes. Dangerous? Yes, and another of the quirky events that makes Britain's annual calendar of festivals so fascinating.

> SCOTLAND

BELTANE FIRE FESTIVAL
Edinburgh

Edinburgh gets seriously pagan during this ancient fertility rite. A Celtic festival marking the passing of the seasons, Beltane (or bright fire) was celebrated all over Ireland and Scotland, and involved the lighting of fires to symbolize new life and the bringing of light after the darkness of winter. In the past, people used to leap over these fires. The current festivities date back to 1988, but are rooted in ancient tradition. A noisy and wild flaming torchlight procession featuring dancing and drumming in a celebration of the four elements – earth, air, fire and water – winds its way to the top of Calton Hill, led by the May Queen and the Green Man, a folk figure that occurs in a number of pagan festivals in the British Isles.

Where: Calton Hill, Edinburgh, Scotland
When: 30 April

BRAEMAR GATHERING
Braemar

In a sea of tartan, the Braemar Gathering brings athletes from all over Scotland and beyond to Aberdeenshire to compete in a series of traditional Highland Games and to celebrate Highland culture. These are hard, manly sports – caber tossing, hammer throwing, stone-putting, tug of war and a race to the summit of the 860m-high hill of Morrone – designed to sort the men from the boys. The Gathering has a long pedigree, dating back some 900 years. It was popular with Queen Victoria, who first came here in 1848 and awarded the event her royal patronage in 1866. Members of the current British royal family often attend, and have been

A performer dances a Highland fling accompanied by a piper at the Braemar Gathering in the village of Braemar in the Highlands of Scotland.

known to sport kilts and raise the odd toast of single malt. Other events include bands of pipers, Highland dancing and even a sack race for the 'wee ones'.

Where: Braemar, Scotland
When: First Saturday in September

COMMON RIDINGS
Border towns

In the 13th and 14th centuries parts of Scotland were at war with England, and landowners along the borders organized patrols to guard their land and livestock from Border Reivers (robbers), from both sides of the border. Today, 11 Scottish border towns hold Ridings celebrations between June and August. These follow ancient traditions of horsemanship, local games and music, and some last for a couple of weeks. At the heart of each, though, is a mass cavalcade, often at full gallop, with riders dressed in period costume following the banner of their town, but all working together to maintain the Ridings tradition.

Where: Eleven Border towns, notably Selkirk, Hawick, Lauder and Langholm
When: June–August

EDINBURGH FESTIVAL FRINGE
Edinburgh

Irreverent and often anarchic, the Edinburgh Festival Fringe is the perfect counterpoint to the more institutional arts and culture of the annual Edinburgh Festival. With no selection committee, anyone is free to turn up and take part. The Fringe largely features theatre, music and dance and especially comedy, often at little or no cost. Some performers hire venues, others entertain in the streets. Many famous comics have been 'discovered' at the Fringe and it is a fantastic opportunity to see some of the up-and-coming stars before they become famous.

Where: Edinburgh, Scotland
When: Mostly in August

HOGMANAY
Edinburgh

The city of Edinburgh throws the undisputed mother of all New Year's Eve parties: a three-day extravaganza that blends elements of paganism, dance music and extreme swimming. The party starts on 30 December with a torchlight parade down the Royal Mile to Calton Hill, where it culminates in a massive fireworks display. On New Year's Eve, there is a huge party on Princes Street that features live music, DJs, dancing and a lot of drinking. On the stroke of midnight, the battlements of Edinburgh Castle are lit up by fireworks. For those waking up with a hangover on New

Year's Day, a traditional cure has to be the 'Loony Dook'. Join the Dookers Parade in fancy dress, before 'dooking' yourself in the all but freezing River Forth. It will take your breath away, even if it does little for your hangover.

Where: Edinburgh, Scotland
When: 30 December to 1 January annually

THE FIREBALLS
Stonehaven

It might be a Celtic pagan tradition and is very likely to have something to do with the weather, but whatever the reasons, festivals in Scotland often seem to include fire in some form. Edinburgh has its famous Hogmanay celebration but in the Aberdeenshire town of Stonehaven, the New Year celebrations get hot, hot, hot as up to 45 locals process down the high street swinging massive flaming fireballs around their heads. Participants have their own 'recipes' to create the fireballs, but all have the same basic form: rags, card and wood, soaked in paraffin and contained in a skin of chicken wire. A fence-wire handle is attached, and the length depends on the height and preference of the 'swinger'.

Where: Stonehaven, Scotland
When: 31 December

UP HELLY AA
Lerwick

Lerwick in the Shetland Islands is closer to the coast of Norway than it is to the Scottish capital, which might explain why it goes Viking crazy during Up Helly Aa. The event started in 1881 following the banning of a tradition of dragging flaming tar barrels through the town to mark the end of the pagan Yule season. Today, events culminate after dark when a torchlight procession of a thousand Guizers 'disguised' as Vikings march through the streets to the burning ground. They circle a replica Viking longboat, which has been painstakingly constructed during the winter, before the torches are thrown aboard, sending the whole lot up in flames. There follows a feasting and drinking session of Valhallic proportions.

Where: Lerwick, Shetland Islands, Scotland
When: Last Tuesday of January

> WALES

NATIONAL EISTEDDFOD
Various locations

The Eisteddfod, a cultural celebration of all things Welsh, travels from place to place, giving communities across the country the chance to participate. An eclectic mix of old and new, it comprises eight days of performances of literature,

A bog snorkeller, using only flipper-power, inches his way along a peat bog to the finishing line, described by contestants as being like swimming through a thick pea soup.

music, dance and all forms of the visual arts – with a particular emphasis on the Welsh language. One of the main events is the presentation of a carved chair to the poet who is to be crowned the Bard of the Festival. It is thought that the whole festival is named after this moment, *eisteddfod* meaning 'a sitting' in the Welsh language. The first Eisteddfod was held in 1176, when Lord Rhys of Cardigan invited poets and musicians to a gathering at his castle. The current Eisteddfod was re-established in 1880.

Where: Various locations around Wales
When: First week of August

WORLD BOG SNORKELLING CHAMPIONSHIPS
Llanwrtyd Wells

One of the oddest sporting events in the world was dreamed up in a public bar in 1985. Bog snorkelling involves contestants kicking, splashing and writhing their way along a flooded 55m trench cut into a peat bog. They can wear a snorkel, mask and flippers, but are not allowed to use any swimming strokes. The water is so dark with peat that they are allowed to stick their heads up for navigation, but all propulsion has to take place with their heads underwater. Contestants are timed over two lengths of the course.

Where: Waen Rhydd Bog, Llanwrtyd Wells, Wales
When: August Bank Holiday Weekend

Bravado

ACTS OF BRAVADO, LAUGHING IN THE FACE OF DANGER, ARE A FEATURE OF FESTIVALS IN EVERY CULTURE. DIFFERENT SOCIETIES HAVE CREATED A VARIETY OF TESTOSTERONE-FUELLED CHALLENGES FOR THOSE EAGER TO DEMONSTRATE THEIR COURAGE OR THEIR WORTH. IN GENERAL BOTH THE PARTICIPANTS AND THE MOTIVE ARE PRETTY MUCH THE SAME. THEY ARE ALL YOUNG MEN, STRUTTING THEIR STUFF AND SHOWING OFF – FOR BRAGGING RIGHTS, STATUS AND TO IMPRESS THE GIRLS.

ABOVE At Janmastami, as part of the celebrations to mark the birth of the Hindu god Krishna, young men in areas of northern India form human towers in order to reach and break open a pot of butter.

OPPOSITE Participants run ahead of the released bulls to tempt them into the sea at the festival of Santísima Sangre at Denia in Spain.

Men on the island of Pentecost in Vanuatu dive forward from a high tower, attached only by vine ropes at their ankles, at the Naghol ritual.

BELOW Human towers (*castell*) are a feature of Catalan festivities at Les Festes de la Mercè in Barcelona, Spain.

Dictionary definitions of the word bravado include 'show of courage, bold front', 'show of boldness intended to impress', and 'swagger'. I have to say that I displayed none of these when running with bulls in the streets of Pamplona, or when facing a galloping *abrivado* (bull run accompanied by horse riders) in Nîmes. But then apparently the word can also mean 'a pretence of bravery', which is what I was showing when being chased across the arena at Saintes Maries de la Mer by a feisty Camargue bull.

One of the most breathtaking feats of bravado takes place at the Naghol (see p. 264), or land-diving festival on the Vanuatuan island of Pentecost. In this age-old ritual, men and boys climb up a twenty-to-thirty-metre wooden tower and hurl themselves off it, secured only with a vine tied to each ankle to break their fall. It is hard to watch, but impossible to look away, as the divers dice with death. On the occasion when I was watching this ritual, one of the vines broke, leaving the diver attached to just one, to break his fall. He hit the ground hard, then stood up and looked at the snapped vine ruefully. He was lucky. One diver was killed when performing the Naghol out of season, for the Queen of England, when the vines weren't supple enough to take his weight. The Naghol is performed in part to guarantee a good yam harvest, but also as a rite of passage: the higher the platform the participants jump from, the braver they are thought to be and the greater their status in the village.

The word bravado derives from the Spanish *bravata*, and Spain seems to have its share of festivals that put people to the test. When you realize that the Spanish also gave us the word macho, from *machismo* (exaggerated manliness), then their approach to festivals seems somewhat more understandable.

There is the tradition of building human towers to demonstrate skill, strength and courage. At the Fiesta de la Virgen de la Salud (see p. 222) near Valencia these towers can be as high as six storeys, while at Les Festes de la Mercè (see p. 224) in Barcelona they can be even taller. The climbers at the top are often children, because they are lighter. However, when the towers inevitably collapse they have the furthest to fall. At the Menorcan Fiesta de Sant Joan (see p. 222), villagers try to place their hands over the heart of a rearing horse, and at Las Luminaries de San Anton (see p. 224), daring riders gallop through the streets and alleyways of the town, jumping through flaming bonfires as they go.

The bull has been considered a worthy opponent for millennia. Reputedly the first bullfight was recorded in the Mesopotamian *Epic of Gilgamesh*; Minoan frescoes in

ABOVE Participants put themselves in danger as they try to touch the heart of a rearing horse for good luck at the Fiesta de Sant Joan that takes place in Menorca, Spain.

Crete show young people of both sexes grabbing the bull by the horns and vaulting over them; and bull sacrifice was a feature of the Ancient Roman cult of Mithras. Bulls are both feared and admired wherever they are raised, and many rural communities all over the world test their courage and speed against their bulls, especially at festival time when there is more than an element of 'pot-valour'.

Of course, the Spanish have a lot of festivals that involve reckless members of the public running away from, and generally tormenting, bulls, in a display of unbridled machismo. In the days before motor vehicles, fighting bulls were herded to the bullring, escorted by a group of horsemen. Over the years the tradition arose of local youths showing off by leaping in front of the bulls as they passed, and the *encierro* (bull run) was born. The most famous of these is the running of the bulls at the San Fermin festival in Pamplona (see p. 225). Each morning during the fiesta, the fighting bulls are run through the town and white-clad males (traditionally) run in front of them. Once the bulls are 'safely' tucked up in their bullpens, cows called *vaquillas* are released into the arena to give the runners another chance to be heroes, but more often to be knocked flying.

It is not just the Spanish who goad bulls to prove their manhood; there is also a great bullfighting tradition just across the border in south-western France. As well as the Spanish-style *corrida*, where the bull is killed, the French also have the *course de cocade*, in which *razatteurs,* also dressed in white, compete to break the strings that have been tied between the bull's horns. The bull is not hurt, but the *razatteurs* sometimes are. The cities of Nîmes and Arles both have bullfighting festivals (see pp. 198–9) that feature *abrivados* of the local Camargue bulls escorted by the *gardians*.

ABOVE At the Onbashira Festival at Lake Suwa, Japan, participants try to 'ride' a massive, felled tree trunk on its journey down the mountain to the shrine where it will be symbolically raised.

ABOVE RIGHT The dance of the *voladores* in Mexico is not for the faint-hearted; suspended by their feet, upside down, the participants spin to the accompaniment of the flute and drums which are played by a man who remains stationary atop the 30m pole.

Pole dancing is not usually regarded as an act of bravado, but when the pole is 30 metres tall, and the pole dancers, or *voladores*, leap from the summit attached by ropes that unwind as they fall, spinning them around the pole, it does take a lot of courage. This ceremony, which has its roots in the ancient Mayan religion, is performed at a number of festivals in Latin America, including the Fiesta de Santo Tomas in Guatemala (see p. 56) and the Vanilla Festival in Mexico (see p. 68).

Japanese culture traditionally prizes male bravery, and a number of Japanese festivals feature tests of strength and courage, none more so than the Onbashira Festival at Lake Suwa (see p. 99). Here the brave and foolhardy ride massive logs down a steep hillside. As the logs, destined to be raised as sacred pillars in Shinto shrines, can weigh up to twelve tonnes, the riders really are taking their lives in their hands.

A typical feature of many of the festivals involving bravado is that there is nothing material at stake, the only prize being the undertaking and survival at the finish. One example of this is the tradition of leaping twenty-one metres into the river from the Stari Most (bridge) in Mostar, Bosnia. The custom began in 1566 as a rite of passage for young Bosnian men, and stopped when the bridge was destroyed during the Balkans war of 1993. It was rebuilt and reopened in 2004, since when the revival of the Ikari Bridge Jumping (see p. 174) tradition has become a symbol of the bravery and resilience of the Bosnian people.

For some, of course, there's no need for an elaborate show of bravado when a straightforward dust-up will do. It may be a simple case of too much alcohol and too much testosterone, but there are some celebrations around the world where the fight

LEFT The proximity of the bull sends some runners to scale the barriers, while others, displaying more bravado, steam on ahead in one of the many bull runs that take place at the Festival of San Fermin in Pamplona, Spain.

ABOVE A diver takes flight from the Stari Most (bridge) and will plunge 21m into the Neretva River in Mostar, Bosnia and Herzegovina.

ABOBE The Pasola requires outstanding horsemanship as well as spear-throwing skills. Sumbanese men engage in this ritual battle at the start of the rice-planting season.

is the point, and ritualized conflicts are used to preserve traditions and hold societies together.

This is the motivation for two particularly gruesome festivals in Bali. The Pukul Sapu festival (see p. 148) aims to promote a sense of brotherhood between the menfolk of the villages of Mamala and Morella by having them beat each other's backs with rattan brushwood switches until they draw blood. The Usaba Sambah (see p. 148) in the walled Bali Aga village of Tenganan is even more bloodthirsty. A ritual fight called *makare-kare* is held between bare-chested men dressed only in sarongs. They whip each other with *pandanus* leaves and the sharp serrated edges cause deep cuts and plenty of blood to flow. The fights are staged for the age-old reason of attracting the attention of the watching unmarried girls of the village.

The Pasola festivals (see p. 147) on the nearby Indonesian island of Sumba involve a series of violent horseback fights in which combatants fling bamboo spears at each other in honour of Nyale, goddess of the sea and of fertility. As the horsemen engage in bloody combat, the villagers cheer them on and the atmosphere builds up to a frenzy. Spears are also the weapons of choice in the Wogasia festival (see p. 264) on the remote island of Santa Catalina in the Solomon Islands. In a ritual aimed at ridding the island of problems and discord from the previous year, so that it is ready for the coming harvest, men from two local tribes meet on the beach to do battle with sharpened sticks.

Tinku (see p. 87), which euphemistically means 'encounter', is a ritualized punch-up among the Quecha and Aymara people of the Andes. The womenfolk, dressed in traditional costumes, form a circle, singing and chanting, while the men gather in the middle and start to fight. They crouch low and swing punches at each other rhythmically in what is essentially a dance. Although meant purely to be a symbolic combat, Tinku regularly get out of control and turn into full-on battles. There are even cases where the police have had to break up Tinku with tear gas, and sometimes people are badly hurt – even killed.

The spirited townspeople of Vrontados on the Greek island of Chios certainly take the prize when it comes to taking combat to extremes with the annual Rouketopolemos festival (see p. 204). This sees the parishioners of two churches firing rockets at each other across a valley at midnight before Easter Sunday, scoring points each time they hit their opponent's belfry. Some believe the tradition began as a way to scare off Muslim soldiers during the Ottoman occupation, so that the forbidden Easter services could be held. Others believe it was a case of nose-thumbing at the Ottoman authorities, who had confiscated the town cannons in order to prevent an insurrection.

BELOW Surrounded by cheering onlookers and womenfolk, the men from various communities engage in an ancient Andean custom – Tinku, ritual battles – said to release the frustrations that may exist between them.

>> OCEANIA

> AUSTRALIA

BEER CAN REGATTA
Darwin

To be eligible to compete in the annual Darwin Beer Can Regatta your boat must be constructed from empty 'tinnies' (aluminium beer cans), the more elaborate the better, and entrants must follow the Ten Can-mandments set by the organizer, the Lions Clubs of Darwin. Number Four of the Ten is probably the most important: 'Thou shalt not drown', and participants are required to wear flotation jackets when out to sea in their dubious crafts. Drinking the cans empty in the first place is only part of the fun. The highlight of the day is the Battle of Mindil in which teams of four people race to find the hidden underwater object. Whichever team finds it first claims the winner's pennant. To add to the general mayhem and excitement of the event, competitors can indulge in rowdy water fights to force their opponents off course.

Where: Mindil Beach, Darwin, Australia
When: Sunday in July

GARMA
Gulkula

The Yolngu Aboriginal people have been living in the north-eastern Arnhem Land region for over 40,000 years and the annual Garma festival is a spectacular celebration of their rich cultural heritage of language, art, dance and music. The festival is held at Gulkula, which is a traditional Yolngu meeting ground, and includes performances of *bunggul* (traditional dance), *manikay* (singing) and ritual ceremonies. There is a forum for academic presentations and to discuss Aboriginal issues. The event is set in a forest of stringybark trees, where some believe the *yidaki* (didgeridoo) was given to the Gumatj people by their ancestor Ganbulabula.

Where: Gulkula, Australia
When: End of July to August

HENLEY-ON-TODD REGATTA
Alice Springs

Beer has been responsible for some of the world's most eccentric festivals, like this one which sees a 'regatta' held on a dry river bed in Australia's Northern Territory, almost 1,500km from the nearest significant body of water. Conceived in 1962 in the pub by local resident Reg Smith as a way of raising funds for charity, the regatta features a series of madcap 'boat' races and surfing events, the day ending with a wild sea battle between Vikings and pirates. Most of the events involve different-shaped boats that are worn or carried by the 'rowers', who run the course with

their legs sticking out of the bottom, but some are actually paddled through the dirt using shovels.

Where: Todd River, Alice Springs, Australia
When: Third Saturday in August

LAURA ABORIGINAL DANCE FESTIVAL
Laura

A growing number of Aboriginal festivals have been established over the past years. The biennial Laura Dance Festival is held at the Ang-gnarra Festival Grounds on the site of the ancient Bora assembly grounds (where initiation ceremonies take place) of the local Kuku Yalanji people. As many as 500 performers from 20 different Aboriginal communities present traditional dance, song, arts and crafts with the intention of passing on their culture across the generations, and showcasing the strength, pride and uniqueness of Aboriginal people.

Where: Ang-gnarra Festival Grounds, Laura, Australia
When: Third week of June, odd years only

MELBOURNE CUP
Melbourne

As the richest prize in Australian sport, the Melbourne Cup, the highlight of Melbourne Cup Week, is part of the national psyche, enjoyed by race-goers, horse lovers and even those who really aren't aficionados but enjoy a flutter. Hailed, even in poetry, as 'the race that stops a nation', Melbourne Cup Day is a public holiday in its host city and in many parts of the state of Victoria, and much of the country will stop work and play to listen to or watch the race. Over 100,000 people flock to Flemington Racecourse for a day of racing, fashion, music and floral displays, with each race day having a different signature flower. Melbourne Cup Day is also a great social occasion away from the actual racecourse, with a range of parties, social gatherings and, of course, the great Aussie 'barbie'.

Where: Flemington Racecourse, Melbourne, Australia
When: Usually 1st Tuesday in November

MOOMBA FESTIVAL
Melbourne

Overseen by the Moomba Monarch, a traditional Australian send-up of the British monarchy, this annual festival has been entertaining Melburnians since 1954. An irreverent and lively combination of unique events, parties and musical performances, Moomba is fun and it's free, and lives up to the official meaning of its name – 'let's get together and have fun'. Three days of concerts with a top-quality line-up of local and international bands are presented on various stages across the city. Traditional highlights include the

Performers at the Laura Aboriginal Festival on the Cape York Peninsula in northern Queensland come together to share their traditions and customs with more than 20 different Aboriginal tribes.

costumed Moomba Parade, with themed floats put together by local community groups, and the Birdman Rally, in which contestants try to cross the Yarra River by leaping off a 4m platform with wings attached to their costumes. Each night also sees a spectacular fireworks display.

Where: Melbourne, Australia
When: Labour Day long weekend (March)

SYDNEY GAY AND LESBIAN MARDI GRAS
Sydney

The biggest and undoubtedly the gayest party in the southern hemisphere, Sydney Gay and Lesbian Mardi Gras attracts people from all over the world to celebrate diversity and acceptance – and, of course, to party. Over three weeks, visitors can choose between an eclectic series of gay, lesbian, bisexual, transgender, queer and intersex orientated arts, community and sports events. There is, naturally, a large social aspect to the Mardi Gras, with a number of official parties and club nights. Led by the so-called Dykes on Bikes, the final Saturday of the festival sees the Mardi Gras Parade where around 10,000 extravagant, colourful and often outrageously dressed participants make their way through the centre of town, cheered on by hundreds of thousands of residents and tourists.

Where: Sydney, Australia
When: Three weeks in February/March

TUNARAMA
Port Lincoln

Although it sounds like an Aboriginal word, Tunarama is

actually a free festival in honour of the tuna fish. The tuna is king in Port Lincoln in South Australia, and the festival was established in 1962 to recognize and promote what was then an emerging industry. The festival coincides with the Australia Day weekend. The Port Lincoln foreshore is covered in a mix of stalls and sideshows and plays host to a costumed procession of floats and decorated vehicles celebrating both the foundation of Australia and the sleek and speedy tuna fish. The highlight of the events is the World Championship Tuna Toss – much like the athletic hammer throwing, but using an 8–10kg tuna as the missile of choice.

Where: Port Lincoln, Australia
When: Long Weekend around Australia Day (26 January)

> MELANESIA

ALOTAU KENU AND KUNDU FESTIVAL
Alotau, Papua New Guinea

The Milne Bay region of Papua New Guinea is peppered with over 600 islands, and the people who live in the area rely on canoes for their day-to-day existence. Naturally canoes are an integral part of this annual festival. Many of the participants come from outlying islands and spend a number of days paddling to reach the festival site in canoes laden with garden food and pigs for feasting, and dance groups and drummers who will be performing. A variety of craft are used, including long war canoes, which seat 50 paddlers. Canoe races are held, and there are traditional food exchanges. A number of dance performances are organized, including a 'sing-sing' where tribal warriors compete in a series of traditional war dances.

Where: Alotau, Papua New Guinea
When: First Friday to Sunday in November

GOROKA SHOW
Goroka, Papua New Guinea

The Goroka is one of the oldest and certainly the best known of all of the tribal gatherings of Papua New Guinea. First held in 1957, it was originally organized by the administering Australian authorities in an effort to promote inter-tribal harmony. Today, it attracts members of up to a hundred tribes from all over the Eastern Highlands who demonstrate their dancing, singing and other rituals and customs over three days of festivities. Participants cover themselves in body paint and wear traditional dress, sporting shells and great feathers from birds of paradise. Although now in part a tourist event, the Goroka still performs an important social function as it provides a rare opportunity for tribes, which have over 30 languages between them, to get together.

Where: Goroka, Papua New Guinea
When: Weekend nearest Independence Day (16 September)

MOUNT HAGEN SHOW
Mount Hagen, Papua New Guinea

Tribal enmity in Papua New Guinea was not confined to the Eastern Highlands, and this festival at Mount Hagen in the Western Highlands performs a similar function to the Goroka. First held in 1964, it provides as many as 50 tribes with a neutral setting in which to meet in celebration of their cultural and tribal diversity. The festival takes the form of a traditional 'sing-sing' in which tribal dancers and drummers perform in cultural rather than physical competition with each other. Crowds gather to watch the truly fearsome tribesmen, decked out with bright body paint, colourful feathers and shells and carrying spears as they perform their traditional dances.

Where: Mount Hagen, Papua New Guinea
When: Third weekend in August

WOGASIA (SANTA CATALINA SPEAR FIGHTING FESTIVAL)
Santa Catalina, Solomon Islands

There are different ways to settle scores – mediation, conciliation or even simple forgiveness – but the Ataua and Amuea tribes on Santa Catalina in the Solomon Islands settle differences by hurling sharpened sticks at each other. The aim of this four-day festival is to cleanse the island of all discord before the coming harvest season. Warriors, carrying spears and small wooden shields, assemble on the beach and start to argue, goading each other into a fighting frenzy. Finally, the first spear is thrown, and the battle is on. There are a number of rules: fighters are only supposed to throw spears at people with whom they have bad blood, and they are not supposed to fight their fathers or uncles. Village elders oversee matters, breaking up fights before anyone is seriously hurt and making sure that grudges are forgiven.

Where: Santa Catalina, Solomon Islands
When: Late May/early June

NAGHOL
Pentecost Island, Vanuatu

This extraordinary ritual takes place on Pentecost Island in Vanuatu, and sees young men throw themselves off great wooden towers with no safety equipment apart from vines tied around their legs to break their fall. The Naghol performs many functions: as a rite of passage from boyhood to manhood, to ensure good health and to guarantee a good yam harvest. Villagers in traditional dress, including *namba* (penis sheaths), dance and chant to encourage the divers to take the plunge from different heights. Divers can fall at speeds of up to 72kph. Also known as land diving, the Naghol is generally understood to be the forerunner of bungee jumping.

Where: Pentecost Island, Vanuatu
When: Usually Saturdays in April and May

> MICRONESIA

YAP DAY
Greater Yap

Greater Yap is a group of four islands in the south-west of the Federated States of Micronesia. The population of the islands – the Yapese – hold an annual celebration of their cultural and spiritual traditions, which centres on dancing. Each year a different village hosts the event and provides free food and drink for visitors to a cultural gathering known locally as a *mit-mit*. People come from all over the area to compete and watch as dancers in traditional costumes – often colourful grass skirts – perform dances that may be sitting, kneeling, standing or with sticks. Yap Day dances can be performed only once in public and then once in the village before being retired forever. There are demonstrations of local crafts. On the last day the local tourist authority holds a reception in honour of the visitor who has travelled furthest to get there.

Where: Greater Yap, Micronesia
When: First weekend in March

ANGAM DAY
Nauru

The people of the tiny Pacific island nation of Nauru cannot forget the two occasions in the 20th century when their population dropped to dangerously low levels. Following a flu epidemic in 1920 their number fell to 1,068. Twelve years later it reached 1,500 and a national holiday was declared. Called Angam Day (*angam* means 'jubilation' or 'home-coming'), the celebration continued until 1941 when the population dropped again below the sustainable level. Recovery was quicker this time and in March 1949 the 1,500th Nauran was born. The Nauruan people have been celebrating Angam-style ever since. The festivities include folk dancing in traditional Nauru costume, as well as feasting, drinking and community games.

Where: Nauru, Micronesia
When: 26 October

> NEW ZEALAND

GOLDEN SHEARS FESTIVAL
Masterton

New Zealand is famous for its sheep, which at times outnumber the human population by as much as 50 to one. New Zealanders are said to be very competitive, as anyone who has seen the All Blacks rugby team will attest to the truth of this. Put these two factors together and you get the Golden Shears Festival, hailed as the premier world shearing and wool-handling event. Over three days, a series of competitive sheep-related events are held, including

Traditional crafts, food, storytelling, dance and song are celebrated on Yap Day by the residents of the islands of Yap, Chuck, Pohnpei and Kosrae of the Federated States of Micronesia.

shearing for all ages and abilities as well as events for handling and pressing the sheared fleeces. The festival was first held in 1958, but became known as the Golden Shears in 1961 when it attracted so much local attention that the army had to be called in to maintain order.

Where: Masterton, North Island, New Zealand
When: Three days in March
....

WAITANGI DAY
Bay of Islands
....

Marking the official signing of the Treaty of Waitangi between the Maori of New Zealand and the Pakeha or European settlers, that led to the formation of the nation, Waitangi Day is marked each year with events all over the country. Official celebrations are held at the Waitangi Treaty Grounds in the Bay of Islands on North Island. The treaty was signed in 1840, but Waitangi became a public holiday in 1974. Three days of activities include a military tattoo, sports and cultural events as well as displays of the traditional dance, food and customs of the Maori people. However, some Maori consider the Waitangi Treaty to have been stacked against them and regard this celebration as a symbol of their unfair treatment.

Where: Nationally: officially at Bay of Islands, New Zealand
When: 6 February
....

> POLYNESIA

FLAG DAY
Pago Pago, American Samoa
....

Commemorating the day in 1900 when Captain Benjamin Franklin Tilley of the US Navy raised the American flag on Samoa to claim the island for the United States. Flag Day on American Samoa is a celebration of Polynesian culture. The week leading up to 17 April is a riot of traditional singing, dancing, music and lively parades, food stalls sell Samoan specialities and there are parties in late-night bars. The American Samoan flag is flown all over the island, not the original Stars and Stripes, but still bearing the American eagle in acknowledgment of its relationship with the Land of the Free. Of particular interest to the islanders are the *fautasi* or longboat races in which boats crewed by 45 rowers compete over a punishing 8km course.

Where: Pago Pago, American Samoa, Polynesia
When: 17 April
....

HEIVA I TAHITI
Papeete, Tahiti
....

The iconic Tahitian 'assembly' (*heiva*) coincides with the granting of French Polynesia's autonomy at the end of June and Bastille Day in July. It brings a flamboyant celebration of Polynesian culture to the waterfront To'ata Square of the capital Papeete. Originating in a festival called Tiurai, which was organized by the occupying French in 1881 to win over the locals after they had wrested control of the islands from the English, the festival is a major celebration of the traditional music, dancing and singing of Tahiti and the rest of French Polynesia, including the Marquesas, Austral and Gambier Islands. Heiva i Tahiti is also a sporting occasion, boasting a number of traditional Polynesian sports events including outrigger canoe and banana races, stone lifting, archery and javelin throwing.

Where: Papeete, Tahiti, Polynesia
When: Throughout July, especially 14 July
....

Index

Figures in italics indicate captions.

Picture credits

All of the images in this book have been supplied through the Alamy photolibrary (www.alamy.com), except for those by Steve Davey and those marked (JNTO), which have been supplied courtesy of the Japan National Tourism Organisation (JNTO).

Accent Alaska.com: 77; Africa Media Online: 22; A Howden - Japan Stock Photography: 105; Alamy Celebrity: 2, 82, 117 left; Alan Haynes: 78 left; Alissa Everett: 31; Alpha and Omega Collection: 44; Andy Buchanan: 178, 181 left, 184 bottom, 185; Arco Images GmbH: 202; Art Directors & TRIP: 110; Arterra Picture Library: 40 right; Asia Images Group Pte Ltd: 166 top; Asnar: 216; Aurora Photos: 40 left, 226; Barry Lewis: 208; Bert Hoferichter: 59; Bjorn Svensson: 219 left; Black Star: 37; Blaine Harrington III: 12, 47, 48; Blickwinkel: 41 top, 53; Brian Harris: 195; Buzz Pictures: 251; Cattle: 112; Charles Bowman: 76; Chichibu Kanko Kyokai (JNTO): 102 flash, 107 bottom; Choups: 190, 206; Chris Illemassene / Expuesto: 33; Chris Robbins: 221, 253; CuboImages srl: 49, 113, 197, 231; Dan Callister: 78 right; Dan Vincent: 260; Danita Delimont: 62; Dave Stamboulis: 145, 146; David Lyons: 250; David Pearson: 182 bottom; David South: 24, 25; David White: 187; Dennis Cox: 23 right, 46, 80 top; Dinodia Photos: 213, 217 top, 252; Ed Endicott / WYSIWYG Foto, LLC: 67, 84 right; Eddie Gerald: 166 bottom; Emil Pozar: 52 bottom; EmmePi Images: 115; EPA European Pressphoto Agency b.v.: 23 left, 55, 81, 90, 101 right, 111, 171 bottom, 180 left, 181 right, 188, 192 left, 227, 229, 230 bottom, 232; Eric Lafforgue: 214 top right; Eric Nathan: 174; FocusJapan: 98; Frans Lanting Studio: 60; Frans Lemmens: 54; Gallo Images: 17, 18; Galopin: 191; Geoffrey Robinson: 243; Giles Moberly: 32; Glen Allison: 64 left; Golden Richard: 74 flash, 75; Hemis: 21, 43, 66, 101 left, 169, 193, 199, 205, 211; Homer Sykes: 248; Imagestate Media Partners Limited - Impact Photos: 16, 165; INSADCO Photography: 173; ITAR-TASS Photo Agency: 177, 180 right; J.Enrique Molina: 212, 218 right; Jameshj: 150; Jan Sochor: 88; Japan National Tourism Organisation (JNTO): 178 flash, 106, 108, 182 top left, 182 top right; Jim Holden: 246 right; John Warburton-Lee Photography: 34; Jon Arnold Images Ltd: 50, 51, 214 bottom, 244 top; Jorge Blanco: 261; JTB Media Creation, Inc.: 36, 97, 103, 123, 257 left; Judy Bellah: 60 flash, 64 right, 65; Juergen Hasenkopf: 259; Kanuma City (JNTO): 109; Kevin Foy: 153, 184 top; Kim Kaminski: 210; Koji Kondoh, Hakata Gion Yamakasa Promotion Association (JNTO): 104; Konstantinos Tsakalidis: 157 inset; LatitudeStock: 15; LOOK Die Bildagentur der Fotografen GmbH: 57, 154 bottom; Loop Images Ltd: 183; Loren Holmes: 71; Luciano Leon: 85 right; M. Timothy O'Keefe: 92; Manca: 184 inset, 172; Mauro Spanu: 52 top; Michael DeFreitas: 56, 61; Michel Friang: 72; Mitja Mladkovic: 41 bottom; National Geographic Image Collection: 215; Neil McAllister: 152; NORMA JOSEPH: 116; Odyssey-Images: 118 main; Paul Brown: 233 bottom, 233 top; Paul Gapper: 155; Paul Kingsley: 152; Pawel Bienkowski: 143; Pegaz: 192 right; Phil Rees: 242; Prisma Bildagentur AG: 45, 79 right, 235, 257 right; Richard Ellis: 80 bottom; Richard Wareham Fotografie: 209; Richard Wayman: 230 top; Robert Estall photo agency: 20; Robert Fried: 68; Robert Harding World Imagery: 1, 19, 29, 74, 87, 156, 194 top, 241; Roger Arnold: 157 main; Roger Bamber: 245; Roger Cracknell: 244 bottom, 246 left, 247; Saitama Prefectural Tourism Division (JNTO): 107 top; Sandy Young: 170; Scott B. Rosen: 255; Shaun Flannery: 237; Stefano Paterna: 89, 158, 159; Steve Davey: 4 flash, 6 flash, 10 flash, 18 flash, 26 bottom left, 26 bottom right, 26 middle left, 26 top left, 26 top right, 27, 34 flash, 35, 38 left, 38 right, 39, 42 bottom left, 42 bottom right, 42 middle left, 42 middle right, 42 top left, 42 top right, 48 flash, 112 flash, 117 right, 119, 122, 125, 127, 128, 128 flash, 129, 130 bottom, 130 top, 131, 132, 133 left, 133 right, 134 left, 134 right, 135, 136, 138, 139 bottom left, 139 middle left, 139 right, 139 top left, 139 top right, 140 inset, 140 main, 142, 149, 152 flash, 154 top left, 154 top right, 161, 164 flash, 164 main, 167, 168 bottom, 171 top, 190 flash, 196, 201, 212 flash, 217 bottom, 218 left, 219 right, 223, 226 flash, 228 bottom, 228 top, 239, 242 flash, 249 inset, 249 main, 252 flash, 254 inset, 254 main, 258, 272; Toni Vilches: 194 bottom; Travel Pictures: 102; Travelib: 63; Travelscape Images: 224, 256; TRV/imagerover.com: 163; Urbanmyth: 95; Visual&Written SL: 179; WaterFrame: 265; Will Steeley: 263 Yadid Levy: 168 top; ZUMA Wire Service: 79 left, 83, 84 left, 85 left, 114, 214 top left.

This book is dedicated to fathers and sons.
To my father Eric, who quietly triumphed over cancer while I was working on this book,
and to my son Alexander Rishi. Sometimes it is comforting to realize that for all the sound and fury,
you are just a small link in a very long chain.

Pilgrims crossing pontoon bridges over the River Ganges during the Maha Kumbh Mela in 2001, Allahabad, India.

Skyhorse Publishing books may be purchased in bulk at special discounts for sales promotion, corporate gifts, fund-raising, or educational purposes. Special editions can also be created to specifications. For details, contact the Special Sales Department, Skyhorse Publishing, 307 West 36th Street, 11th Floor, New York, NY 10018 or info@skyhorsepublishing.com.

Skyhorse® and Skyhorse Publishing® are registered trademarks of Skyhorse Publishing, Inc.®, a Delaware corporation.

Visit our website at www.skyhorsepublishing.com.

10 9 8 7 6 5 4 3 2 1

Library of Congress Cataloging-in-Publication Data is available on file.

Cover design by Jane Sheppard
Interior design by Bobby Birchall, Bobby&Co
Additional research by Orly Kuperard

Print ISBN: 978-1-5107-0591-3
Ebook ISBN: 978-1-5107-0592-0

Printed in China